THE IMAGE OF THE FUTURE

The Jossey-Bass / Elsevier
International Series

 Elsevier Scientific Publishing Company
Amsterdam

The Image of the Future

FRED POLAK

Translated and Abridged by ELISE BOULDING

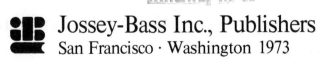 Jossey-Bass Inc., Publishers
San Francisco · Washington 1973

THE IMAGE OF THE FUTURE
by Fred Polak
translated and abridged by Elise Boulding

For the United States of America and Canada:

Jossey-Bass, Inc., Publishers
615 Montgomery Street
San Francisco, California 94111

For all other areas:

Elsevier Scientific Publishing Company
335 Jan van Galenstraat
Amsterdam, The Netherlands

Library of Congress Catalogue Card Number LC 72-83209
3 -13-74
International Standard Book Number ISBN 0-87589-152-7

Manufactured in The Netherlands

FIRST EDITION

Code 7237

Foreword

My first acquaintance with the work of Dr. Fred Polak came in the year 1954—5, when we were both fellows at the new Center for Advanced Study in the Behavioral Sciences at Stanford. Dr. and Mrs. Polak lived in a little house at the back of the garden of the house that the Bouldings rented and participated very cheerfully in the life of the Bouldings and their four young children. Many exciting things came out of that year at Stanford, such as the Society for General Systems Research and the *Journal of Conflict Resolution*. But looking back on the experience after nearly twenty years, I think the most important impact on the thought of both Elise Boulding and myself were the many conversations that we had with the Polaks around the dining table and in the garden. In my own case, many aspects of my subsequent work, including *The Image*, which was written at the Center that year, owe a great deal to Polak's ideas. Polak, indeed, was a pioneer in what has come to be called "futurology," an ugly word, which, however, represents an important movement in human thought. One is tempted to say, indeed, that we are all futurologists, and in this respect the impact of Fred Polak's thoughts is much greater than is usually recognized.

The human condition can almost be summed up in the observation that, whereas all experiences are of the past, all decisions are about the future. It is the great task of human knowledge to bridge this gap and to find those patterns in the past which can be projected into the future as realistic images. The image of the future, therefore, is the key to all choice-oriented behavior. The general character and quality of the images of the future which prevail in a society is therefore the most important clue to its overall dynamics. The individual's image of the future is likewise the most significant determinant of his personal behavior.

I have long felt that the original version of *The Image of the Future* was one of the most significant works of the twentieth century, and that it has never received the attention which it deserves, perhaps because of its length. The condensed version is a new opportunity for readers to become acquainted with it, and I am convinced that no one who becomes acquainted with it will fail to be profoundly influenced by it.

Kenneth Boulding

Institute of Behavioral Science
University of Colorado

Translator's Preface

When Fred Polak came to the Institute for Advanced Studies in the Behavioral Sciences in Palo Alto as a Fellow in 1955, his recently published *Die Toekomst Is Verleden Tijd* had just received the Council of Europe Award. Since the Bouldings and the Polaks kept a joint household that exciting first year of the Institute's existence, Kenneth Boulding and I had ample opportunity to become acquainted with Fred Polak's unique ideas. The effect of that year on Kenneth Boulding can be traced to his *The Image*, which bears little surface relationship to *The Image of the Future*, but which did in fact first take root in Fred Polak's thinking, and was written at the close of that golden California year as a summing up of a rather special kind of intellectual journey.

My own response of Fred Polak's ideas was to learn Dutch in order to be able to translate his book and make it available to the English-speaking world. I translated it in full, since it was too difficult to translate and condense at one and the same time from a language I was just learning, but I knew that the leisurely intellectual pace of the original would not find many readers in the hurried American scene. Therefore I had from the beginning intended eventually to produce a condensation that would render Polak's ideas on the future more intellectually accessible to American colleagues, particularly in the social sciences. Other things intervened, and it took ten years to get back to the condensation project, but I find that the book has a new kind of timelessness now that man has entered space.

In the intervening decade there has been a sudden proliferation of theories, books, societies, and institutions all dedicated to the study of the future. Very few people are aware of the intellectual debt that this future-oriented scholarship and activity owes to Fred Polak, who was the first in the post-World War II period to undertake the difficult conceptual work of clarifying the role of the image of the future in the social process at the societal level. Much of the recent work is of a strictly empirical nature, which Polak himself welcomes, but to focus on these empirical studies without a knowledge of the broad sweep of the underlying historical processes involved is to sell mankind short at a very crucial time in history.

Polak is very explicit that in this book he is concerned with the future in Western culture only, and that he is analyzing images of possible futures *on this world*. Taking the task of image-making for the future very seriously, he ruled out fantasies about other worlds as just that — fantasies. The timeliness of Polak's book today is that it marks the end of that part of human history in which man could trace out one part of the global cultural heritage and have it make sense, and it also marks the end of the time when thought about human life elsewhere than on earth was only a fantasy. Intellectually and spiritually, man is hardly ready to face the implications of a common global heritage on earth, or of cosmic belongingness in the universe. Polak's *Image of the Future* can help disoriented Western man get his bearings, understand the road he has traveled, and thus help him face the task of image-working for the now-incredible futures which lie before him.

The pessimistic tone of the second part of *The Image of the Future*, as Polak depicts moment-ridden man trapped in a moment-bound culture, never gives way to despair. At every turn, the author reminds us that there still is a turning possible, that new vistas can open up. Today we are glimpsing these new vistas, and Polak's work will help us make both more realistic and more daring use of the new chances that history is offering man.

It is no small thing that a man who as a Jew had to live in hiding in the German-occupied Netherlands all through the war, emerged from that shattering experience with a vision of man as a future-creating being, and that he has been able to marshal all his own intellectual and spiritual energies to communicate this vision to precisely that generation of young men and women who need desperately to know that it is possible to create other and better futures.

Elise Boulding

Contents

PART TWO: ICONOCLASM OF THE IMAGES OF THE FUTURE

Part One
The Promised Land

I. The Future as a Work of Reconstruction

Chapter 1. Basic Concepts: Time, Images, and the Future

Every great thinker who has concerned himself with the historical process has speculated about the meaning of time and its flow in history. Marx, Hegel, Spengler, Toynbee, and Sorokin, each with his own variation on the theme of time-flow as mechanically patterned fluctuation, predict the future but ignore its dynamic interaction with the past and the present. This book will give an added dimension to our understanding of the historical process by including the interaction between completed and noncompleted time. Social change will be viewed as a push-pull process in which a society is at once pulled forward by its own magnetic images of an idealized future and pushed from behind by its realized past. Poised on the dividing line between past and future is man, the unique bearer and transformer of culture. All of man's thinking involves a conscious process of dividing his perceptions, feelings, and responses, and sorting them into categories on the time-continuum. His mental capacity to categorize and reorder reality within the self (present reality) and in relation to perceptions of the not-self (the Other) enable him to be a citizen of two worlds: the present and the imagined. Out of this antithesis the future is born. Man's dualism is thus the indispensable prerequisite to the movement of events in time, and to the dynamics of historical change.

Every man leads a double life, though the duality may go by different names, according to historical circumstance. The perception in antiquity of a unity of opposites has, in the twentieth century, given way to a sense of irreconcilable opposites. The theologian sees the duality as the separation between the *eschaton* and this world, the student of ethics as the distinction between the is and the ought, and the philosopher as the awareness of the transcendental. The artist identifies art with the Other by definition; he works with the not-seen and the not-yet. The historian sees the unfolding of history as the working out of man's inner dualism in space and time, while the psychologist sees man as a battleground of his own conflicting drives.

It is not difficult to recognize the duality of the now and the Other as a continuous theme in history, but how this dualism functions in any given period is a more complex question. Of the many ways in which man has approached the problem of his own dividedness, the following five summarize his major orientations to the realm of the Other:

1. Life cannot be purely transitory: there must be something more enduring. Man hopes for future grace.

2. Life cannot simply end in imperfection. There must be an Other realm into which man can enter.

3. Life should not be transitory and imperfect. Man rebels out of despair, but without hope.

4. Life is not as it appears to be. This world is an illusion and the essential reality is veiled from man.

5. Life does not have to be the way it is. Man can reform and re-create the world after any image he chooses.

The first of the routes into the Other emphasizes flight and may involve a pathological separation from reality. The second may be dionysian or apollonic: drugs or fasting can equally lead to spiritual ecstasy. The third route, most pertinent to our study, may be thought of as the normal, simultaneous sojourn in two worlds. Man "hears" the inaudible and "sees" the invisible at the same time that sound and light waves from the physical world reach his senses. This acoustical-optical synchronization can be achieved only with the help of the imagination. The image must first be received before it can be broadcast. Image-reception refers to a whole range of phenomena such as dreams, visions, and all forms of imaginary encounter with the Other. It is a highly personal and individual experience, often limited to an elite in a given society. The broadcasting that follows image-reception is our central concern, especially insofar as mass media are used to extend the effect of the image. Symbolic-poetic presentations of images, destined for the public, abound in myths and legends. Usually the image-rich secret language of the initiated must be translated in order to be understood by the layman. The visual image may have the most direct impact on the general population, particularly if it stimulates its active participation in the imaging process. Art is the medium par excellence for transposing images from the Other world into this world: not only pictorial art, but also drama, from miracle play onward, and the rich and varied combinations of music and dance that have evolved through the centuries. Finally, Nature herself, great schoolmistress of all the arts, has always provided man with images of the Other world. Man has ever busied himself with interpreting her signs and portents, trembling before eclipses of the sun, and reverent before the rainbow.

Time and Space Consciousness

The more sophisticated man's time-consciousness becomes, the more skilled he is at finding paths to the Other. The initial discovery of space and time as independent units, each capable of being divided into that which is present and that which is not present, was, however, a process of enormous complexity. Once man understood that "here" could be yesterday or tomorrow, he had discovered the two formal Kantian categories of the temporal and the spatial. These became the tools with which he shaped his images of the future, both in another time and in another space. As man's sophistication increased, he was able to conceive of these Other dimensions as a new category, a new regulative idea. The result of this macrocosmic splitting of the spatio-temporal dimension was the opening up of vast new concepts for men's minds to play with.

Spatial images of the Other have taken many forms through time. They may be roughly classified in the following seven categories:

Before this world: Images concerning an original state of nature, a lost paradise, Eden, Arcady.

This world: Images of the Promised Land, the New Jerusalem.

Below this world: Images of Hades or Tartarus, an oceanic or volcanic kingdom, a land of the dead, a land of shadows, hell.

Above this world: Images of the beyond, a Kingdom of Heaven, Olympus, empyrean.

Outside this world: Images of the *isles of the blessed*, Atlantis, never-never land.

After this world: Images of Elysium, Valhalla, a hereafter, a resting place for spirits of the departed.

Beyond all worlds: Spatial images of a metaphysical-cosmic nature, which are essentially nonspatial and ethereal: The All-One, infinity, nirvana.

Temporal images of the world have been variously projected into the distant future or, as in classical mythology, into the past. At certain times in history, eschatological images of the future have shouted "Soon! " Images projected into the past represent romantic idealizations of that past: the biblical paradise, the Renaissance image of antiquity. The age of romanticism looked to bygone times, and our own century reveres the Middle Ages, a period despised by the Enlightenment. There is also a tendency today to idealize the wisdom of primitive man. The aching nostalgia for the time of unspoiled beginnings represents a kind of vision of the future—an image of unattainability. These dreams of the past operate on the future, though indirectly. Mostly, however, it is the future that has attracted man's dreams, hopes, and fears. The future rather than the past is seen as holding the key to the riddle of his existence. Death itself, the one certainty, is the chief inciter of our thirst for knowledge of what is to come. Man has never been able to accept *Ignoramus, ignorabius* as his motto.

The domain of the future, however, is without boundaries. Yet it is only by drawing boundaries in the thought-realm that man can produce a problem that can be grasped and worked with, and it is only by redrawing the boundaries of the unknown that man can increase his knowledge. No problem so persistently defies our skill at drawing boundaries as the problem of the future, and no problem presses quite so hard on our intellectual horizons. In the act of searching out the future, Homo sapiens crosses the frontiers of the unknown and is transformed from the man of action, who responds to the moment, to the man of thought, who takes account of the consequences of his actions. He leaves behind the familiar universe of sight and sound and surveys the universe of the unseen and unheard, continually bringing small fragments of the unknown back with him out of the darkness and adding them to the known. Who can say whether this building up of the known diminishes the unknown?

Man is not easily discouraged, however. Everything drives him to accept the challenge of the unknown. The instincts of preservation and reproduction demand it. All economic activity is an answer to this challenge; the primitive nomad gathering fruits and nuts and the modern industrial magnate are alike answering the call of the unborn tomorrow; so are the men who chart the seas and those who chart the heavens. No man, not even the suicide, can leave tomorrow alone. The suicide but hastens tomorrow in his impatience.

In exploring his own future, man has always been haunted by the sense of doing the forbidden. The Greeks knew well the dreadful consequences of *hubris*, the sin of challenging the omnipotence of the gods. And yet, throughout history, man has never ceased to explore these bounds. He has suffered as a result, but he has also succeeded in pushing the bounds far out into the realm of what was once considered impossible. This spiritual overstepping of the boundaries of the unknown is the source of all human creativity; however, man has not always been bold in approaching this frontier. Folk migrations and adventures of daring and discovery have always been countered by the longing for one's home and hearth. Nevertheless, crossing frontiers is both man's heritage and man's task, and the image of the future is his propelling power.

The Path from Idea to Image

We have already indicated that man has met the challenge of the unknown by carving from it images of the future. How has he done this? The task has two aspects: the splitting of time into the now and the Other, and the creation of an Other world to fill the Other time. We are concerned here with the breach man has made in time: the astrologer of ancient Babylonia kept a double clock for this world and the Other; Hegel saw the future locked in the present, mystically complete in the Great Pyramid; and Pierre de Laplace worked out a railway timetable from the present into the future.

The future not only must be perceived; it also must be shaped. The myth has from earliest times served this function of giving shape to perceptions of the Other. The Promethean myth united a creation story with a vision of the future through the gift of fire. When Pandora opened the fabled box and let sorrow and trouble loose in the world, she was still left with the spirit of hope, the possibility of visions. The course of the stars has been made to write man's future from time immemorial, and eschatology has contributed its visions of the next world. The animal world has always provided man with symbolic material for portraying the Other. In the dawn of time, man did not differentiate so sharply between himself and the animal world as he does now. The phoenix, rising out of its ashes, symbolizes the new, Other time. The vulture that daily ate away at the vitals of the immobilized Prometheus symbolizes the binding of man to the past, as the fall of Adam and Eve through the serpent's wiles represents the chaining of mankind to original sin. Prometheus was redeemed, however, giving us the prototype of the image of the future: a story of salvation. This image always operates as a projection backward, from the future into the present. Even if it is, or

5

seems, a dim memory out of a distant past, it acts at the same time as a foreshadowing of a distant tomorrow. Paradise and the Golden Age are in this way transplanted from prehistory to the final stage of man, who dreams not so much of his beginnings as of his end. The products of this work of the imagination are highly diverse: philosophic and historical images, replete with ready-made meanings; ethical images, typified by the charismatic figures of Socrates and Jesus; socio-political images, such as Plato's *Politeia* or al-Farabi's *Model City*[1], and religious images that give form and substance to messianic expectations.

The concept of a vision that guides the actions of men is very old indeed. The Sumerians and the Babylonians conceived of the sky as the dwelling place of the gods and believed that man's actions were directed from these heavenly headquarters, with the movements of the stars and planets foreshadowing events on earth. Early man expressed himself in pictures and images, and expected the same from his gods. Given the assumption that the gods did reveal the future, what could be more natural than to regard the course of the stars as a kind of divine picture-writing?

Eventually, man emancipated himself from the picture-writing of the gods and created new images, sometimes in terms of the will of God, sometimes out of his own humanistic striving. Once he became conscious of creating images of the future, he became a participant in the process of creating this future. While it is not possible to trace here the complex process of emancipation from the doctrine of absolute determinism it should be noted that astrology, neoplatonic cosmology, neopythagorean numerology, the Jewish Cabala, the mysticism of the Middle Ages, natural philosophy, and white magic played a part in this development. Out of all this there emerged the idea of man as a microcosmos and as a microtheos. Paracelsus, for example, conceived of man as created out of the four earthly elements, but also out of a fifth, *quinta essentia*. This is the stuff out of which the stars are made, and which constitutes the "quintessence" of the human spirit. Man himself, synthesis of star-stuff and earth-stuff, is the keystone of the universe.

At the same time, if man is really a microcosmos, he may use the divine potential within him to bring about his own fulfillment and his own integration with the universe around him. Here the concepts

---

[1] Robert Hammond, *The Philosophy of al-Farabi and Its Influence on Medieval Thought* (New York: Hudson Press, 1947). (Al-Farabi, who died ca. 950 A.D., was a brilliant Arab scholar, scientist, music theorist, and theologian.)

of freedom and responsibility emerge. Jakob Böhme's *Aurora oder Morgenröte im Aufgang*[2] describes very well the transition to a new point of view that took place at the close of the Middle Ages and on through the whole of the Renaissance. During this period there was an increasing recognition of man's influence on his own destiny, a bridging over of the chasm between man and his future, and a fuller insight into the dignity and worth of man and his images of the future.

The images of the future that man has created are intimately related to the time-concepts he has held. If his view of himself as a free agent has affected a radical change in his images, so have his changing time-concepts had their impact on these images. All of the images of the future that carry man out of and beyond himself also contain a time-concept that is outside of and beyond existing time. This concept is often labeled eternity and as such is used in various ways by religion and philosophy. Retained in its original wholeness by Plato and Spinoza, eternity later begins to disintegrate; in Kant, for example, the category of time is limited to a human mode of perception. Einstein takes Newton's absolute time and makes it relative in a space-time continuum. Bergson brings time firmly down to earth as "duration." Existentialism, finally, reduces time to the continually disappearing moment.

Paradoxically, while the philosophic concept of time is becoming more cramped and narrow, the scientific concept of the time-span is expanding with explosive rapidity. Biblical time reckoned in thousands of years from the Creation to the end of time. Today, the origin of the earth has been pushed back to between two and five billion years, and the existence of life on earth now covers a period of hundreds of millions of years. The clock is set between half a million and a million years from the first appearance of the genus Homo. Earth is only a tiny satellite of a second-rate star clinging to the edge of the dazzling carpet of the Milky Way. Moreover, there may be millions of Milky Ways, millions of light years apart, and new ones always in the process of creation in a constantly expanding universe. Magnitudes of this order may not be intrinsically unmeasurable, but they are certainly beyond the grasp of man's mind, and lead straight back to the nearly lost concept of eternity.

For the purposes of our study, the boundary outside of time is drawn at that point where comprehension fails and wordplay sets in.

---

[2] Jakob Böhme, *Aurora: That is, the Day-spring, or Morning-Rednesse in the Rising Sun*, trans. by John Sparrow (London: J. Steator for G. Calvert, 1656).

But where does the boundary lie inside of time? Temporal reckonings have always been highly relative. The thousand and one nights of the Arabian princess stretched into an eternity of nights, while the year 2000 seems an eternity away to moment-bound man of the present. The chiliastic sects which have been awaiting the Second Coming of Christ ever since His First Departure await an eternally receding future, just as many of today's intellectuals await the decline of the West with similar fervor. We face the paradox that man's life expectancy is approaching the century mark, but the century itself becomes as eons when its beats are counted in the modern tempo.

In contrast to the emphasis on the imminent is the preoccupation with the ultimate extinction of the human race and the death of the planet that has been its habitation.[3] We are not concerned here with a secularized end of time, however, but with the future of Western man in the face of the meteoric bursting forth of new centers of political power and the increasing acceleration of social and technological change.

Since there have been more new scientific discoveries in the past fifty years than occurred in the previous five thousand years, we cannot make simple projections into the future from the present. Our thesis is that we are faced with a literal breach in time. The breach has forced Western man to leap from what we now call modern times into ultramodern times, into what might well be for him last times. These ultramodern times may not be sufficiently jelled for purposes of observation until the turn of the century. It is the future from that point on that will concern us in the second part of this book, especially as this future lies concealed in today's images of the future. Before examining our own future, however, there is still much to be done. We must examine the nature of the image of the future, study how it is formed and propagated, and ascertain its relationship to the historical time-flow. The next chapter will deal with the theoretical aspects of this problem, followed by a historical analysis of the development of images of the future in Western civilization.

---

[3] W. O. Stapledon, *Last and First Man* (London: Metheun, 1930); George Gamow, *Birth and Death of the Sun* (New York: Viking Press, 1940); E. J. Slijper, *Het Lot der Mensheid* (Groningen: T. B. Wolters, 1952).

Chapter 2. Image and Actuality

It was but a small step for man from realizing that he had a future to wanting to know what that future would bring. The impulse to propitiate the powers of the future in order to avoid catastrophe and procure blessings may well have been part of the drive to know from its early beginnings. Both magic and religion probably arose at least in part out of this twin drive for certainty and control. For many centuries man struggled to obtain a reliable reading of signs and omens, both in the heavens and in the world around him. It seems likely that dependence on the direct inspiration of gifted specialists, whether priest or prophet, came somewhat later. Sometimes prophet and propitiator were the same, at other times the two functions were separate. As man the maker embarked on the adventures of agriculture, navigation, and his first large-scale engineering projects, such as pyramids and waterworks, the need to predict and control the future became of still more practical urgency. The beginnings of science grew out of this urgency: astrology and its more sober offspring, astronomy, alike served this need to know the future.

In attempting to blueprint his own future, man has been forced to deal with the concepts of value, means and ends. As long as the prophet propitiator was acting only as a transmitter of messages from on high, man accepted his ethics ready-made, with no alterations allowed. In a later stage man staggered under the double load not only of having to construct his own future but of having to create the values that will determine its design. To primitive man, the task of looking into the unknown must have seemed terrifying enough. As modern man gains an increased understanding of the complexity of interplay between attitudes and values and technological know-how in the process of social change at all levels of society, the terrifying aspects of the unknown are scarcely diminished. However, between this initial period and modern times there have been many ups and downs in man's attempts to push back the frontier of the unknown. This attempt can be seen as a twofold process: the development of ideas concerning the ideal future as it ought to be, and the unfolding of the real future in history, partly as a result of man's purposeful intervention. Awareness of ideal values is the first step in the conscious creation of images of the future and therefore in the conscious creation of culture, for a value is by definition that which guides toward a "valued" future. The image of the future reflects and reinforces these values. The relationship between conceptions of the time-dimension, the future, and the idealistic ethical objectives of mankind for that future, has been a neglected one and offers a fruitful field for research.

As a society develops a common set of values and norms in its ethics and moral philosophy, this leads to a more or less stable set of expectations regarding the future behavior of its physical environment, as it develops practices in the realm of magic, religion, and science in order to deal with natural or supernatural phenomena. These two trends of expectations merge and crystallize into systematic projections toward the future, or images of the future. We have already indicated that our concerns center on those crystallized expectations that picture a radically different world in an Other time, and that are imaginatively shaped in such a way that they can be applied on behalf of mankind.

The resurrection of Israel as preached by the Old Testament prophets has been one of the most powerful and persistent images of the future ever evolved, as has the Kingdom of Heaven proclaimed by Jesus. In *The City of God*, St. Augustine spells out still further this potent image of the future, to be fulfilled by the grace of God and mediated through the Christian church. Plato's *Politeia* opened the way for a series of projections which, via Thomas More's *Utopia*, culminated in the socialistic and humanistic utopian images of the Enlightenment.

In a se se it is the prophet, the projector of images, who may write in advance a considerable part of the history of the future, but the materials out of which he creates his images are drawn largely from the cultural heritage of the social group or society to which he belongs. The images themselves may be thought of as time-bombs that explode somewhere in the future, although the men and societies who create them have little control over when, where, and how they will explode. These explosions release masses of concen-

10

trated energy, and radioactive particles load the heavily tidal time-stream between past and future.

Theory of the Image

In this work we are, in a sense, taking the existence of images of the future as given and tracing out the effects of their existence on the course of history. In doing so we are deliberately starting in the middle of the story, so to speak, and apparently ignoring the beginning, the problem of images in general and how they are formed. We offer no excuses for this, because it is the business of the mind to begin work at the point of major insight. The image of the future does represent such a major insight, and carries within itself its own intellectual imperatives for a further working out of the idea. This procedure seems all the more justified since, according to our thesis, it is the image of the future that forms a dynamic factor par excellence and an extremely powerful force contained in the working of all images as such. Therefore, the dynamics of the images of the future, which we treat separately in this book, have a special relevance for a theory of the image in general. We cannot and do not wish to ignore the problem of a systematic theory of the image, however, and would like to consider this work as a small contribution to a more general theory.

The more general theory of images may be thought of as "eidetics." This concept, derived from the Greek *eidelon*, "image," has a long history. Plato, Epicurus, and Democritus used the term to refer to knowledge and the learning process. Francis Bacon made similar use of it. The term *eidetisch* appears in the writings of the German psychologists, especially E. R. Jaensch, who specialized in research on children between the ages of thirteen and fifteen. Jaensch related certain types of eidetic endowments to physical constitution *(Körperbau)* and to personality type. On the basis of this he later outlined a theory of the development of culture. The concept recently appeared in slightly changed form in a book by the economist Kenneth E. Boulding.[1] Though very welcome, these developments are only a beginning and leave many questions unanswered. Nor do they put enough emphasis on the significance of the time-

---

[1] The Dutch original of *The Image of the Future* preceded Kenneth E. Boulding's book, *The Image* (Ann Arbor: University of Michigan Press, 1956) by several years.

dimension in the dynamics of image formation and image propagation. They shift the focus away from the image of the future as such, which served as the initial center of interest and inspiration, and which we view as a basic element in the operational activity of all images.

In a general theory, attention must be given to the dynamics of image formation, both in the private and the public mind, and the function of images in the economy of the individual personality and the social, national, or cultural group. What do images mean, how are the meanings transmitted, and how do they affect individual and social behavior? Under what conditions do images change, and why? What can accelerate or retard these changes? How amenable are they to purposeful manipulation, in both the short and the long run? We hope that some light is thrown on all these questions by our study of images of the future.

One of the strongest links between images and the image of the future is contained in the Book of Genesis, where we are told that God created man in His image. It would be wrong to suppose, however, that the use of images to capture the future is limited to the spheres of religion and mythology. Such images are always present and operative in all social groups, and social science is increasingly making use of these images to increase its analytic power, but without fully understanding the implications of adding the time-dimension to its analysis. Images are at work everywhere, individually and collectively: private and public images, images of ourselves and others, of our own group and of other groups. We hold images of our own nation, race, profession, party, and belief-system, and likewise of other nations, races, professions, parties, and ideologies. Images are formed and changed of producers and consumers, capitalists and communists; of artists, bohemians, and scientists; of entrepreneurs and workingmen; of right and wrong behavior, good and bad guys, hipsters and squares, organization men and rugged individualists; of husbands, wives, and children; and of fathers and mothers.

Public relations men are powerful image-makers and manipulators. They build images to influence buyers and voters; they sell attractive public images and self-images with which people, whether consumers or citizens, can easily identify. The secret of their being able to persuade the masses to buy certain brands, symbols, ideas, or politicians is hidden in the almost unlimited potential of selling an image of the future with modern techniques of merchandising and marketing. It is, however, a rather long way from the classic image of the future to today's cheap imitations. Later on the implications of this assertion will become clear.

Images and Their Dimension of the Future

We have already stated that this work singles out the image of the future because we are convinced it is the time-dimension of the future that acts as a pre-eminently dynamic force in the working of all images. In analyzing how the concept of the future has operated in the historical process, there are six main aspects that come into play:

1. *Images of the future are always aristocratic in origin.* The author of the image invariably belongs to the creative minority of a society. He moves in the company of Isaiah, Socrates, Rembrandt, the French *philosophes*, and nearer to our own day, such men as Henri Bergson and H. G. Wells. The formation of images of the future depends upon an awareness of the future that makes possible a conscious, voluntary, and responsible choice between alternatives. This means that the development of images of the future and ethics are intimately related. Human judgments can, to a great extent, be explained in relation to the striving toward a highly valued future goal. The development of ethics and moral philosophy is one aspect of the development of techniques for visualizing and controlling the future, and the image of the future receives much of its driving force from ethics. Kant's ethics—reduced to his famous categorical imperative, the whole field of *Sollen*, "ought," as distinct from *Sein*, "is," and *Wirklichkeit*, "reality," as opposed to *Wert*, "value,"—are all based on a time-dimension hitherto never clearly delineated. They can all be effectively translated into the language of the image of the future. They all express the underlying philosophy of what we call influence-optimism. Man, in this process of ethical development, is no longer simply "split man," capable of dividing his perceptions into two realms. He now becomes "moral man," responsible for the use to which he puts his perceptions and powers for reaching the Other and better. At this point the positive image of the future in its classic form becomes one of the main instruments of culture, providing both a vision of civilization and the tools for realizing it.

2. *The propagation of images.* The force that drives the image of the future is only in part rational and intellectual; a much larger part is emotional, aesthetic, and spiritual. The appeal of the image lies in its picture of a radically different world in an Other time. Psycholo-

13

gists will term this variously as escapism, compensation mechanisms, and projection. It is above all the spiritual nature of the ideals embodied in the image of the future that infuses the image with power. As between two opposing schools of thought, historical materialism and historical idealism, we favor the latter. The primary forces in history are not propelled by a system of production, nor by industrial or military might, but rather by the underlying ideas, ideals, values, and norms that manage to achieve mass appeal.

3. *Image-effect, or the relationship between the projected future (whether positive or negative) and the actual future as it passes into history*, is discussed in the next chapter.

4. *Self-elimination of images* becomes central to our discussion in Chapter 18, "Timeless Time." Self-elimination takes place in a natural way through the historical process of succession of images, and through the dialectical changes they themselves provoke.

5. *The periodic adaptation to time-change through self-correction, renewal, and change on the part of images of the future in the continuous interplay of challenge and response* forms the underlying connecting thread of Part One. It is only when we come to the turn of this century that we must for the first time examine the last aspect:

6. *The loss of the capacity for adequate self-correction and timely renewal of images of the future.* It is a main thesis of this work that for the first time in the three thousand years of Western civilization there has been a massive loss of capacity, or even will, for renewal of images of the future. There are few signs of constructive images, and no generally accepted idealistic images, forthcoming today. There is a contraction of time-consciousness to the momentary present and a blurring of a specific sense of the future. The dualistic mental structure that is essential for eschatological and utopian thinking about the future has been severely crippled.

We do not discuss private images of the future, but only shared public ones, not because there is a difference in the operational principles involved, but because we are primarily concerned with the larger social and cultural processes. The kind of images that we discuss are shared public images of the cosmos, God, man, social institutions, the meaning of history, and others of similar scope. Again, in all these images it is the time-dimension of the future that gives them their special force. For example, the dimension of the future exercises a dominating influence on the image of the world, the *Weltanschauung* (see Chapter 18, "Timeless Time"). The image of God is a concept that is related to the future in its very essence, since God lives as a promise in the minds of hopeful men (see Chapter 17, "De-eschatologizing," and Chapter 19, "The Future of the Christian Belief-System"). The future dimension in the image of man is related to the concept of the dignity of man in terms of man's responsibility for his own destiny (see Chapter 9, "The Renaissance as a Renaissance of Utopism"). We deal with the impact of the future on the image of social institutions, both implicitly (see Chapter 10, "The Image of the Future: Guiding Star of the Age of Enlightenment") and explicitly (see Chapter 24, "New Perspectives"). The nationalistic image of the future is discussed in connection with the regression of the once universal utopian ideal (see Chapter 10). The image of the processes and meaning of history is also treated in its relationship to the dimensions of the future (see Chapter 14, "The Image of History and the Image of the Future").

In focusing on the time-dimension of dominant public or collective images of the future, it becomes obvious that these different images are structurally interrelated. The image of the future as such may therefore be an important tool for an interdisciplinary social science. The possibility that science may be able to predict and control social processes through analysis of existing images of the future, both private and public, and direct a change of these images, is a thought-provoking one. Granted that we may still be a good distance away from effective prediction, it is still not too soon to begin pondering the problems of controlled image-change. How could such a possibility be fitted into a democratic system of government? The whole question of public policy in relation to image-change may be a matter of life and death for Western civilization. If we pause to think what can be done with the minds of men through the public school system, public health policy (which is increasingly concerned with mental health in its educational and preventive as well as remedial aspects), economic policy, censorship, and a foreign policy based entirely on secret negotiations, we cannot accept the idea of controlled image-change as a social good per se. We not only need to give a great deal of thought to practical methods of image-change and the kinds of images that our society needs, we must examine and be as fully aware as possible of the influence on society of those images of the future already existing in the minds of political planners, scientists, and professional practitioners in every field. If we find that these influences are bad or weak, how can we redirect them? If we find that the creative minority of our culture is no longer constructing positive and idealistic images of the future,

15

what then? These are some of the questions that we hope our historical analysis helps to answer. However, the whole truth does not reside in the image of the future alone. These images do not act on the historical process in a vacuum. They are in a constant state of interaction with the past and present. Thus, we will now examine the interplay between the time-dimensions of past, present, and future.

Dynamics of Interaction Between Past, Present, and Future

How can we account for the diversity of images of the future that emerge from history? Why does this image arise in this time and this place, and another elsewhere? Why does each society have a characteristic type of image? It will not suffice simply to describe split man and state that his unique mental capacities enable him to divide his experience into two realities. Nor can we be content with a conception of man as a completely free, independent being who can choose his images of the future at will. He is—or conceives himself to be—opposed by certain forces of the time that are perhaps themselves the ultimate shapers of the future.

Beside the antithesis in the human mind between the here-and-now and the Other we must place a second antithesis, that of human potency or impotence as opposed to divine or supernatural omnipotence. Man can visualize the Other, but can he do anything about it? The entire history of philosophic and religious thought is significantly marked by man's tragic conflict between the dream and the power to act on the dream.

Optimism and Pessimism

Who or what really dominates the future, and how is the domination accomplished? Man's images of the future have depended on his changing answers to these questions. The psychologically inclined observer comes face to face with the riddle of societies that seem either basically optimistic or basically pessimistic, seeing the world through either rose-tinted or smoked glasses. These changing attitudes relate both to the idea of supernatural dominance and to the concept of the power of man to rule over his own future—to superhuman versus human power. Would the explanation of these succeeding waves of optimism and pessimism give us a key to history, or would it be just the reverse? And is the struggle for power between man and the supernatural a real one, or only a figment of the imagination?

This raises the point of the functional relationship between the image of the future and optimistic and pessimistic attitudes. Which of the two is the independent variable? This question compels us to examine more closely the various feelings societies have had about the position of man in the cosmos, and how he stands in relation to time. When we include the element of power, the mere opposition of optimism and pessimism becomes an oversimplification. There have always been degrees of feelings of human impotence combined with a kind of optimism, and feelings of human potency mixed with a kind of pessimism. Optimism and pessimism are then used in a different sense, one which conceals the very problem on which we wish to throw light.

It will be helpful to make distinctions between optimism and pessimism along the lines of the concepts of *Seinmüssen*, "what must be," and *Seinsollen*, "what ought to be." It would then be possible to speak of *Seinoptimismus* or *Seinpessimismus*, which we shall refer to as essence-optimism or essence-pessimism, and *Willensoptimismus* or *Willenspessimismus*, which we shall refer to as influence-optimism or influence-pessimism. The essence categories refer to an unchangeable course of events; the influence categories refer to the supposed or rejected possibility of human intervention. The first point of view sees history as a book that has already been written; the second sees history as a process that man can or cannot manipulate.

The correspondence between essence-optimism and its accompanying image of the future is fairly direct. Man has scarcely any role to play in the image of a universe that operates by divine and faultless harmony. He is a sojourner in a world progressing steadily toward perfection. Various schools of thought have identified different primary mechanisms in this evolutionary process. The physiocrats looked upon agriculture as the key, nineteenth-century liberalism emphasized the doctrine of self-interest, and Marx saw the proletariat as the crucial instrument that would bring about the last stage of perfection. Basic to all these systems is a combination of doctrines of determinism and automatism. Human power is usually eliminated as superfluous. Here we observe a combination of essence-optimism and influence-pessimism, with a net positive effect upon the image of the future.

The most negative image of the future grows out of a combination of essence-pessimism and influence-pessimism. In this view of life chaos overrules cosmos from beginning to end, and man can do nothing except resign himself to the inevitable. Examples of this view are found in the concept of original sin, in the ideas of eternal recurrence, and in the concept of the evanescence of all human culture. All that is left to man is the possibility of a stoic *amor fati*, "love of fate," or suicide. The pendulum of history constantly swings between the two extremes. There is an extended area between these poles, however, where the thoughts of men are more wont to come to rest. Here we find the several possible configurations of essence-pessimism and influence-optimism, and the separate streams of thinking and doing converge. Certainly, existing reality is both precarious and disgusting. It is possible, however, to imagine a much better future, and it is even possible for man to work for this future. The conception of the nature of this work and the manner of approaching it may be one of relatively passive submission to a higher power, or an active exercise of the human will.

We can discern two main types of influence-optimism in these configurations, with two corresponding types of images of the future. In the one, man's role is indirect; the accent is on supernatural power and man's reconciliations with it. In the other, man's role is direct; the accent is on natural events and human effort. In these two different conceptions, the mandate of work is set against the mandate to pray. These are the two main paths to victory over the unknown. The religious route offers man the help of a savior. The secular route offers the philosopher's stone. They result in parallel images of the future—one eschatological, the other utopian—but they are not always separate: there are times in history when the two routes merge into one main highway.

Man and Culture

The most interesting problem is not so much the various modes of attack on the future, but the question of how various hierarchies of goals come to be established, and why certain means to chosen ends are valued in one historical period, and different means are valued in another. At any given period one finds a coherent culture-pattern into which the means-ends scheme of a given society fits. Each cultural epoch has its own uniquely fitting images of the future. It is also possible to relate the psyche of a people to their images of the future: "Tell me what your vision of the future is, and I will tell you what you are." This is, however, only a tautology. How do we account for the fact that each phase of culture, each type of human personality, appeared on the historical scene just when it did and in just that form? Why do cultural patterns and social attitudes change? What is the relationship between these shifting patterns and the changing images of the future? Specifically, why do we see such changes within the images of the future regarding the role of man and his feelings about the attainability of his goals?

Historically we are faced with a continuous process of transformation, sometimes gradual, sometimes in a series of abrupt shifts, from a passive and indirect influence-optimism to a more direct and active one, until at a given moment man suddenly seems to be bereft again of his will power. Thus, in the development of Western civilization we have seen man shift from a passive drift toward a future Kingdom of Heaven to a sudden seizing of the rudder with full mastery of the arts of navigation. His increasing skills in agriculture and medicine gave him a new power over life and death. Now, unexpectedly, the hand on the rudder wavers. Man continues to try to steer, but apathy has overcome him, and life seems to be but an "existence to the death." Was the faith in human power but a bubble, to be pricked so soon?

Any student of the rise and fall of cultures cannot fail to be impressed by the role played in this historical succession by the image of the future. *The rise and fall of images of the future precedes or accompanies the rise and fall of cultures.* As long as a society's image is positive and flourishing, the flower of culture is in full bloom. Once the image begins to decay and lose its vitality, however, the culture does not long survive. The secret of Greek culture, which came to its second flowering in the Renaissance, lies in the imperishable harmony of its image of the future. The endurance of Jewish culture, reborn today in Israel, lies in its fervently held image of the future, which has survived diaspora and pogrom alike. The prognosis of the dying Christian culture—if it can be said to be dying—lies in its dying image of the future. The primary question then is not how to explain the rise and fall of cultures, but how to explain the succession of shifting images of the future. How do virile and forceful images of the future arise, and what causes them to decline and gradually fade away? Furthermore, how do the successive waves of optimism and pessimism regarding the images fit into the total cultural framework and its accompanying dynamics?

19

Challenge and Response

Historical forces operate not only out of the past but also from the future. That man exercises influence over his future through the image he projects of it is only half the truth. The other half is that the future itself in its turn exercises a special influence over man and his images of the future. This kind of personification of the future can easily lead to mystification, so Toynbee's challenge and response thesis will be helpful here. According to Toynbee, that culture survives which can give timely and adequate responses to the ever-new challenges that are presented to it. But who makes the challenge? Toynbee would answer that the times make the challenge on the basis of the response a society has given to the previous challenge, and so the causal chain recedes into the infinite distances of the past. However, it is possible for man to look forward as well as backward. The challenge of the times can also be based on the future, which may challenge us to examine and prepare in advance to solve the problems it has in store for us. Certain possibilities out of an infinity of potential futures throw light or shadow on the present and can be further illuminated or darkened by the influence-optimism or influence-pessimism of the man who looks ahead. Out of the reverberations of the clash of past and future in the present, the image of the future emerges.

The future works upon the present only to the extent that the present can receive the challenging images it broadcasts. Man has to be tuned in to the right wave-length. Image-reception varies widely, however, not only from historical period to historical period, but from individual to individual during the same period. This is inevitable, since the shape of the future is not yet an objective reality, but a vision subject to the temper and spirit of whoever sees it.

Second, we must give closer attention to the manner in which the response to the challenge of the future is made. Toynbee maintains that just as the challenge varies in nature and severity, according to circumstance, so the adequate response must vary. It is in forging a response to a challenge that the members of the inventive and creative minority either pass or fail their crucial tests of competence. This is indeed true, but we would add that this adequate response can be nothing less than a comprehensive and inspiring vision of the future.

The challenge of our times consists in building up for the real future that which the possible future, by virtue of its relationship with the most recent past, is trying to demolish: images of the future inspired by a renewed influence-optimism, which can lift us out of the lethargy of our present essence-pessimism. So far, our generation has made precisely the wrong response to the challenge of our future. Nihilistic images are paralyzing us into an inability to forge more positive and constructive ones. Western man must never stop thinking and dreaming the materials of new tomorrows, for he has no choice but to dream or to die.

Definition of the Problem

In trying to give a systematic history of man's thinking about the future and the influence of this thought on the actual course of events, we have had to adopt criteria in order to select from the overwhelming amount of material available, and to stay close to our purpose.

Out of the vast array of historical images of the future, we shall be concerned with those that have sifted down through history into the receptacle we term Western civilization. We shall be especially interested in the influence the siftings from earlier periods have exercised, by dominating current attitudes and beliefs, on the development of this civilization. Specifically, we will try to ascertain whether the critical condition of still-revered current images of the future out of our own past is a factor in the present critical condition of Western culture. In general we will treat those images that best illuminate the problem of the future of our civilization.

In a systematic study of the future we must unfortunately exclude one of the most important sources of all knowledge, human experience. We can experience what has been, but not what is to be. We can experience what has happened to those images of the future and their anticipated futures, which now belong to the past. However, as soon as we want to change our knowledge *ex post* into an *ex ante* knowledge we have to tap supplementary sources. Only with the help of reason can the experience of the known provide a basis for a useful extension into the unknown. Science has already taken a long stride in the direction of predictions of the future by using models based on assumptions of specific periodicities or trends. Concepts of determinism have given way to concepts of probability. At the same time, specialization in science has led to an examination of more and more minute segments of reality, moving further and further away from total patterns of any kind. Irrational tools have contributed more to thinking about the future. Faith has been the most impor-

21

tant factor, with its ample tool-chest containing all the instruments of sacred knowledge. Next come philosophic thought, meditation, and speculations, sometimes coupled with asceticism. Last comes the realm of emotion, particularly those aspects concerned with hope, longing, and expectation. Intuition and ecstasy belong here, and most of all the power of the free creative imagination, which is indispensable to all thinking about the unknown. Thinking about the future requires faith and visionary powers, mixed with philosophic detachment, a rich emotional life, and creative fantasy.

What sources can we turn to in order to feel our way into thought about the future of other times and peoples? The symbolic language of the myth will tell us much. Religions and sacred writings and teachings will be helpful. We can also feel our way into the images of the future by studying the philosophers, scientists, and artists of the past who helped to create them. History itself will give us the broad picture of the image-life of a society.

The Problem Restated

By focusing on the idea of the future as the Other, the perfect antipode of the imperfect here-and-now, we automatically eliminate all those predictions of the future which do not stand in polar antithesis to the present. This elimination implies a basic distinction between utopian and eschatological visions on the one hand, and short-term or even long-term social planning on the other. The position here is that bold visionary thinking is in itself the prerequisite for effective social change, even when piecemeal amelioration is involved. We also reject the vaguer phenomena of thought about the future and focus instead on crystalized images of the future.

We are treating the image of the future both as an object for research and as a statement of the problem. In this time of culture-crisis the social scientist must be made aware of his role in the creation of the future, and to achieve this awareness he must also consider the image of the future as an object for research. It is time that the image of the future be introduced into the social sciences as a conceptual tool, adding to their diagnostic powers. The anticipatory image of the future is tested in the present book for its value in helping to write the history of the future, at least for the coming century. The concept of the personal equation is relevant here. The observer influences that which he observes. The formulation and description of images of the future may influence the future

22

itself, and the social scientist may rewrite the history of the future.

In addition to considering only those concretely expressed images of the future that are the antipodes of the present, we will further delimit our field by including only those historical images that are positive: those images that express optimistic belief that the Other world is not only different but better. These positive images may vary widely in content and orientation, ranging from the area of supernatural and personal salvation to the humanistic reconstruction of earthly societies. In every case they represent a high idea of a realm of the future: the Thousand Years' Reign of Christ, the Golden Age, or the New Zion. The special characteristics and functions of the negative image of the future typical of our own time will be examined in Part Two.

A sociological study of this kind must inevitably touch upon philosophy, theology, psychology, history, and anthropology. However, even in his capacity as a generalist, the sociologist is no less a specialist. He must give special attention to the dynamics of social change, particularly as they function in revolutionary changes in social institutions, cultural patterns, the spiritual climate, and the world-view.

Stated in sociological terms, the problems are these: what is the relationship between fundamental changes in the social structure and changes in the reigning images of the future? Is there interaction between images of the future and the future itself? More specifically, what are the implications of a disintegrating image of the future of Western culture for the future of that culture?

II. Images of the Future from Western Civilization

Chapter 3. Oldest Sources

In the last half-century the researches of archaeologists, biblical scholars, and cultural anthropologists have brought to light ancient cultures that were previously unknown. These discoveries have muddled orderly timetables of historical development that these same scholars have been at such pains to construct. Categories once assigned to the Assyrians and Babylonians, for example, have had to make way before a bewildering array of Sumerians, Aramaeans, Akkadians, Chaldeans, and other peoples. It is now even disputed that the Nile is the cradle of civilization. This continuing regression to ever-older sources of civilization is interesting, but not relevant to our purpose. Our main concern is with the process of transfer of images of the future; how far into the past the chain extends is of less interest to us than the demonstration of those links that are still relevant to our own present and future. Egypt and Mesopotamia, which have added to the fusion of ideas in Hellas, Persia, and Israel—historically, the three great cultures leading to our own—thus provide convenient places to begin our historical journey.

The influences from the Land of One River and the Land of Two Rivers have not been entirely the same. Both the Egyptians and the Mesopotamians were intensely preoccupied with the future, although their attitudes and motivations differed. The Egyptian preoccupation with death, evidenced by the *Book of the Dead* and the pyramid tombs, suggests that the prevailing attitude of the times was a very somber essence-pessimism. Nevertheless, the Egyptians believed in life arising out of death and faced the future with faith and self-assurance. The calm is the calm of a pyramided bureaucracy in perfect equilibrium, built to support the royal dynasty on top. The philosophy of life, then, is actually characterized by what we have called influence-optimism, both in its indirect form of achieving control over the environment through scrupulous attention to religious ritual, and in its direct form of unmediated and rational exercise of human power, as exemplified in engineering feats of irrigation control in the Nile Valley. The Pharaoh, son of the gods and high priest of his people, is the citizen of two worlds par excellence. As one who is initiated into the mysteries of the future and who mediates between the gods and men, he is able to work for the benefit of his people.

The reverberations we get from Babylonia sound a different theme. Here we become aware of what was to grow into the wailing tones of Genesis, Job, and Ecclesiastes, of the tragedy of man's fall and his curse, and of the punishing flood. The predominating notes are those of doubt, insecurity, and the feeling of human impotence. The belief in astrology, with its strongly deterministic character, encourages passivity. The distance between mortal man and the immortal gods can never be bridged. The accent falls on an essence-pessimism, although there is a seeking after salvation in the mystery religions of Ishtar and Temmuz, linked with the recurrent seasonal fruitfulness of nature. The astral double image of Ishtar is that of the morning and the evening star, symbolizing respectively war and love. Ishtar is both queen (power) and mother (life). Man is dependent on her supernatural power for his own life and power, but in this very conception of anthropomorphic dualism the split nature of man's mind is actively at work and becomes manifest. The struggle between man and God for control over the future has begun. Hellas, Persia, and Israel each witness this contest in its own way.

Chapter 4. Hellas

Everyone knows that classical Greece was a unique creator of beauty—in art, in human character, and in clarity of thought. But how many students of Greece are aware of its image of the future? Hellas *is* an image of the future, and the greatness of Greece lies in the fact that our modern Western civilization has been modeled on that image. Why, then, is it commonly held that Greece had no clearcut vision of the future?

In our discussion of Hellas, we will focus on the flowering of Greek culture that occurred between 1000 B.C. and 400 B.C. The Greek image of the future that matured during this period is such a harmonious expression of all the existing cultural elements that it blends imperceptibly into the overall cultural pattern. Hellenic man became the ideal representative of the harmonious split personality, living simultaneously in the here-and-now and in the Other world.

Another reason why the Greek image of the future has not been singled out as such is because that which was taken for granted by the average man of antiquity scarcely even occurs to the man of today. The unperceived Hellenic vision is but the mirror of our own decline, in which our own lack of vision stands revealed. The imaginative reconstruction of another world, which came easily and naturally to the Greeks, is hard to conceive of for technology-minded man. The entire Hellenic culture is suffused by its image of the future; the statues, the temples, the myths, and the intensely practical city-states are symbolic of the basic harmony between two worlds.

The Humanistic Image

The Greek image of the future is a positive vision of man's struggle
to fulfill his inborn potentialities in the face of divine sanctions and
inner weakness. The unique quality of this vision lies in the fact that
on the one hand the struggle is depicted as being tragically unequal,
while on the other the duty is laid upon man to take up the
challenge. At the height of their power, the Greeks relied relatively
little on magic and astrology. They took fate into their own hands
and boldly overstepped the permitted bounds of human behavior,
despite the punishments they knew the gods would have in store for
them. In a drama of tragi-heroic dimensions man perpetually struggles upward, is perpetually struck down by the gods, and is perpetually exalted even in his downfall. The sculptor molds the physically
perfect man. The poet sings of the ideal hero, perfect in courage. The
teller of legends and myths recounts the unceasing struggle of man
against his fate. The cults encourage man, who strains all things to his
own measure, to aspire to the divine. The ethic of the ideal man of
the future is socratic virtue, and the politics of the ideal state of the
future rests on platonic justice.

The Hellenic image is, above all, humanistic. Man is at the center.
It is man who strives to realize his *own* image through his struggles.
During the flowering of Greek culture, the locus of the image of the
future shifts from the realm of the gods to the world of men. This
makes relatively little difference to the content of the images, because the gods always personify distinctively human qualities, and
the ideal man always has distinctly divine qualities. There is, however, a shift in emphasis from manlike gods to godlike men as the
Greek image begins to materialize in the course of history. A corresponding shift takes place from emphasis on the relationships between gods and men to emphasis on the relationship between man
and man. Greek philosophy, striving to relate human thought and
cosmic harmony, has had an incalculable influence on Western
thought. Greek art, religion, political thought, and science, based as
they are on the values of the ideal human community, have been
fruitful both in creating images of the future and in creating the
future itself.

The Myth

The oldest components of the Greek image of the future can be found in mythology, a heterogeneous collection of material representing many layers of history. It is in the myth that the split personality first succeeds in conceiving the Other world and crystallizing its image of the future. The elementary forces of nature are represented as deities, and gradually Greek man creates a second nature for himself in which all geographical phenomena are animated by the supernatural. Every rock, river, and hill is the dwelling place of a specific god, and often of his family too. Gradually a complex world of gods evolves, not unlike the world of men, even to the point where the ruler of this Other world, Zeus, is not omnipotent.

The Greeks had a concept, inherent in all mythological thought, of an unchangeable natural order—what later Western thinkers were to call "natural law"—that stood above and beyond the unpredictable Olympian world. The Greeks called this *anagkè* or *heimarmenè*, "fate." *Anagkè*, however, is only one of the many personalities the Greeks made use of to symbolize fate. Probably no culture has ever created as many different images of fate as did Hellas. There is Moira, daughter of the Goddess of Night. There are the Three Fates, who tirelessly draw out the threads of life: Clotho holds the spindle, Lachesis draws out the thread, and Atropos, the oldest and grimmest of the sisters, cuts it off. When a thread is to be cut, Zeus himself cannot stay Atropos's hand. There is the goddess Tychè, symbolizing the vicissitudes of fortune; Nemesis, who metes out reward and punishment; and the Erinyes, the three avenging furies. Hellas would not be Hellas, however, if the ancient Greeks accepted destiny as final. The vision that was to become the Greek image of the future developed in the process of the struggle against this destiny. Strife is the father of all things.

In Greek mythology the creation of the world is accompanied by much tumult and fighting. Cosmos is created out of chaos through battle. Everyone fights—gods, demigods, giants, Cyclopes, hundred-armed monsters—and only after a long time is a new god, Zeus, able to establish and maintain order. This is not the end of fighting, however, but only the beginning of a new kind of rebellion, symbolized by the Promethean myths. Prometheus's desire to protect and defend men from the jealousy of the gods arouses the wrath of Zeus. Prometheus, after enduring an unendurable punishment bravely and worthily, is set free.

There are other myths with this same theme of *hubris:* the boundaries of the natural order cannot be overstepped without grave consequences. Icarus, who wanted to fly to the sun, and Phaeton, who wanted to drive the sun's chariot, are both destroyed. Mythol-

28

ogy delivers the prologue and sets the stage in readiness for the appearance of the chief actor, man. The gods stand aggressively in the wings, ready to interfere at any moment. Behind and above them lurk the inscrutable forces of fate and destiny. Against this background and in the face of these protagonists, man develops his own personality and his image of the future concerning his full humanity.

Poetry and the Drama

The *Iliad* and the *Odyssey*, singing of the adventures of immortal heroes, are the bibles of Hellas. They describe the ideal warrior and the ideal man, who combines in his character the beautiful and the good *(kalos kai agathos)*. But they are more than lyrical exaltations of heroes. Notes of fate and suffering, daring and despair, rebellion and utter defeat run through the epics. Man's consciousness of himself as a free agent has been awakened, and he butts his head against the stone wall of his own limitations. Man's struggling, suffering, and bending in the face of overwhelming forces are tragic, and yet his tragedy is the essence of the heroic way of life.

Hellenic man's conception of his struggle becomes ever sharper and more incisive. The conflict waxes hotter, the suffering becomes more intense, man more human, fate more threatening, and the vision of the future more exalted. In the tragedies, encompassing both the grief and the more lighthearted moments of man, Greece reaches its zenith and provides the irresistible momentum for Western culture.

In the Greek drama we find examples of voluntary and involuntary sinners, both held in the grip of fate. Innocent or guilty, the tragic man is doomed in the battle with supernatural power or with daemonic forces within his own soul. The overbold hero who tries to storm the gates of heaven is no more sternly punished than the quiet home-loving man who inadvertently treads on forbidden ground. Fate acts indiscriminately, according to its fixed standards. However, the noble man who is driven to evil deeds through the curse of his descent, retains his nobility and his heroic character to the end.

Sophocles plays on the theme of the accursed innocent in *Oedipus, Antigonè*, and *Electra*. An important shift takes place here in that the chorus, at once sympathetic observer and voice of warning regarding the doom to come, recedes into the background, and the spotlight falls on the fully responsible individual actor. The prospect of suffering and ultimate doom does not alter the task set before man, to live nobly and to die nobly. A different note is sounded by

Euripides, especially in *Medea*. The accents of resignation grow weaker, those of rebellion grow stronger. There is a sharp protest against injustice toward man, particularly against the infliction of divine punishment on the innocent. When the gods do evil they are not gods, says Euripides, thus bursting the bonds which tied men to an antiquated, anthropomorphic image of the deities.

Overall, Greek drama appears to carry a pessimistic message, as impotent man sinks under the weight of unmerited doom. But closer inspection reveals a layer of optimism beneath the surface. Tragedy does not consist simply in the downfall of man. That is not the main point of Greek tragedy, which in fact forcefully propounds a vision of the future for mortal man. It is Prometheus *unbound*. It is learning wisdom through suffering. If the hero dies, he dies master of his own soul, and thus triumphs over the future he does not live to see.

Death and Immortality Cults

Courage may overcome destiny, but it cannot overcome death. The very attempt to conquer death results in terrible punishment. Asklepios, who successfully practiced the art of healing, is tossed into Tartarus by Zeus for his pains. Sisyphus, who succeeded in keeping Thanatos, god of death, at bay for a time, is condemned to a task of eternal futility. Orpheus, a mere mortal, almost succeeds in rescuing his beloved Eurydice after she has already passed from the earth into Hades by the sheer power of his love and the beauty of his song. But the fateful human capacity for doubt interferes: Orpheus looks back at the critical moment and thus fails in his mission.

Although the final, insuperable barrier always remains, we see in these motifs of love, suffering, and doubt the milestones on the long road to the victory of life over death through the vision of things to come.

This profound revolution in Greek culture developed in three ways. First came the concept of the immortality of the spirit. Doomed by destiny, a hero becomes immortal in his very doom. Second came a change in the attitude toward death, reflected in the mystery cults. The Eleusinian mysteries, centering around the worship of Persephone, daughter of the goddess of fertility, who is carried off to the underworld to be Pluto's bride, created a vital link between death and life. Zeus decrees that Persephone shall spend six months of each year above ground with her mother, to ensure the

30

fruitfulness of the earth, and six months of the year below with her husband. Although the Eleusinian mysteries began as simple fertility rites, they gradually acquired a highly spiritual character. The once-drastic resolution in ending physical death was transformed into rebirth and a cycle of eternal recurrence.

The third and last transposition is symbolized in the dionysian and orphic mysteries. Dionysos, the exuberant god of wine, brings ecstasy to a society previously dominated by the sterner Apollo. As the god who is cruelly torn limb from limb only to be reborn again in glory, Dionysos is symbolic of the torn spirit of man, which is also reborn. In the end the dionysian mystery cults are fused with the more purely Hellenic orphic cults. Dionysos Soter reappears in the orphic mysteries as a savior who can bestow the gift of an immortal soul on his initiates if they follow the way. Now the religious image of the future is complete.

If Hellenic man is not the first, he is at least the most adaptable and versatile of that species, the citizen of two worlds. Thoroughly human, realistic to the core, he nevertheless has complete freedom of movement in a second realm and reaches his artistic zenith in combining the two.

It is no coincidence that the concepts of metamorphosis and of the amphibian, a creature who can lead a double life, are crucial in Greek thought. The gods can assume countless shapes, and men are turned into animals, trees, or whatever an avenging or rescuing god can think of at the moment. This fluid boundary between animals and men, and between animate and inanimate nature, symbolizes the two-in-one character of the here and the beyond.

The Philosopher Citizen of Two Worlds

Thus we have the ancient Greek before us: sober and boisterous, disciplined and passionate. Hellenic man faces squarely the ambivalence of his own nature and of reality in his search for ultimate values. Side by side with the religious image of the future, a philosophic image has also been developing as an intellectual liberation from the mythological world view. At first the Greeks scarcely distinguish between the wisdom of men and the wisdom of gods. The Delphic oracle, for example, is supposed to enable men to act on the basis of the wisdom of the gods. The temple of this oracle, however, is also inscribed with sayings of the seven sages of early Greek history, including "Know thyself." The train of thought from

"Know thyself" to Protagoras's words, "Man is the measure of all things," and to socratic man, who searched for truth above all, forms an unbroken line of development in man's search for power over his own destiny. The same progression follows in the history of Greek science.

Thales, who could foretell solar eclipses and crop failures, stood in no magical fear of the course of the stars. He replaced the mystery-shrouded, fatalistic concept of mythology with the unambiguous symbols of natural law. Once systematic relationships have been established, it is only a step to prediction of the future. Attempts to deal with the paradoxes of immutable being and ceaseless becoming again reveal the Greek genius for synthesis. Plato postulates a real, nonearthly world of eternal ideas of which the observable and changing phenomena of this world are but reflections. The human soul has perceived the ideal world before birth, and when it enters mortal man it carries images of the Other world of ideas with it as a dowry. Thus Plato fused religious and philosophical conceptions that are essentially images of the future.

In a second major synthesis, Plato fuses abstract metaphysics and social policy into a single model, the *Politeia* (actually "the body politic," misleadingly translated *The Republic*). This blueprint of an ideal society visualized within the framework of the existing city-state represents an attempt to escape the processes of change and deterioration, which the Greeks considered inevitable for human society. As Prometheus brought fire to earth from the heavens, so Plato brought the idea for the preservation of human culture. With this doctrine supernatural power is transformed and put at the disposal of human power.

How Image Worked on Actuality

Hellenic man acted on the course of his own future by shifting his focus in two respects. First, there was a gradual transition from indirect to direct influence-optimism. The idea that man could determine his own destiny and achieve his own liberation dominates the thinking of both Socrates and Plato. Second, there was a change in emphasis from individual determination of one's own destiny to collective determination of mankind's destiny. The concept of collective destiny is not new, but its initial appearance was limited to the curse afflicting all succeeding generations of a man who offended the gods. It was not horizontally conceived as affecting contemporaries, nor was it a destiny that could be worked for. It could only be accepted. A new kind of vision of the future emerged as man's focus of concern expanded from his own immediate family to the family of mankind. The transition to humanity as a whole and to the idea of man as such is made via the Promethean myth and the emerging conceptions of Greek democracy and justice. The Greek historians mirrored this transition. Herodotus still took a mythological view of destiny, while Thucydides, twenty years his junior, gave a genuinely historical insight into the limits of human control over events. Socrates made the last great leap to human autonomy at the cost of his own life, a price he *chose* to pay. Plato, finally, wrote the Greek "Ninth Symphony," outlining the ideal human community attainable by man's own efforts.

The last stage in the evolution of Greek culture represents a coming of age in the discovery of the highest human values, which in turn represent the Greek images of the future. They point to a coming *paideia*, the vision of a glorious civilization created by human effort. This *paideia*-creating man, who first emerged from the cocoon of Hellenic thought, was destined to be twice rediscovered in later eras: first by the Renaissance and then by the Enlightenment.

The denouement in the drama of Greek culture is tragi-heroic in typically Greek style. Suddenly the thread of life of Hellas was snipped, not because the Greek image of the future was decaying but, on the contrary, because of its rampant flowering. Greece went under because of the fatal weaknesses inherent in its own best qualities, as free personal development degenerated into unbridled individualism. The closed nature of the city-state was too constricting for the surging Greek spirit within. Individual fought against individual, city-state against city-state. Hellas disintegrated as a political entity at the very zenith of external unity and dynamic power. But even in political decline, Hellas achieved its greatest triumph: the spatial diffusion of Hellenism. The spiritual riches of Hellas and its unimpaired images of the future now spread throughout the whole Mediterranean world. Both of its major images, the utopian and the eschatological, participated in this diffusion process. The utopia of the ideal state lived on in the Hellenistic world-empire of Alexander the Great, gradually assuming the form of an ideal reign of peace. The eschatology of a future state of grace, developed in the Greek mystery cults, came in contact with Persian and Judaic images of the future, in a process of mutual influence. It also had its impact on the then-budding Christian faith.

33

Note on the Roman and Byzantine Empires and on Russia

The question may be raised as to why the two great Hellenistic concentrations which became the Roman Empire and the Byzantine Empire are not given special treatment in this work. In the case of Rome, no independent vision seeing beyond the present into the future ever developed, apart from the primarily geographic concept of a universal empire and its corollary of the Pax Romana. Since our study is concerned with images of the future that have shaped modern Western society, Rome clearly offers no test of our theory. In our view, the problem of Rome is not the problem of why it fell, but how it ever rose to such heights, and why it didn't fall sooner, since it lacked a positive image of the future. Was it merely moving along under the momentum gathered by Hellas, or were there other forces at work? We suggest that there were indeed other forces, which in turn point to the second reason why the Roman Empire is not included in our study.

It can be maintained that the Roman Empire never really fell, but lived on in its single vision of a universal world-empire until well into the Middle Ages, with Constantinople as its cultural capital and the Hagia Sophia as its religious center. The fact that the so-called Eastern Roman Empire maintained its vitality while other Hellenistic centers of culture gradually declined, and that Constantinople functioned as a meetingplace for East and West and as the citadel of Christianity a thousand years after the fall of Rome, presents a challenge to the historian. It offers a more stringent test for theories of cultural dynamics than does the Roman decline. Nowhere else do we find the messianic-apocalyptic imagery and the prophetic strains of primitive Christianity, including its original eschatology, so vigorously kept alive by official theology and dogma, even at the cost of a break between Constantinople and Rome.

In our opinion (and here we differ from Arnold Toynbee) this vision of the hereafter was the source of vitality of the Byzantine Empire, which enabled it to stand against fellow Christians and "heretic" Rome as well as against Moslems and barbarians. The waxing and waning of the Byzantine Empire is closely related to its ability to maintain and adapt its prevailing images of the future. There is some justification for saying that the Byzantine Empire never fell completely and finally, any more than did the Roman Empire, for it did not simply disappear, either as a temporal idea or as a physical entity.

Eastern and Western Europe did not form two separate compartments. Byzantine scholars were constantly drifting into Western Europe via Italy and enriching its culture, especially during the Renaissance. It makes sense to distinguish these two cultural entities, however, despite the interaction between them, and Eastern Byzantium thus must fall outside the scope of our study.

When Constantinople fell, Russian czarism took over Byzantium's holy mission, becoming the third Rome. Russian nationalism and internationalism continue to be pursued on the basis of this unchanged Byzantine image of the future. Russia has successfully given new life to this old vision. The Marxist image, also powered by eschatological and utopian forces, was skillfully grafted on as a new branch of the old vine. The Russian world outlook is not an artificial top layer superimposed upon the preceding development of the Hellenic-Byzantine-Slavic state of mind, but a quite natural and consistent outgrowth of a long historical process. One finds this unshakable and optimistic belief in the future rising over the whole range of Russian literature, even when the undertone is pessimistic, as in the writings of Gogol, Dostoevski, Pushkin, Vladimir Solovev, and Nikolai Danilevski.

The image of the future is the source of energy that powers Russian politics and policy. At the moment it contains an explosive charge which is upsetting the equilibrium of the international force-field. The final result of this flood tide of energy and particularly its repercussions on Western European culture depend on the potentialities of the counterforces. In the end, the future may well be decided by that image which carries the greatest spiritual power. The real contest is between ideological images of the future, perhaps particularly between the ideal American and the ideal Russian image. The further development of the older Western European images of the future and of newer Asian or African images may possibly cause the scales to tip either way. As yet, the course of history from the fallen Roman Empire that resulted in the unique mingling of Hellenic-Byzantine and Slavic-Marxist elements in Eastern Europe, has not modified the pattern of Western culture.

Chapter 5. Persia

Relatively little is known about Persia. There is no consensus on geographical extent, historical dates, or the degree of autonomy or development. In general, however, one thinks of the lands reaching from the Caspian to the Arabian Sea, and of a period between 1000 B.C. and 500 B.C. The little that is agreed upon by scholars concerns Persia's cosmic-religious image of the future, and consists of the following descriptive features.

1. A prophetic religion ascribed to Zoroaster, stemming from an old nature religion. A personal God now reveals himself and his intentions in regard to the future.
2. A fundamental strain of dualism, even deeper than that of Hellas, represented by the two kingdoms of light and darkness arising from one primeval source.
3. The concept of the end of the world with the final conquest of darkness by the god of light. A method of calculating time and dividing history into periods is developed within this framework.
4. The Day of Judgment, presided over by a messiah known as Saoshyant, which introduces the victory of the kingdom of light and brings in the additional concepts of reward and punishment.
5. The concepts of reward and punishment, which presuppose that man plays some role in achieving his own salvation. This doctrine of choice between the alternatives of good and evil testifies to a direct influence-optimism. Through purification and ritual, man can preserve himself from the influence of evil spirits.
6. In one offshoot of Mazdaism, Manichaeism, the emphasis shifts to future salvation in another world. The prophet Mani keeps the dualism of the kingdom of light and the kingdom of darkness. But

this world and man are seen as a creation of the prince of darkness and as a breach in the kingdom of light. Only through penitence and asceticism can man free himself from evil and ascend into the kingdom of light.

The prophetic religion of Zoroastrianism, in all its variations, owes its strength to its vision of what lies ahead. The worship of fire is symbolic of the fiery belief in this future. In the midst of many historical uncertainties this Parsee vision has exercised an enduring influence on human thought, particularly through its effects on Judaism and Christianity.

Chapter 6. Israel

Although the literature on Judaism could flood out many libraries, the people of Israel and their God remain shrouded in mystery. The scholars who came closest to dealing with the aspects of Judaism with which we are concerned are the German sociologist, Max Weber, in his work on the sociology of religion,[1] particularly his study of the Jewish prophets, and the Jewish theologian Martin Buber.[2] The Old Testament is, of course, the best source for the materials we need. Its wealth of imagery, sociological analysis apart, gives the sympathetic reader a vivid picture of the Jewish image of the future.

The known history of ancient Israel, in the broadest sense, extends from 1250 B.C. to 150 A.D., encompassing the fortunes of a number of different tribes in different geographical areas. To the oft-repeated question, "How did this people achieve such overwhelming importance in history?" we answer, "Because of the immortal quality of its image of the future." This answer implies that Israel had a unique image of the future, that this image had an imperishable quality, and that it had an unparalleled influence on the course of history. These images, which evolved a thousand years before Christ, have remained operative for three thousand years, specifically through the figure of Christ himself, affecting both Christendom and Islam.

---

[1] Max Weber, *Gesammelte Aufsätze zur Religionssoziologie*, Vol. III, *Das antike Judentum* (Tübingen: J. C. B. Mohr [Paul Siebeck], 1921), with a foreword by Marianne Weber.

[2] The following books by Martin Buber are of special interest: *Israel and the World* (New York: Schocken Books, 1948) (see his essay on "The Faith of Judaism," pp. 13 ff.); *The Prophetic Faith* (New York: MacMillan, 1949) (see Chap. 7, "The Turning to the Future"); *Israel and Palestine: The History of an Idea* (New York: East and West Lib., 1952).

The world-impact of Judaism presents a paradox. On the one hand, Israel was only able to exercise such enormous influence because its ideas and images were so different from those of its contemporaries. On the other hand, as in the case of Hellas, it was only after Israel's national identity was destroyed and the Jewish people were driven from their homeland that the full spiritual impact of the Judaic image of the future was felt. When this image ceased to represent the national unity of the Jews and came to represent an idealized unity, it achieved its fullest potency. We must first understand the nature of the ancient Jewish image of the future before we can fully grasp our own.

The Covenant Between God and Man

The key to understanding the Otherness that typifies Israel is to be found in the concept of the Covenant, the archetype of an Other relationship between God and man. The Covenant has two aspects: it unites a number of different tribes into Israel, and it binds this united Israel to a deity of its own. The first articulation of the Covenant comes in Genesis, with God's promise to Noah that floodwaters shall never again destroy the earth. The first negative foundation develops gradually into a positive, mutually binding contract. The Covenant is renewed and extended during the time of the patriarchal fathers—Abraham, Isaac, and Jacob—and again with Moses and Joshua.

The Covenant represents a give-and-take relationship between equals who arrive at an agreement through free mutual consent, backed by guarantees and sanctions on both sides. Jehovah binds and pledges himself to Israel, Israel binds and pledges itself to Jehovah. The conditions and commitments of the contract are made very clear. God promises salvation and blessing to Israel; in return, the people of Israel promise to believe. They will put their faith in this God only, and will serve no others. They will live according to his laws (set forth in the Torah), though the Covenant itself is not a written contract. Vows are binding on the basis of the spoken word alone, first in face-to-face encounters between Jehovah and man, later in dreams or in waking visitations to chosen individuals.

The Covenant, although concluded by word of mouth, is characterized by two special tokens, one offered by Jehovah, the other by Israel. As a token of his Covenant with Noah, Jehovah placed the rainbow in the sky, to reach to the earth. As a token of his Covenant with God, Abraham was ordered to institute the circumcision of every infant male born to Israel. Here we see the contours of the Jewish image of the future beginning to take shape. The rainbow symbolizes not only the promise of rain, so essential to the desert-dwelling Jews, but also the portal of hope. Through this radiant arch, the hand of God touches the earth. The circumcision seals this Covenant of hope with blood and pain. Not only does this rite set Israel apart from all other peoples, but it guarantees the fulfillment of the central promise of the Covenant: the continued existence of Israel as a people through the ritually dedicated male organ of fertility.

The Covenant, then, lays the foundation for the unique Jewish image of the future. In its own remarkable way Israel developed an original system of self-determination of fate, which was to determine the fate of the whole Western world for a long time to come, in the form of a pact with a self-assigned supernatural power. Everything in this image of the future speaks of Otherness: the Other God, the Other man, the Other destiny.

The Other God

The ancient Jews came in contact with many gods in the course of their nomadic wanderings. They did not deny the existence of other gods, but chose their own. And just as the Jewish vision foretold, the surrounding realms and their gods were eventually destroyed, whereas for three thousand years Jehovah has remained the God of Jews, Christians, and Moslems.

Jehovah is not a chthonian deity, concerned with the harvest cycle, nor is he a remote god, residing only in the heavenly spheres. Although his dwelling place is generally designated as being in the heavens, his field of operations is just as unmistakably here on earth. The God of Israel stands completely alone. His origins are not revealed. Lonely and solitary, he has neither wife nor child. For a long time he was the Nameless God: "I am that I am." Even as Yahweh he remains the hidden, invisible God, veiled in darkness. He is the God of whom, in his Otherness, no image may be made. Nevertheless, this God without an image stands central to the Jewish vision of the future.

In the beginning Yahweh was in some respects a kind of tribal king. He had anthropomorphic traits, which were strongly reminiscent of the Jewish patriarchs. Above all he was mobile, and he led the Jews in their wanderings. He was both far off and near. A military protector, he pitched his tent with his tribe like any commanding officer on the field of battle, and knew how to unleash the forces of nature against the enemy when the safety of his people was at stake. Like a good leader, he guided his people to the two great goals established by the Covenant: the spatial goal of the Promised Land, and the temporal goal of an enduring name, a perpetual national existence. The worship of Jehovah involved strict adherence to his laws, which covered every area of life, including political justice, social ethics, and community hygiene.

The relationship of Israel to this Jehovah is essentially a reconciliation of opposites: he is loved and feared, a stranger yet intimate, impenetrable and yet constantly revealing himself. The only certainty in the relationship is the movement toward the final goal, and Israel exalted above all other peoples.

The Other Man

Having the Other God, the Jew becomes the Other man, clearly set apart from Greek, Egyptian, or Babylonian man. In emphasizing the difference, the Jew inevitably awakens enmity in his neighbors. It is in the act of hearing and obeying the Other voice that he becomes the Other man. Although this double task is basically one, it contains the tragic seed of the struggle between split-man and supernatural power. The command to hear implies free, intelligent action in the present, according to the currently expressed will of God. The command to obey, however, implies the acceptance for all time of certain imperatives and taboos. Significantly, the text in Joshua speaks first of obeying God; only afterward is his voice mentioned.

Obedience to God's commands is the most basic trait in the Jewish religion. Infidelity to Jehovah is not just a betrayal of trust. It is a violation of his monopolistic rights and a turning to other gods. The whole concept of idolatry, of serving false gods, is for that time new and unique to Israel.

It has been remarked that Hellas was the spectator on the world scene, and Israel the listener. Greek man was predominantly visual-minded; the Jew was largely auditory minded: not the retina but the eardrum is the instrument of image-reception. Repeatedly Jehovah's presence is announced by thunder or the sound of trumpets, but only Moses actually looked on God, and that from behind. To Samuel he said, "I will do a thing in Israel, at which both the ears of every one that heareth it shall tingle." For Israel the divine encounter is entirely on the basis of the spoken word. It is the voice of the Lord that bridges the gap between "obey" and "hear." In Jewish history, these two worlds have always coexisted in delicate balance. At its best this balance represents a synthesis of human and superhuman power. On the one hand the written law, on the other the spoken word—together they shape the Other man, under the authority of the Other God.

The Other Destiny—What It is Not

The destiny of Israel is Other, both in what it is and in what it is not. The elements that are notable by their absence are primarily Eastern in character, while those that come to the fore emerge later as typical features in Western culture.

The Hebrew idea of destiny bears little relationship to the Egyptian, Babylonian, Greek, or Persian concepts. Most significant is Israel's lack of receptivity to the prevailing ideas in mythology, astrology, and eschatology. The mythical materials in the first twelve chapters of Genesis played a much less important role in the Old Testament than one would think from a study of the New Testament. Israel itself was much more concerned with historical reality, such as the flight from Egypt and the entry into the Promised Land. Nor did Israel possess a theogony for Jehovah. He simply appears out of nowhere to Abraham, a new and unknown divinity who justifies his existence through promises and establishes his legitimacy by fulfilling them. All Hebrew mythology is concentrated in the one all-embracing myth of the Covenant, and every myth is directed toward proving that Israel has been chosen by an omnipotent Jehovah to be his people.

The Old Testament is not lacking in symbolism borrowed from the magical lore of the East, but in general, magical practices are regarded coldly, since they threaten Jehovah's omnipotence. Although Abraham, the father of Israel, was born in the Chaldean city of Ur, cradle of astrology, cosmology had little interest for the Israelites. It is possible that in choosing to listen to Jehovah's voice, Abraham was making a deliberate break with the recognized supernatural forces of his time. The mysticism of the orgiastic cults stood in evil repute among the Jews, whose rocklike belief in Jehovah was more of a businesslike contract than a mystical experience. Although the prophetic tradition contains elements of individual ecstasy, the prophet's openness to the word of God is a far cry from the alcoholic delirium induced in other cults as a means to mystical union with the divine. Jehovah's appearance on earth, and especially his practice of speaking directly to chosen individuals, may be regarded as mystical events in the narrower sense of the word, but these phenomena all stem from the practical, verbal nature of the Covenant.

The function of eschatology is to round off and fill in the gaps left by mythology. Together they answer the ultimate questions, whence and whither. These questions never really arise in Hebrew thought, however. Israel is essentially agnostic concerning the ultimate meaning of human existence and the possibility of life after death. The promises of the Covenant refer to Israel's future on earth. Rewards and punishments are meted out here.

The Other Destiny—What It Is

The positive aspects of the Other destiny flow from the unique bipolar relationship between Israel and Jehovah. Three distinct factors in the determination of destiny may be identified: the Covenant, the religious observances, and the prophetic tradition connecting past and future.

The concluding of the Covenant is historically a unique act of human determination of destiny. But how can a man know what Jehovah's requirements for his behavior are, and keep up with Jehovah's changing moods and commands? This is the task of the priests and scholars. They study and interpret the Torah to obtain systematic knowledge of Jehovah's will for his people, and they study his signs and tokens in order to predict his plans. It is the prophets, however, who make Israel. The prophet is God's herald: more than a king, better than a priest. He shows the way to both ruler and ruled, and is chief interpreter of the Covenant. He is also a revolutionary: the champion of the poor and the oppressed, and the leader of the opposition. The prophet fosters the idea of personal responsibility: everyone must answer to his own conscience for carrying out the Covenant's commands. He does this the more effectively because he is usually of the people, rather than of the priestly élite.

Israel's repeated breaking of the Covenant brought about a breach in time. Between promise and fulfillment now stood the chasm of rejection and judgment. In the end, however, would come the day of which Isaiah speaks, "the day that the Lord bindeth up the breach of his people, and healeth the stroke of their wound." This is not to be a gradual evolution toward perfection. Rather, there would be a second temporal breach, this time in Israel's favor. Man has it in his own power to hasten or postpone the day of salvation. Thus, the prophets replace the idea of an arbitrary or hostile fate with a rational concept of man's role in shaping his own destiny.

Utopia and Eschatology

Originally the Judaic image of the future was utopian, but eschatological characteristics were gradually added to the point where it is impossible to draw sharp distinctions between the two traits. We will first examine the original image and then consider the transitional eschatological forms.

The Judaic utopia is implicit in the promise contained in the Covenant. Jehovah's prophets, especially Isaiah, Second Isaiah (chapters forty to sixty-six of the Book of Isaiah), and Ezekiel, were the first to paint a clear picture of this ideal society. Despite the major historical influence of this work, it is rarely mentioned in the extensive literature on utopism.[3] Isaiah and Second Isaiah give fragments of a more complete description of an ideal society, and Ezekiel systematically constructs an ideal state. While the Judaic utopia was conceived differently by the various tribes of Israel, there are features common to all the utopian images of the Jewish prophets. They are:

The World As It Is: The Jews expected their paradise on earth. The Promised Land could be geographically located and described: it flowed with milk and honey. Their vision focused on that part of this world which Jehovah was to apportion to them.

The World As It Will Be Remade: Not only is salvation to take place on earth, but earth is to be made new. The image of the future does then indeed contain a concept of an Other world, a world strikingly like the original paradise—reinstated by Israel.

The World of Israel: Israel has been promised perpetuation of its name and race. The house of Jacob and the house of David will be

---

[3] One exception to this is J. O. Hertzler's *The History of Utopian Thought* (London: G. Allen and Unwin, 1922), which contains a section on "The Prophets as Forerunners of the Utopias." Oddly enough, Martin Buber, the prophet of modern Judaism, makes no mention of the prophets at all in his recent *Pfade in Utopia* (Heidelberg: L. Schneider, 1950).

restored, Judah and Israel reunited, and Zion and Jerusalem reestablished. But that is not all; as the Chosen Nation Israel will be the center of the universe.

Israel, the despised and rejected, will be exalted above all nations. Small and undistinguished, it will nevertheless exceed other nations in glory, as Joseph exceeded in glory the brothers who sold him into slavery. Banished by all peoples, Israel shall become a beacon beckoning them back to her. "And there shall come forth a rod out of the stem of Jesse, and a branch shall grow out of his roots which shall stand for an ensign of the people; to it shall the Gentiles seek."[4]

The World of the Here-and-Now: The fact that the moment of realization is thought to be at hand gives a highly realistic character to the prophetic proclamation. It reveals Jehovah's short-term plans, so to speak, for the very near future.

The World of Man: The concept of responsibility for one's own destiny is firmly rooted in the Jewish prophetic tradition. Merely to wait in passive expectancy for the promised joy is not enough. There can be no salvation without conversion, no conversion without repentance, and no ultimate re-creation without the Last Judgment. The prophet's task, then, is to sound the call to a new life of righteousness.

It is these exhortations to Israel by the prophets, more than the laws and the commandments, which strengthen the social and ethical elements in Judaism. They bring into being a part of the utopian society that they anticipate.

At this point utopian concepts undergo a subtle transcending process that opens the door to eschatological concepts. The first step in this direction is a progressive spiritualization of promised joys that were originally earthly in nature. Jeremiah places more emphasis on the inward spiritual state of man than on the external features of the New Jerusalem. The change is even more pronounced in Second Isaiah and Ezekiel.

Two cornerstones of the Covenant are the circumcision of the flesh, and the concept of Israel as an enduring collectivity bound by the Covenant. Jeremiah employs "circumcision" metaphorically, not literally: "Circumcise yourselves to the Lord, and take away the foreskins of your *heart*, ye men of Judah and inhabitants of Jerusalem: lest my fury come forth like fire, and burn that none can quench it, because of the evil of your doings."[5] The same subtle

---

[4] Isa. 11:1.
[5] Jer. 4:4.

transition from fact to symbol, from purity of the body to purity of
the spirit, befalls the idea of a collective destiny for Israel. The old
Covenant united the tribes of Israel as one party to the contract with
Jehovah. This meant that every Israelite was personally responsible
for prior and succeeding generations as well as for his own. But
Jeremiah proclaims a time when men shall no longer say, "The
fathers have eaten a sour grape, and the children's teeth are set on
edge. But every one shall die *for his own* iniquity."[6]

At the same time that every Jew is made responsible for his own
acts and not for those of his ancestors, the sufferings of Israel as a
whole continue and increase. The historical caesure of the destruction of Jerusalem compels another interpretation of evil. Second
Isaiah provides a new theodicy in which, with axiomatic reversal, the
guiltless sufferings are represented as the will of God. The suffering is
no longer punishment for sins, but a sign of pre-election to a coming
salvation. To this end Second Isaiah introduces the figure of the
suffering servant: the sinless one, bearing the sins of many. The idea
of vicarious suffering now becomes incorporated into the image of
the future.

If Jehovah has chosen Israel to atone for the sins of all people,
including the Gentiles, this implies that Jehovah has grown from a
tribal God to the God of mankind. If Israel is to be the salvation of
all, this salvation can no longer include the idea of the earth as
especially reserved for Israel as the Chosen People. This salvation
acquires a nonearthly character, beyond space. Jehovah himself no
longer dwells in Israel, but on high, and his salvation shall be forever.
Ezekiel adds significantly to this concept of eternity: "Thus saith the
Lord God; Behold, O my people, I will open your graves, and cause
you to come up out of your graves, and bring you into the land of
Israel . . . And shall put my spirit into you, and ye shall live, and I
shall place you in your own land."[7] The spiritualization of salvation
reaches a new level in this proclamation of existence beyond time.
Before, death had been the end; immortality had applied only to the
name and race of Israel. Now the portal to eschatology has been
opened.

Much light has been cast on Jewish messianic thinking by scholars
looking back to the Old Testament from the New. But of greater
significance for the image of the future is the origin and development
of that thinking which looks forward out of the Old Testament. The

---

[6] Jer. 31: 27—31.
[7] Ezek. 37: 12—14.

46

Covenant provides the key to understanding this development. It establishes and maintains the expectation that Jehovah will one day again take the reins into his own hands. Just as the oldest prophecies about a coming salvation were related to prophecies about a coming king, so the oldest messianic expectations are built around the kings, the anointed ones of Jehovah. A king will come who, representing Jehovah, will be the perfect general, the perfect judge, and the perfect prince of peace.

Concurrent with this shift toward more eschatologically oriented ideas, another transition takes place, one that is closely allied with the repeated disappointments Israel suffered from the kings of the House of David. Slowly the messianic hope is liberated from this royal stranglehold. Such statements as "Behold, a king shall reign in righteousness" imply that this king might come from anywhere. Isaiah also speaks of Cyrus, a gentile king, who is to be his shepherd and work for the salvation of Israel.

As the concept of universal salvation becomes increasingly established as a process taking place beyond space, it also comes to be conceived as taking place beyond time. In times of disappointment with the royal house, the Jewish people remembered God's promise to raise a new prophet like Moses or Samuel. However, if he could raise a new prophet he could also bring back an old one. Once the redeemer is conceived to be supernatural, man drops the familiar crutch of all his racial yesterdays and trusts to that which is to come.

The relationship between Israel and Jehovah in the course of this spiritualization becomes at once more vague and more inward. Jehovah was never a god who begot children of his own, as did the Greek gods. The messiah to be sent by him was represented as human, though having no human father. Isaiah prophesied that a virgin would conceive and bear a son, to be called Immanuel. Daniel's vision of the Son of Man shows what a long road has been traversed from a trivial paradise for Israel on earth to a spiritual kingdom for mankind beyond space and time: ". . . Behold, one like the Son of man came with the clouds of heaven, and came to the Ancient of days, and they brought him near before him. And there was given him dominion, and glory, and a kingdom, that all people, nations, and languages, should serve him: his dominion is an everlasting dominion, which shall not pass away, and his kingdom that which shall not be destroyed."[8]

---

[8] Dan. 7:13, 14.

The apocalyptic visions to be found in the Apocrypha and other pseudoepigraphic writings represent both a continuation of and a divergence from the prophetic tradition. Written in the centuries immediately before and after Christ, these texts are deliberately predated so that they can accurately prophesy that which has already happened and thereby lend both credence and authority to the additional prophecies the writers put into the mouths of the Hebrew ancients. These latter prophecies are of great importance because of their influence on the subsequent flow of history. We are interested in those characteristics of the Jewish apocalypse that deviate from the picture we have built up so far of the Jewish image of the future. There is a sharpening of the dialectic idea. The new time represents a complete break with all previous time. The contrast between good and evil is also more sharply drawn, and the apocalyptic catastrophe achieves cosmic dimensions. There is a preoccupation with last times and with the esoteric knowledge that enables man to decode the cryptic plan and timetable of salvation. Finally, there is an intensification of the Other-worldly character of the image of the future.

The one utopian characteristic that is retained in the apocalyptic image is the Thousand Years' Reign, or the millennium. This chiliastic concept of a period which is to precede the Last Judgment represents an intermediate stage between utopia and eschatology. The movement toward eschatology introduces elements of determinism into the image of the future. In Nebuchadnezzar's dream about a colossus with feet of clay, for example, the giant was broken by a stone cut out of a mountain without the aid of human hands, after which the Kingdom of God was established. Not only was the grand finale predetermined, but the intervening acts were also laid down from the beginning.

The Cabala is a continuation of the apocalyptic tradition in the same sense that the latter is a continuation of the prophets. It contains a profound cosmology interlaced with a pseudoscientific number-symbolism; applied to the Holy Writ it results in predictions of the future. In its own peculiar way the Cabala preserves and passes on the Judaic image of the future as a living thing. In the nineteenth-century Cabalism found a modern mystical continuation in Hasidism, a movement of religious revival among the oppressed Jews of Eastern Europe. The legends and tales of the Hasidim, the "wise and pious men," deal with the deepest mysteries of life. The original core of the Covenant, between the Jews and God as between equal partners, is reactivated. As man wanders over the face of the earth pursued by suffering, God wanders and suffers with him. In this mystical atmosphere of reciprocity between God and man, the image of the future becomes a vital, dynamic longing for final deliverance. Every good deed brings this salvation closer.

Israel's Image of the Future

We said at the outset that Israel presents an enigma. How were a few nomadic tribes able to develop this unique religion, and how were the Jewish people able to remain spiritually intact over centuries of adversity? From our point of view there is no mystery at all. Israel's power is in her living image of the future. The power of the prophets and the revolutionaries, of Maccabees and Zealots, of Chiliasts and Hasidim, all came from this burning expectation for the future. With equal logic we may say that as soon as this image of the future dims or moves out of focus, the salvation it mirrors will also fade.

Chapter 7. Christianity

The image of the future revealed in the Gospels of Matthew, Mark, and Luke resemble in broad outline the Jewish utopia, to which Jesus places the crowning touch. Although the teachings of Jesus are concerned with future salvation in a re-created earth, and give less emphasis to a transcendental salvation than did the Jews, His appearance does not represent a breach in time, but rather a high point in the development of Israel. The disciple Paul was the first to try to interpret the arrival of Jesus as a breach in history. In doing so he encouraged the transcendentalizing of the image of the future, as we see both in his epistles and in the fourth Gospel. But a return to the Jewish prophetic-apocalyptic image of the future is unmistakable in the Revelation of John.

All of the Gospels are rooted in the Judaic matrix, and Jesus, the circumcised, is in spirit a typical Old Testament figure. He considered Himself, and was considered by His disciples, the Messiah of Jewish prophecy—Immanuel, the long-awaited Son of David, the King of the Jews, the Son of Man, the Christ. Both Jesus and His disciples knew the books of the Covenant intimately. At the beginning, Jesus founded a new Jewish sect, and directed most of His teaching to His fellow Jews. He was accustomed to attending synagogue on the Sabbath, and His first preaching took place in the synagogues of Galilee and Nazareth. The early Christian communitites were, in fact, patterned after the synagogue. Christian teachings were spread abroad largely through the Jewish diaspora, and the language of Jesus, especially in His use of images, is very consciously the language of the Jewish prophets. If Jesus can only be understood as a link in the chain of succession from the Jewish prophets, whom He described as the "key of knowledge,"[1] the same must be true of the image of the future that was central to His teachings.

The God of Jesus is unquestionably the One God, the Other God of the Jewish Covenant. The multitude, beholding His miracles, "glorified the God of Israel."[2] But with Jesus a new and gentler Covenant, proclaimed by the prophets, has been introduced. The Other God undergoes a further change. The accent is the love of God and love toward God: "You shall love the Lord your God with all your heart, and with all your soul, and with all your mind. This is the great and first commandment."[3] Unconditional obedience is not absent ("Thy will be done"), but the relationship of God to His people is more that of a generous and loving father to His children.

The sparseness of references by Jesus to the nature of the Kingdom He proclaimed may be explained by the fact that the people of His time understood so well what He meant that no explanations were necessary—the Kingdom proclaimed was basically the then-current Jewish image of the future. This implies that for Jesus the divine Kingdom of the future must have had the same strongly utopian characteristics as the Jewish prophecies.

A few words should be said about "Kingdom of God" and "Kingdom of Heaven." Matthew always refers to the Kingdom of Heaven, which could be misunderstood as excluding the Kingdom of God on earth. The Jews, however, avoided using the direct word for God, and often replaced it with the spatial circumlocution "heaven," where the throne of God was supposed to reside, as in "The Lord is in his holy temple, the Lord's throne is in heaven."[4] This did not mean that His Kingdom was only in heaven. Even Paul, who tended to spiritualize the teachings of Jesus, speaks of Him as delivering "the Kingdom to God the Father after destroying every rule and every authority and power."[5]

Jesus translates some of His own symbolism as referring spatially to this world. He explains the parable of the weeds in the field by calling the field the world, the good seed the sons of the Kingdom, the harvest the end of the world, and the reapers the angels. It is not to be wondered, then, that Jesus compares the Kingdom of God to a wedding feast, a pearl, a vineyard, or a field, nor that at the Last

---

[1] Luke 11:52.
[2] Matt. 15:3.
[3] Matt. 22:37, 38.
[4] Pss. 11:4.
[5] 1 Cor. 15:25.

Supper He foretells that "I shall not drink again of the fruit of the vine until that day when I drink it new in the Kingdom of God."[6] Jesus was not an ascetic. Nothing human was strange to Him. Whoever leaves house and field for His sake will be repaid a hundred-fold in houses and fields. These things are not surprising when considered in the context of the Jewish image of the future, which speaks of material abundance side by side with spiritual perfection.

No later interpretations or conflicting texts can erase the fact that Jesus thought the Kingdom was coming very soon. The Jewish prophecies and the apocalypses also contain this idea, but in the teachings of Jesus it acquires urgency and tangibility. When He sends His disciples to preach the Kingdom to the lost sheep of the House of Israel, He tells them that the Son of Man will come even before they have gone to all the cities of Israel and returned again. Jesus drastically shortened the time-span between present and future; everything points to a fast-approaching climax.

The image of man as seen through the teachings of Jesus is the mirroring of Christ's image of God: "You, therefore, must be perfect, as your heavenly Father is perfect."[7] Only a holy man is fit for the new Covenant with the holy God. In principle this was true under the old Covenant too, but the concept of holiness has changed. Jesus requires more than a yearning after the great moment. No prophet or teacher ever demanded so much activity or set such high goals for men to fulfill before they could be accounted worthy to enter into the Kingdom. Beyond deeds, Jesus makes clear that the God of love asks love from man. Repentance and conversion, the unreserved, passionate turning or returning to God are basic in the new view.

It is in His teachings about the relationship between man and man, however, that Jesus most clearly defines His utopia. The "reversal of the signs"—of minus into plus, of plus into minus—the turning upside down of all the usual social behaviors, is so radical and complete that religious scholarship has bent all its efforts through the ages to blur the openly utopian character of these teachings and blunt their impact by transferring them to the realm of eschatology. The teachings of Jesus are startling because He inverts everyday assumptions and thus shows them in a completely new light. Man must learn to think and act in an entirely different way, as if he lived in another world. He must love his neighbor as himself, and treat every man,

---

[6] Mark 14:25.
[7] Matt. 5:48.

including the enemy, as a brother. He must give, lend, and ask nothing in return. He must be merciful and judge not. The requirement is perfection in love, forgiveness, justice, and piety.

Jesus travels the road first taken by the prophets of Israel to its ultimate destination, utopia. His concern, too, is for the humble and the oppressed, and it is above all among them that He finds true devotion. Preaching good news to the poor, Jesus emerges as the great revolutionary, as differences of class and condition fall away. Before God all men are equal, the children of one Father. Jesus stresses in a new way the old Jewish proverb that God "makes his sun rise on the evil and on the good, and sends rain on the just and on the unjust."[8]

Christ preached the brotherhood of man and the community of possessions as it would be practiced by the first Christian collectives. The feeding of the five thousand becomes the model of sharing. As a social idealist and utopist He had no equal. He was concerned also with the exercise of human power of man over man: "Blessed are the meek, for they shall inherit the earth."[9] And again they will inherit it by a reversal of the usual behavior; instead of the armed rebellion practiced by the Zealots, Jesus preaches the opposing of violence by nonviolence. Passive obedience to the temporal authorities (incarnation of the Evil One) who placed an image of the Emperor in the imageless temple of Jehovah, was far more effective than open rebellion and disobedience. Pontius Pilate sensed this. Here indeed was "truth."

For a place in the Kingdom man must stake nothing less than his whole life. The puzzling text "From the days of John the Baptist until now the kingdom of heaven has suffered violence, and men of violence take it by force,"[10] makes sense in terms of this concept of strenuous exertions on behalf of the Kingdom. No man is exempt from the responsibility to take up his own task and follow in the path of revolutionary leaders like John the Baptist and Jesus Himself. Jesus completes and perfects the indirect influence-optimism of the Jewish image of the future, the unshakable faith in God coupled with invincible human determination. He who asks will receive, he who seeks will find, and he who knocks will find the door opening.

---

[8] Matt. 5:45.
[9] Matt. 5:5.
[10] Matt. 11:12

Transcendence in the Image of the Future

In the New Testament we see the same process of transcendence and spiritualization taking place in the image of the future as was observed in the Old Testament. The Gospel of John and the Epistles of Paul provide the main supports. Jesus no longer recognized the authority of dogma laid down by the Jewish priesthood. Christology and the cult of the church were, of course, developed well after His time, as His simple teachings were interpreted and elaborated. Avoiding as far as possible the theological problems of Pauline and other interpretations, we will confine ourselves to a few observations directly pertinent to our theme.

Paul systematically went about separating the teachings of Jesus from their Jewish antecedents. Most of his Epistles reflect this, particularly those to the Romans and the Hebrews. He sets Jesus above Moses, for Christ is the end of the law.[11] He is the new priest of the new Covenant: ". . . Christ has obtained a ministry which is as much more excellent than the old as the covenant he mediates is better, since it is enacted on better premises. For if that first covenant had been faultless, there would have been no occasion for a second."[12] Jesus, then, is the caesura between Judaism and Christianity.

For Jesus the Kingdom of God is central, but for Paul, Christ and the Kingdom of Christ stand central. Jesus taught the triptych of repentance-conversion-forgiveness, but Paul taught that of suffering-resurrection-redemption. Paul provides the point of departure for a Christology that overlays and eventually stifles the Judaic image of the future. For Paul the new order has already arrived with the appearance of Jesus. He who lives in Christ is already another man, even under the present earthly dispensation.[13] With Paul, the future passes into the background. Already, in accepting Jesus, man comes to fullness of life in Him.[14] The proximity of the time has been exchanged for the proximity of the person.

Along with the emphasis on the person of Christ comes the doctrine of original sin. Committed by one man and visited upon all, it is now taken away by one man for the sake of all. The first Adam was of the dust, the second Adam is of heaven.[15] This doctrine

---

[11] Rom. 10:4.
[12] Heb. 8:6, 7.
[13] 2 Cor. 5:17.
[14] 2 Cor. 2:10.
[15] 1 Cor. 15:45—7.

strengthens the concern for salvation and weakens the individual will to action. To live in Christ through baptism and to be crucified with Christ in the flesh gives a new life now, immediately, and a promise of resurrection with Christ and eternal life after death. The emphasis on life after death is in deliberate contrast to Jewish agnosticism on this point. Salvation of the human spirit from its earthly chains, or immortality, becomes of more importance than salvation from suffering on earth. When the Kingdom comes it will be by the hand of God, and not as a result of man's striving. Good works, retained by Jesus from the Jewish tradition, make way for faith and grace. Paul's influence-pessimism leads directly to the Augustinian teachings of predestination.

Is the Kingdom of God to come on earth? The Kingdom of God, says Paul, does not mean food and drink, but righteousness and peace and joy in the Holy Spirit.[16] Flesh and blood cannot inherit the kingdom of God.[17] Little is said about the signs of an earthly advent. The tendrils from the vine of Jewish prophecy that were entwined in the teachings of Jesus begin to wither away.

"Now faith is the assurance of things hoped for, the conviction of things not seen."[18] Again and again the early Christians are told to persevere in hope. Had Paul perhaps grown wiser through the unrealized expectations of Jesus for the near future? Was he himself disappointed over the Second Coming that never came? In his Second Epistle to the Thessalonians he tries to quiet the rising excitement over the Coming, but nevertheless still writes as one who in principle shares these expectations.[19] Four or five years later,[20] these expectations are still very real to him. He writes with urgency to the Corinthians not to waste time in dealing with matters of this world, for "the appointed time has grown very short . . . the form of this world is passing away."[21] The tone of one of his last letters, written to the Ephesians, is very different. Expectations of an imminent Coming are not even mentioned, and the letter is full of

---

[16] Rom. 14:17.
[17] 1 Cor. 15:50.
[18] Heb. 11:1.
[19] 2 Thess. 2:1, 2.
[20] The chronology of the epistles is not the same as their order of appearance in the New Testament. Thus, the Epistle to the Thessalonians comes first historically, probably written in 52 A.D. The first Epistle to the Corinthians has been dated at approximately 56 or 57 A.D., and the Epistle to the Ephesians at 62 or 63 A.D.
[21] 1 Cor. 7:29—31.

long-range advice concerning how the Christians ought to conduct themselves on earth.

Is Paul then no longer primarily concerned with the future? This can certainly not be said. "One thing I do," he writes to the Philippians, "forgetting what lies behind and straining forward to what lies ahead, I press on toward the goal."[22] The goal, however, has shifted its focus from earth to heaven.

While Paul is passionate enough in his zeal for the Kingdom, his view of man's role in determining his own destiny and bringing about this Kingdom is passive to an extent that later opened the way for the development of Quietism. The heroic, revolutionary, and utopian ethic sinks gradually to the level of a comfortable middle-class outlook on life. The utopia of Jesus makes way for the nonworldly eschatology of Christ. This line of development is drawn even more sharply in the Gospel of John. Not only does Christology become increasingly the central focus of the teaching, but other elements are added through Hellenistic influences. One can now speak of the Christ-mysteries and the *logos*-metaphysics.

Jesus is no longer primarily the Prophet who announces the renewal of human society on earth, but rather the Redeemer. It follows that the center of gravity of the future shifts into the past (the time of Jesus), with a corresponding emphasis on the life of the present as rooted in history. This regression is pointed up by the fact that the Kingdom of God is only mentioned twice in the entire Gospel of St. John. Its earthly aspect, as well as the idea of a coming breach in time, have been completely sublimated. The well-known text "My kingdom is not of this world"[23] has, moreover, been further narrowed by the interpretation "My kingdom is not for this world." The net result is that the eschatological expectation of a cosmic re-creation at the end of time, already stripped of its utopian content, becomes a spiritually empty expectation. The realm now referred to is not a new order, but is rather the eternally existing divine order. Both the utopian expectations for the future, and the eschatological ones, welded together by Jesus, are seriously weakened hereby. Jesus, Prophet of the future, has, according to this Gospel, prophesied Himself. For this reason John is able to portray Jesus as saying "I have overcome the world" in the past tense. The Jesus of John does not cry out on the cross the messianic laceration, "My God, my God, why hast Thou forsaken me," but breathes the

---

[22] Phil. 3:13, 14.
[23] John 18:36.

serene words of fulfillment, "It is finished." The great overturning has already taken place; the *kairos* is behind us.

We may ask of John, as of Paul: Is he no longer concerned with the future? Again, this can not be said. John's mysticism, however, no longer has a cosmic, but rather an individual, focus. Expectations for the future become concentrated on the individual soul and on the ecclesiastical community, to which the coming spirit of truth will reveal all things. This is a thought which will find its completion in St. Augustine. The later church sacrament of partaking in the mystical body of Christ is suggested here: "He who eats my flesh and drinks my blood has eternal life, and I will raise him up at the last day."[24] The symbolic body of Christ thus comes to obscure His actual reign. The radical ethics and social utopism of the Sermon on the Mount are no longer visible.

Perhaps the fate of the image of the future would have been sealed for once and for all, if it had not flamed up with renewed intensity in the Book of Revelation, that much-disputed last book of the New Testament which after a long struggle was finally accepted into the canon. Revelation, generally assumed to be of the same date as the earliest gospel writings, is probably a Jewish apocalypse in a Christian adaptation.[25]

Written in esoteric language, the revelations in this book of St. John the Divine parallel the traditional apocalypse. The descriptions, with many quotations from the prophets of coming catastrophes, are also true to the tradition of "blessings through doom." Here they are related both to the battle with the Antichrist (the dragon with seven heads) and to the struggle with Rome (represented as Babylon, the mother of harlots, and also as the Great Beast).

What is unique in Revelation, however, is the remarkable synthesis between Jewish and Christian delineations. The first four chapters, with the seven letters to the seven churches, and the final admonition in Chapter 22, form the Christian framework. In between stands Jewish mythology with Christian interpolations. They do not always form a harmonious whole. The threads of two different conceptions of the Messiah seem to run right through the book; one is the Jewish vision of "he who is still to come," the other is the Christian image of "he who has come." The first is a portent, a woman with child (Israel), "clothed with the sun, with the moon under her feet, and on

---

[24] John 14:2—7; 12:32.
[25] This is also presumed by some scholars to be true of such pseudoepigraphic writings as the Testament of the Twelve Patriarchs and the Sibylline Oracles.

57

her hand a crown of twelve stars."[26] The second, which has already appeared, is the Lamb. It is the Lamb that is meant in the repeated call for return, *mara natha*, Come, Lord Jesus; and in the repeated affirmation, "I am coming soon."[27]

In addition to the image of a return at the end of time to earthly paradise, Revelation contains an analogous expectation of a utopian intermediary stage, which will provide a foretaste of eternal bliss: the Thousand Years' Reign of peace during which Satan will be seized and chained, finally to be released and thrown into the pool of fire with the people of Gog and Magog at the time of the Last Judgment.

This divine interim, with its first judgment and first resurrection, was what most captured the fascinated attention of believers as coming first and soon. The final end was much more remote. The Revelation of St. John thus became a continuing source of inspiration for all later chiliastic and adventist movements. It was the smoldering fire that blazed forth again and again, particularly in the Middle Ages, in fiery expectations for an imminent earthly Coming.

The Christian Image of the Future

To speak of *the* Christian image of the future, as we have spoken of *the* Jewish image of the future, is impossible. There are several Christian images of the future, differing in character and influence.

At two extremes stand the Gospel according to St. John, with its strongly Hellenistic orientation, and the Revelation of St. John, with its intensely Jewish strain. In the first, the horizon of the future does not extend far beyond individual salvation and the Christian community, and this Gospel becomes the bastion of the established Church. In the second the horizon expands to include both the descent of God's Kingdom to earth and the Thousand Years' Realm which is to precede it; Revelation thus provides authoritative support for the more dynamic sects.

In the exegesis of the New Testament, according to the point of view, either the Gospel of St. John or Revelation is devalued. It is not possible to do this with the teaching of Jesus in the Synoptic Gospels. Instead, His teachings are skillfully shunted aside by reclothing the rebellious Jesus, who turned the world upside down, in the garments of Christology. Thus Jesus the violent revolutionary, as

---

[26] Rev. 11:15 — 12:17.
[27] Rev. 22:7, 20.

described by Flavius Josephus, is hidden behind the mystical mask of the Christ.

Paul, whose position lies midway between the two extremes, makes the best of both worlds. He is indeed the first Jewish-Christian theologian. His theology, however, contains the elements which in their further development will undermine Jesus's image of the future, both in its utopian and eschatological aspects. But not yet. Not in the time of the earliest Christians, when the visions of Jesus and Paul evoked the spiritual transports of martyrs and saints, the potent witness of the Christians of the catacombs.

Such is the propulsive power of these images that it brings about a new era, in which all the signs are reversed again: a time in which the church can claim to incarnate the Kingdom of Christ on earth, whereas Jesus Himself had inveighed strongly against the Jewish tendency toward ecclesiasticism; a time in which the Roman Empire is granted the attribute of divinity as the Holy Roman Empire, whereas the teachings of Jesus contained a liberation from temporal power and the Book of Revelation had directly attacked Rome. So phenomenal was this original power that the centuries-long process of watering down the core of the image of the future that Jesus evoked has to all appearances not damaged the future of Western Christianity. To all appearances!

When Nietzsche flung his fell accusation at the world, "There was in fact only one Christian, and he died on the cross," it was, in a certain sense, an understatement. After Christ's bodily death on the cross His own disciples executed him once more spiritually.

At first it was Jesus, the Nazarene, that was preached. On the road to Damascus Jesus transformed Saul into Paul—and then Paul in his turn transformed Jesus into Christ. Jesus, the mortal man, had His share of human imperfections and failings. During thirty years He grew toward his inescapable future, into the Christ sent by God. Later the picture is reversed, and the eternal Christ, infallible, divine, and omniscient, becomes the predestined and metaphysical Jesus, appearing on earth in the flesh. In the first centuries baptism was done in the name of Jesus; after the Council of Arles in 314, it was performed in the name of the Trinity. The hope is no longer for a return of Jesus in the flesh, but for a return of Christ in the spirit. The gospel, the Glad Tidings of Jesus, is painfully compressed in the transition, and possibly in the long run doomed to death.

The Jewish image of the future has managed to survive throughout centuries of historical ups and downs and even of fundamental alterations in structure, with its power and elasticity unbroken and its core basically unharmed, or perhaps even better adapted and strengthened. Christianity, on the other hand, we will see undergoing serious crisis after a history of less than two thousand years. First it purified itself of Jewish and apocalyptic utopism and then tried to rid itself of synoptic and mythical eschatology. The resulting crisis would have dangerous consequences both for the Christian faith and for the foundations of our culture.

Chapter 8. The Realm of the Future in the Middle Ages

The passage of more than a thousand years from the first beginnings of Christianity through the Middle Ages encompasses a variety of developments which defy brief description. Even when the Middle Ages are viewed as a structurally unified cultural period, great contrasts present themselves. It is a period of growth from immaturity to overripeness, from grossness to refinement. The contrasts all stem from the basically split nature of the era. The very term Middle Ages, the idea of a *media tempestas*, comes from an outdated classification, product of the humanistic Protestant image of the future that divides historical time into antiquity, the Middle Ages, and modern times.[1] The Middle Ages are clearly stamped with Roman Catholicism, a fact that predisposes to oversensitivity on the one hand and undervaluation on the other.

One or another of the preceding facts may in part account for the scant attention that medieval images of the future have received. The gap cannot be closed here, but we do wish to stress that this period forms an indispensable link in the historical chain of ideas concerning the future and to summarize certain aspects of the era:

1. Any evaluation of the Middle Ages as a static period is unjust. On the contrary, it was a dynamic epoch with its own special picture-gallery of the future.

2. The expectation of the coming Kingdom of God is central to

---

[1] Most historians of utopism pass lightly over the Middle Ages or ignore it entirely, jumping nearly two thousand years from Plato to More. W. J. Aalders in his *Toekomstbeelden van vijf eeuwen (Images of the Future of Five Centuries)* (Groningen: J. B. Wolters, 1939), deals almost exclusively with modern times.

medieval thought, though these expectations underwent remarkable undulations, with alternations of tension and relaxation. Irreconcilable views of the relationship between man and the world, man and the church, and man and God existed side by side.

3. It is the medieval images of the future that carry the Hellenistic-Persian-Jewish-Christian heritage over into Western culture. These projections become the building blocks of the new postmedieval culture.

4. In counterpart to the aforementioned continuity is a dialectic which carries the potential of the dissolution of medieval images of the future. The same images that represented a religious integration of transcendent and eschatological points of view gave rise to the later areligious or even antireligious humanist and socialist images of the future. Through its images, the Middle Ages begot not only the Reformation but the Renaissance and even the Revolution, as well as the later romantic Neomedievalism.

In order to gain a comprehensive grasp of the image of the future of the Middle Ages, we will limit ourselves to the study of only two outstanding, partly parallel lines of development, which are medieval extrapolations of biblical images already described. One image stems from the Apostle Paul and the Gospel according to St. John blended with a Gospel-like evangelism and Hellenistic ideas. The other has the Book of Revelation as its Magna Carta, blending Jewish and Persian influences. Two independent images of the future are finally crystallized. In the first, the thread moves from this world toward the Other; through the image, the world is remade and raised to heaven. In the second, the thread moves toward this world from the Other; through the image, heaven spreads like a tent over earth. The first represents an increasing spiritualization, the second an increasing materialization.

Related to this difference of transcendence versus immanence is another, more profound distinction. In the first image the tone is deterministic; history is preordained, and the role allotted to man a passive one. In the second, history is liable to change through the application of human power, and man's role becomes active. It would not yet be entirely accurate to apply the labels of eschatology and utopia. Despite the essential difference between these two images of the future, each contains a combination of both eschatological and utopian elements. Nevertheless, in one the accent is on eschatology, in the other it falls on utopia. The Middle Ages demonstrate that the current conflict between utopia and eschatology does not exist in logic and has not always existed in reality.

Spiritualization

Spiritualization is not a natural process but an artifact of scholars and metaphysicians. In the Middle Ages the Kingdom of God is spiritualized through the successive operations of a small intellectual elite of theologians, ecclesiastics, and mystics. Three aspects of this process of reshaping the image of the future can be observed in the church, the world, and the realm of the spirit.

The Church

Ideas and concepts from gnostic and neoplatonic philosophies were introduced by the earliest Christian teachers and skillfully woven into the teachings of Paul and John to produce the so-called eclectic *logos*-mysticism. Some of these teachers were sainted, others were declared heretic. The distinction between saint and heretic, which tends to become fluid with time's passage, is not always relevant in assessing the influence of the ideas involved, either on their contemporaries or on posterity. Church fathers sometimes proclaimed false doctrines.

Origen of Alexandria was one of the early spiritualizers. Opposing the Jewish apocalyptic-utopian ideas concerning a material Kingdom of God on earth, his heavenly Jerusalem takes on the appearance of Plato's ideal state and of Homer's Elysian Fields. The Jewish idea in Revelation of the Thousand Years' Reign of Peace is also abandoned. What is important is personal salvation after death. Cosmic eschatology retreats in favor of individual eschatology. St. Augustine brings this idea into sharper focus. There is a pronounced platonic influence noticeable in *The City of God.*

There is much disagreement over the writings of Augustine, [2] whose ideas changed radically during his lifetime. The allegorical terminology in *The City of God* lends itself to divergent interpretations. Historians of utopism and eschatology both claim him for their own. It would be more productive to note the often-ignored duality in Augustine, weighted though it is in the direction of transcendence. Fundamental to the Augustinian image of the future is a split between this world and the Other world. The political kingdom of earth and

---

[2] One of the best nontheological works on this subject is Edgar Salin's *Civitas dei* (Tübingen: J. C. B. Mohr, 1926). An earlier, comparable work by the same author is *Platon und die griechische Utopie* (Munich: Duncker u. Humblot, 1921).

the devil on one hand, and the redemptive heavenly Kingdom on the other, represent, respectively, the fall of Adam and salvation through Christ. During his earthly pilgrimage man is necessarily a citizen of two worlds.

St. Augustine's contribution is his interpretation of the events leading to the mysterious leap into the Other realm. The leap is twofold: first, the leap of the individual man, and only second, that of mankind as a whole. The last day on earth of the individual man takes precedence in Augustine's thinking over the last day for the species man. Death and hell receive increasing attention during this period and ultimately become the major obsessions of medieval man.

To the question "What must I do?" Augustine's frank and outspoken answer is "Nothing, beyond maintaining complete faith in and utter obedience to God." In contrast to Origen, Augustine sees sinful man as helpless in spite of himself and his own will.[3] Since the Fall, every man belongs to the mass of the damned *(massa damnata)*. Augustine's doctrine is symptomatic of a highly important regression; it almost annihilates the nascent idea of independent human power acting for the good. Human faith and divine grace are the poles between which life on earth moves. God determines, through Christ, who shall enter His City.

Does the sin-laden creature thus stand utterly alone in this life? No, on this point the apostolic-charismatic tradition is maintained. The Church dispenses grace for the earthly existence through its mediators, and administers the last sacraments at the time of passing into the beyond. The Church's later attempts at self-deification are firmly based on Augustine. The Church as a kingdom comes to embody the pilgrimage of the Kingdom over the earth through time until the moment of elevation arrives. According to these conceptions the Kingdom of God is at once that which is to come and that which has already come. If the Kingdom of God has already appeared on earth through the First Coming of Christ, and if the Christian Church is really bringing about the evolution of this Kingdom into its ultimate and final state through its dedicated actions— then, says St. Augustine, drawing the logical conclusion, the last times have come!

Augustine is chiliasm's[4] sharpest opponent, not through denial of

---

[3] The term "free will' is intentionally avoided here, since there is great controversy over Augustine's thought on this point.

[4] The Council of Ephesus pronounced chiliasm as a heresy in 431, the year after Augustine's death.

its claims, but by proclaiming that they have already been realized. This point of view relegates the remaining course of history to a minor place in the perspective of imminent divine fulfillment of time and also permits Augustine to remain somewhat aloof from the Holy Roman Empire. The kingdoms of this world come and go. Even Holy Rome could become a second Babylon. The Kingdom of God will come independently of the *civitas terrena* and in conflict with it. The City of God and the earthly city are now existing concurrently, interpenetrating one another, locked in an intense struggle. The last Judgment will bring the final separating out through the establishment of the dominion of the Kingdom of God.

On balance, though Augustine's image of the future is indeed an ingenious mix of utopia and eschatology, as an image it has lost much of its power. The task imposed on the Roman Catholic Church is the utopian striving toward perfection on earth. On the other hand, the doctrine of the grace of a God who intervenes in the course of history is an eschatological one. However, both utopian and eschatological images of the future are weakened. The eschatological system pushes this world into the background as a temporary but necessary evil. This deprecation in advance of all historical kingdoms diminishes the meaning of the human struggle. Further, preference is given to eternal life for the individual, above a renewal of earthly life for mankind.

We are here concerned with very subtle shifts in accent whose effects are only noticed much later. In the Middle Ages proper, as already stated, Christian expectations for the future were still overwhelmingly upward-directed. Also, the Holy Roman Empire, considered the partial crystallization of these expectations, was designed to further this nonearthly goal.

The World

Despite the potential weakening of St. Augustine's modernized image of the future, the older image retained its influence undiminished in one respect, the belief that the end of the world was close at hand. The gradual overvaluing of the present in the thinking of the Church could not extinguish man's profound longings for the future. The hoofbeats of the approaching apocalyptic riders are repeatedly heard as echoes from that Other, coming world.[5] The terrible "How much longer?" was the haunting spectre that tortured the medieval

---

[5] Rev. 3:20.

mind. *Quo usque tandem?*

From earliest times eminent Christian thinkers have pondered deeply the end of the world and the dawning of the last days. Only a few illustrations of this facet of the medieval image of the future can be considered here.

Origen devised a scheme of five periods based on the parable of the workers in the vineyard:[6] the early morning (Adam), the third hour (Noah), the sixth hour (Abraham), the ninth hour (Moses), and the eleventh hour (Jesus). An analogous division of time into six ages based on the six days of Creation received more attention (this idea is Jewish in origin). Each of these six periods is conceived as being one thousand years long, since in the sight of God a thousand years is as a day;[7] the seventh period, corresponding to the day of rest after the act of Creation, is the *tempus ultimae quietis,* the world Sabbath. Many Christian writers, beginning with Barnabas, recorded this sixfold classification. These ideas were so firmly imprinted on the minds of people in the Middle Ages that the approach of the year 1000 gave rise to widespread expectations concerning an imminent end of time.[8]

St. Augustine accepted a similar sixfold classification, inferring a correspondence between the six days of Creation, the six stages in the life of man from infant to graybeard, and six stages of history, consisting of the Creation, the Flood, Abraham, David, the Babylonian Captivity, and Jesus Christ. But he rejected the idea that each epoch has an equal duration, also pointing out that the length of the final epoch, already dawned, cannot be calculated. This view relates to his opposition to chiliasm.

Side by side with these historical classifications we find geographical classifications influenced by Jewish and Hellenic models. The best-known example is that of the four kingdoms in the Book of Daniel. Later Christian interpretations identify these Kingdoms as the successive reigns of Babylonia, Persia, Hellas, and Rome. The Antichrist was to appear at the time of the fourth and last earthly kingdom, heralding the beginning of the end. Augustine also approved and used this classification. The Roman Empire as the penultimate kingdom made a satisfactory geographical counterpart to his

---

[6] Matt. 20:1—7.

[7] Ps. 90:4.

[8] According to Nicholas of Cusa, the world would end shortly after 1700; Pico della Mirandola set the date at 1994, and Melanchthon thought the end would come exactly in the year 2000.

system of temporal classification.

The spatial delineation in the medieval image of the future, pointing toward the idea of an earthly utopia, had consequences that both weakened and strengthened the utopian idea. Hitherto, the end of the Roman Empire had been anticipated as the liberation from earthly chains. Now the Empire was sanctified under Augustine's influence, and man turned toward rather than away from this temporal kingdom.

Augustine is reputed to have written *The City of God* as a reassurance to Christendom after the fall of the earthly city, Rome, in 410. Since the end of the world had not yet come, the Roman Empire, the fourth and last kingdom before the eternal Kingdom of God, could not possibly have ceased to exist. Further, the Holy Roman Empire was obviously the only power that could restrain the Antichrist in this world.

The idea of the need for maintaining and rebuilding the Roman Empire gradually won in strength. (Augustine's *The City of God* is said to have been the favorite reading of the princes of the Middle Ages, especially Charlemagne.) This resulted in the forced prolongation of the Empire at all costs. Probably Augustine neither foresaw nor intended that his efforts to make secure the temporal authority of the Church would result in the compressing together of the two worlds, which he had in fact intended to remain sharply differentiated.

The vision of earthly redemption and renewal was not entirely destroyed by this process of transforming the Kingdom of God into a secular kingdom, however. The old expectations continued, adapting themselves to new circumstances. With the shift of focus to this world, the image of the future once again turned from eschatology to utopism. Since all hope now rested on the maintenance of the present world kingdom, might not a world savior be called upon to bring about the long-awaited liberation of mankind?

Although hopes for a quick return of Jesus faded away, a whole wave of other, and sometimes older, soteriological expectations surged up. Virgil sang of the birth of a wonder child who would set a new world-cycle in motion. Enthusiastic later interpretations made this refer to the Roman emperors. These ideas fused in the later Middle Ages into a body of thought known as emperor-mysticism. The Charleses of France and the Fredericks of Germany competed with one another for the honor of being named the emperor of peace. In a more spiritual variation of caesaro-papism there was a similar expectation of a future angelic pope, *papa angelicus*. The

67

realists, however, seeing how a powerful kingdom could flourish, staked everything on wielders of temporal power. These were the men who prepared the way for Machiavelli's *The Prince*, for François Fénelon's *Télémaque*, and for the so-called mirrors for princes' of the eighteenth and nineteenth centuries. In short, they prepared the way for enlightened despotism.

A typical dialectic had thus unfolded. Beginning with spiritualization, the liberation from worldly power, the spiral now ended in a considerable extension of the temporal power of the ecclesiastical hierarchy. The more the Church flourished on earth, the further the end of time was pushed into the future. And yet the spiritual power of the older images of the future proved to be stronger than the combined supremacy of temporal and ecclesiastical power. Another vision arose out of all these conflicting streams of thought. The time was ripe for a reversal to be led by Joachim, the visionary Abbot of Fiore, who burst open the cocoon of the Middle Ages in the second half of the twelfth century.

The Spirit

Nearly a thousand years before Joachim, the heretic prophet Montanus (ca. 150 A.D.) offered a new division of historical periods in contrast to the three originally postulated: those of nature, law, and grace. His periods were labeled the times of the Father, the Son, and the Holy Spirit, the third having just begun. In Joachim's day these ideas were ready for reincarnation, and Joachim used them to make a new calculation of the end of time based on Revelation.

The first kingdom is that of the Father, Israel, recognizable in the Old Testament and predominantly of the flesh. The second kingdom is that of the Son, Jesus, and identifiable in the New Testament; it is partly of the flesh, partly of the spirit. The third kingdom is that of the Holy Spirit, prophesied by Revelation and purely spiritual in nature. The main difference between the second, currently prevailing, and third, coming, kingdom is a radical change in respect to the Church, although Joachim himself remained faithfully within the Roman Catholic frame of reference. However, the Augustinian image of the future is drastically reshaped. The second kingdom, made secure by Augustine, is the kingdom of the Church, the *ecclesia militans.* The third kingdom, proclaimed by Joachim, is the kingdom of a totally different church, the *ecclesia spiritualis.* In this third, purely spiritual kingdom, the universal Christian brotherhood will come to final fulfillment. In this society there will no longer be any need for the church of the second kingdom. The *ordo clericorum* of the visible and sanctified church, with its priests, will make way for the *ordo monachorum*, in which all men shall be holy. In this new order even the New Testament, its task complete, will no longer be required. The third kingdom will be that of the new, untaught, and unwritten gospel.

When will the third kingdom arrive? According to Joachim's calculations, in 1260, preceded by a two-generation period of preparation beginning around 1200. With this new vision a new future, born of the Middle Ages, indeed begins. With the careful separation between the second and third kingdom, a real boundary seems to have been drawn across time. This becomes very clear when the images of the future of Augustine and Joachim are compared. They both aim consciously at a spiritualization, the one indirectly, through the church, the other directly, through man. They both basically reject the chiliastic heresy. Joachim's third kingdom lacks the paradise-like features associated with earlier images of the millennium. But neither can he accept Augustine's idea that the church had already inaugurated the Thousand Years' Reign.

The fundamental point of difference between them is that Augustine reckons backward from the end of time, and Joachim reckons forward to the final state of man. The one writes history, the other makes it. For Augustine the great turning point came when Christ appeared. For Joachim the decisive turning point is still to come; he reaches into the future and inspires coming generations.

Unlike Augustine's platonic city, Joachim's third reign is a kingdom of flesh-and-blood men, transformed into a new spiritualized type of man. The question is not one of individual salvation, but rather one of a cosmic transformation of mankind in history. In his predictions, Joachim gives expression to his mystical faith in man as a fully historical being. Thus, he undertakes a utopian turning back to this world, and at the same time engages in a "forward-struggling return" to the historical Jesus of the Gospels. Joachim's threefold division of time marks a break with the orthodox position which regards Jesus as the immovable center of history. It represents a revolution of Copernican dimensions, extending man's horizons and broadening his perspective. For Joachim, Christ and the Church are important but incomplete signs of the future. The true meaning of the sacraments lies not in a perpetual reliving of the past sacrifice on the cross but in the pointing ahead toward the unfolding of the Holy Spirit in history. Joachim makes use of the same historical method we are espousing in this book: deducing the past from the future and explaining this past as a movement toward the imaged future.

The central issue here is a recreation by Joachim of the dialectic of historical development. The dialectic is already present in the figure of Jesus—birth and ministry, suffering and death, resurrection and return—and similarly in the development of Christianity itself—the flowering of primitive Christianity, the decline of the Church, the purifying restoration and fulfillment. Joachim therefore presents the transition from the second to the third reign as the death of the Church, foreshadowing the extinction of the State in the later dialectics of Marx.[9]

The transition from Augustine's visible Churchly Kingdom to Joachim's invisible Spiritual Kingdom is revolutionary in potential, if not in fact. Joachim's function was to spell out the future, not to reform it. He envisions, but makes no provisions. It was not Joachim, but the fiery followers who tried to make his predictions come true who met the fate of declared heretics.

Materialization

Breaches were made by others besides Joachim in the bulwark of the Middle Ages, at different times and places. The cumulative result was a gradual crystallization, especially in the later Middle Ages, of new motives and new ideas, which all contributed to the evolution of the image of the future. The following effects may be briefly noted:

1. An increasing reaction against dogmatic and scholastic theology and the worldly hierarchy of the Church. There were signs of a return to the Bible, especially to the Old Testament prophecies, the earliest Gospels, and the Acts of the Apostles. A secular, lay form of worship became increasingly valued as the call to follow Christ in daily life sounded more insistently. Vigorous lay movements developed, some simply outside the Church, others actively opposing it.

2. The pendulum swings back. The spiritualizing of the Kingdom of God, combined with a devaluation of the earthly city, set in motion a counter-trend with interest focused on this world. The idea of the Kingdom actually coming on earth, which had never entirely disappeared from religious thinking, once more gained ground in a very literal sense. Something more was now required than a platonic abode for the soul.

---

[9] This is further discussed in Jacob Taubes, *Abendländische Eschatologie* (Bern: A. Francke, 1947), Book IV.

3. Chiliastic expectations, lurking underground ever since they had been declared heretical, burst forth again. The worse the present misery, the more alluring an intermezzo of peace and abundance would look. After the Thousand Years, time enough for the great flood and the much-feared Judgment Day. But that the Thousand Years' Reign had already come, as Augustine taught—who could believe that with the earth still such a vale of tears?

4. The shift of interest to this earth was accompanied by a shift of interest to this time. Here and now! The time of patient waiting was past. A more critical spirit arose, which bred a more radical and rebellious mentality.

5. This rebelliousness, in turn, led to an altered conception of the relationship of man, not only to Church and State, but to God. A cautious emancipation from subjection led to a search for freedom and responsibility in both sets of relationships. The doctrines of Thomas Aquinas[10] supported this development. Reviving the importance of human reason, reworking the thought of Aristotle, Aquinas was the first to do justice to romantic naturalism and to Abelard's humanistic plea for intellectual freedom. Further support came from the decline of feudalism, the rise of autonomous cities, and the emergence of the bourgeoisie.

Thus, the idea of a transcendent yet intervening God gave way to conceptions of God as a partner. The preceding developments were not systematic, but rather various streams of thought all flowing in the same direction, toward a change in the image of the future, with the accent on a this-worldly utopia. We will discuss three aspects of the countermovement, relating to the cloister, the people, and the sect.

The Cloisters

The cloister grew out of the seclusion practiced by certain solitary individuals known as hermits or anchorites, of whom Anthony the Recluse (ca. 300 A.D.) may be considered the prototype. Organized ecclesiastical monasticism has its origin in the work of St. Benedict at Monte Cassino. After the monastic reforms in following centuries, the cloister was reorganized again by Bernard of Clairvaux in the

---

[10] The revolutionary teachings of Thomas Aquinas met the same fate as the teachings of Jesus, becoming a bulwark of churchly conservatism.

early twelfth century. It was Bernard who transformed the speculative oriental mysticism into an active Western-style mysticism, particularly in the concept of the literal imitation of Christ in thought and deed. This was a new type of teaching and required a good deal more than the following of the old Church formula of consolation in life and blessedness in death. Although it led to heresy in later times, it first developed within the Church. One of the later offshoots of this movement was the Brothers of the Common Life; Thomas à Kempis, author of *The Imitation of Christ*, came from this group.

The cloister, as an isolated island in and yet out of this world, resembles the island-states of utopism:[11] Atlantis, Oceana, Icaria, and Utopia itself. The call of the cloister to the imitation of Christ represents a significant return to utopism. The trend is buttressed by a revival of the early poverty-sharing aspostolic community.

The monastic orders of the Dominicans and Franciscans, founded in the thirteenth century, also exercised a deep influence in this direction. The Franciscan Third Order brought new-old ideas of poverty and service to the world of the common man. The seed fell in fertile soil.

The People

The people, by whom we mean the poor in possessions and in spirit, had all along resisted the spiritualization fostered by the intellectual elite. There was little general acquaintance with the Bible, particularly before the discovery of printing, nor was such acquaintance encouraged by the Church. The poor man's Bible was the image, in all its forms—the pictorial-plastic image in church art, the graphic image in the miracle play, and the auditory image—the enduring image of the future as handed down according to verbal tradition. The people had known all along about the coming Kingdom in a more direct sense. Even if the Bible were not their Book, the people knew its stories. They knew from the Sermon on the Mount, the Beatitudes, and the parable of the rich young ruler how highly Jesus valued poverty and community of possessions. They knew also that the earliest Christian communities, founded by the Apostles, practiced total sharing.[12]

---

[11] Hans Freyer sees in the island-form a specific characteristic of utopias; see *Die politische Insel, Eine Geschichte der Utopia von Platon bis zur Gegenwart* (Leipzig: Bibliogr. Inst., 1936).
[12] Matt. 19:21; Acts 4:32—37.

Indeed, in the first centuries after the time of Jesus it was not only the heretics, such as Carpocrates and Pelagius, who preached such a form of communism; there were also saints who raised their voices against the evil of serving Mammon, Ambrose and Chrysostom among them. When St. Francis of Assisi elevated poverty into a gospel, these ideals of the early Church received new impetus: voluntary poverty movements sprang up all over Europe, and mendicant monks were everywhere. Old ideas of the truce of God, of the brotherhood of man, of equality, of sharing possessions, were all quickened into new life. It was the early Christian utopian ideal of human perfection which these new orders, especially the Franciscan, embodied. As the example of the friars minor spread far beyond the cloister walls, it received a tremendous response from the masses: the poor, the oppressed, and the unnoticed. Religious ideas here blended quickly and easily with those of social utopism and utopian socialism. Socio-economic and political motives added their weight to these trends, which found their strongest expression among the peasants, the very backbone of the earthly city. Their spiritual and earthly horizons coincided. Mother Earth, exploited and enslaved by great landholders (including Church and cloister), plundered by knights and by armies, could long ago have provided an earthly utopia of abundance and peace.[13] The idea of a Thousand Years' Reign was the peasant's unique spiritual inheritance, and one for which he was willing to lay down his life when necessary.

The chiliasm of the Middle Ages was primarily a peasant chiliasm. At first peaceful, it took on a more aggressive character toward the close of the period. Peasant revolts spread from Italy to England, from France to Germany. The new spirit was anarchist and revolutionary. The Reformation was itself the product of these agrarian revolts. Both the image of the future and the future itself were strongly influenced by this blending of secular and religious forces, with the added impetus of the pathos of the sect.

The Sect

Although the literature dealing with sects is largely polemical, the sect played an important role in the medieval transformation of the

---

[13] Note, for example, the typical title of the chiliastic work by Burnet, *Theoria sacra telluris*, cited by Alfred Doren, "Wunschräume und Wunschzeiten," in *Vorträge Bibl. Warburg* (Leipzig: 1927), p. 187, n. 48, from the following source: Corrido, *Geschichte des Chiliasmus*, 4 Vols., (1781—83).

image of the future into a chiliastic one. The word "sect" comes from the Latin *secare*, "to cut," so a sect is literally something which is cut off. The Cathari, sects protesting the corruption of the church, derived their label from the Greek *katharos*, originally meaning "pure" and later acquiring the specific meaning "heretic." "Heretic" comes from the Greek *hairein*, "to choose," thus saying of the heretic nothing more than can be said of anyone who subscribes to a religious belief, that he has made (another) choice. Gradually, however, these terms came to arouse other, antipathetic associations. The religious movement unleashed by Jesus first crystallized as a sect. A given movement can only be labeled sect or heresy in retrospect, according to whether it succeeds or fails.

A peculiar phenomenon also appears when one looks at the dissenting movements of the pre-Reformation and post-Reformation periods. The Catholic Church, of course, draws no distinction between the two—in its eyes all "other" movements are equally heretical. Protestant theology, on the contrary, often identifies as "pre-Reformation" thinkers those heretics who were active before 1517. But after the emergence of Luther, Calvin, and Zwingli, anyone who pronounced these same pre-Reformation heresies is once again labeled heretic. Thus we have pre-Reformation chiliasts and heretic chiliasts. It is true that Protestant chiliasm, disappointed in the Reformation, burst forth the second time with greater virulence than had ever been the case when the initial break with the Catholic Church was made. For this reason a distinction between sects appearing before and after the Reformation makes sense.

1. *Pre-Reformation*

Among the sects that in the very first centuries threatened to overwhelm the Christian Church, and were declared heretic, two are of special interest: Montanism and Gnosticism.

The prophet Montanus appeared in Phrygia ca. 150 A.D. and proclaimed the coming of the Thousand Years' Reign, announcing that the Holy Spirit dwelt within him. Gnosticism, in the form founded by the Persian prophet Mani ca. 250 A.D., revived the ancient opposition between the kingdom of darkness, the earth, and the kingdom of light, or heaven.

Montanism and Manichaeism together form the first links in the continuing chain of images of the Other world as set forth in Revelation—a world which shall redeem this one. These ideas had great staying power in the face of repeated condemnation by the Church. In the twelfth century the Gnostic-dualistic heresy reached a

74

highpoint among the Cathari, especially the South-of-France Albigenses. This group was wiped out in the thirteenth century by the Crusades and the Inquisition. But thoughts of the Other Kingdom persisted, strengthened by the so-called apostolic heretics, who wished to re-create the first apostolic communities here on earth. Further support came through the voluntary poverty movements in Lombardy and Lyons, from which the Waldensian sect originated, to spread all over Europe, influencing the Moravian Brothers and others. The Beghards and Beguines were also related to these groups.

Although many of the above-mentioned movements were declared heretic, the church-bound Dominican and Franciscan orders were nevertheless closely related to them in spirit. The prophetic teachings of Joachim broke through vehemently among the Franciscans. The radical wing, the so-called spirituals, saw the mendicant order as the beginning of the new world-order of the third kingdom. They were close to the Joachimites.

As long as Joachim's doctrines remained in the realm of prophecy, scholasticism knew how to stretch here and squeeze there so they would fit into the teachings of the Church. Younger generations, however, wished to shift the image of the future into the present. They wanted to force their way through to that which for an earlier generation was still to come. Furthermore, before the new world-order could appear, the existing church had to disappear, by force if necessary. We thus find the Joachimites charging that the papal church of the second kingdom is really the Antichrist. Joachim himself never dreamt of opposing the Church. His followers, however, were willing if necessary to storm the gates of heaven.

The Joachimites saw the development of the monastic orders from Benedict to Francis as the fulfillment of Joachim's prophecies. St. Francis was the expected new leader, and the Franciscans were the new holy ones who would replace the priests who had fallen to the world. The Church took a stand of active opposition, for while the Church owed its very origin to its eschatological mission, the nonfulfillment of that same salvation which it proclaimed was the condition *sine qua non* for its continued existence. Living on the proclamation, it would die of the fulfillment. This paradox explains the different attitudes the Church took in long-run and short-run matters.

Gerardo San Dannino collected Joachim's works under the title *Evangelium acternum (The Eternal Gospel)* in 1254; his revolutionary introduction to these writings placed them in obvious contrast to the text of the New Testament canonized by the Church, and yet they were a spiritual continuation of the gospel of Jesus. Gerardo was condemned to lifelong imprisonment. Fra Dolcino, who was burned at the stake as a heretic in 1307, made a contact between the Joachimites and the Apostolic Brethren, who wandered barefoot and begging through the land. These latter considered it their mission to involve the peasants in rebellion against the Church. They wished to arouse the peasants to establish the new state of salvation (which was also a social utopia) with their own hands. The tumult spread as far as England in the fourteenth century, further whipped up by Wycliffe, the "poor priests," and the Lollards; it reached Czechoslovakia, where the flames were fed by Hus and his followers, active well into the fifteenth century, as well as by their offshoots, the Taborites. They all fought to bring about the Kingdom on earth by force of arms, through peasant rebellions—and they were crushed to the last man by the bloody and ruthless methods of the times.

2. Post-Reformation

It was only after the Reformation that chiliasm really blazed up. The chiliasts were not frightened by the persecution and extermination of heretics; the fire and sword of Church and Inquisition did not move them. On the contrary, they were filled with indignation and bitter disappointment by the lukewarm behavior of the Reformation toward the old Church. A new apocalyptic fire burned throughout Europe in the sixteenth century, fed by the faggots of burning heretics. It burned hottest in Switzerland, Germany, and the Netherlands, fanned mainly by the impetuous behavior of the Anabaptists.

Baptists and fanatics tried again and again to institute the Thousand Years' Reign by force, with short-lived success. Their sometimes bestial excesses were on occasion exaggerated by their opponents for their own purposes. Nearly all these activities ended in bloody catastrophe.

One figure rises above the tumult, that of the revolutionary theologian and prophet of Zwickau, Thomas Münzer. This forerunner of Christian socialism was himself inspired by the writings of Joachim and his direct contacts with the Hussites and Taborites. He was first a follower of Luther, then his great adversary. In 1525 Münzer was beheaded as the leader of a peasant insurrection after a defeat at Frankenhausen. This was the signal for great uproar on the part of the multitudes, beginning at the seat of Zwingli's reforming activities, in Zürich. For the Schwärmer he did not go far enough. For Luther, who classed him with the Schwärmer, he went too far.

Wherever a head was knocked off the chiliastic dragon, more heads grew. The English revolutionary movement of Puritans and independents in the seventeenth century was spurred on by chiliastic expectations. Cromwell's army regarded itself as a group of already redeemed saints arousing the masses to the "holy experiment." The radical wing of this band separated off into congregations of nonconformists: there were Fifth Monarchy Men, Seekers, Diggers, and Levelers. All died out after attempting to found communistic-chiliastic societies. The millennialist idea found echoes among the Quakers and many other smaller sects.

Similar sects cropped up in all countries during the seventeenth century. In Czechoslovakia, Comenius emerged as a leader, connected with the Anabaptists of Bohemia and the Moravian Bretheren. In France the Huguenots were the chiliasts. In Germany the pietists carried the banner, via Weigel and Böhme, and here the movement found its main continuation through the apocalyptic mathematics of Bengel in the eighteenth century, leading to provisional termination in Kant. In Russia the echoes resounded until the time of Tolstoy and his followers. In the Netherlands, Johannes Cocceius maintained chiliasm against Voetius, in a somewhat more spiritualized form, with his *Panergycus de regno die.*

There is a strain of chiliasm in later movements which has continued into our own day among the Adventists, the Irvingites, the Methodists, the Revivalists, the Open Bible sects, and the Jehovah's Witnesses. This strain is to be found in all religious groups which take as their point of departure a literal interpretation of Revelation as the proclamation of the Thousand Years' Reign.[14] Let us now examine a few characteristics which are common to all the sects.

Localization and concentration are powerfully at work in all sectarian movements. Various factors force the materializing of the millennium in the direction of pronounced localization; u-topie becomes topie, and isolation becomes urbanization. The desire for the restoration of the Roman Empire with its capital city, the insurrections of the peasants against existing city powers, the conquest of Jerusalem in the twelfth and thirteenth centuries, and the revived memories of the Old Testament promise of a New Jerusalem—all lead in this direction. So do the New Testament promises[15] about a coming city. Thus began a long line of Thousand Year Realms, each with its own city. In the second century Montanus announced that the new realm would be founded at Pepuza, a tiny

---

[14] Their history is written with loving care by Walter Nigg, in *Das ewige Reich* (Zurich: Reutsch, 1944).
[15] Heb. 11:10, 13:14; Rev. 21:2.

village in Phrygia. Cola di Rienzi named Rome as the Eternal City in the middle of the fourteenth century. Tabor was named as the center in 1420, and toward the end of the fifteenth century the Dominican Savonarola elevated Florence to a theocracy and praised it as the beginning of the great overturning. The Anabaptists established the realm in Strasbourg in 1530 and Münster in 1534. About 1600 the Dominican Tommaso Campanella, one of the most famous of all chiliasts, wished to establish the City of the Sun in Calabria. And in 1901 the prophet John Alexander Dowie built Zion City in the United States.

Readiness for revolution is another characteristic of these sectarian movements. The quiet waiting for the appearance of the Kingdom has now given way to an active taking of destiny into man's own hands.

The pathos of the sects lies in the combination of white-heat fanaticism, humane idealism, and the self-sacrificing spirit of the movements, and the fact that many of their followers paid with their own blood in the tradition of the early Christian martyrs.

Utopism is a powerful element in later chiliasm, along with an indispensable, ever-present eschatology. The poverty and compassion of the mendicant orders, and their teaching of the liberty and equality of all men before God, are all translated into a human community in which communism of property, and sometimes even communism of love between men and women, is practiced.

The image of the future is affected both negatively and positively by chiliasm. Once expectations are met, there is a void. The hypertension of the present and the premature reaching out toward the future results in frustration and disillusion. Chiliasm as an idea is also compromised through its own excesses. However, it has also had its revitalizing effect on the Church, even into the present. It challenges both Church and theology. It prepared the way for modern times and laid the groundwork for utopian socialism. Weitling, the German socialist, was influenced by the Baptists, and the Englishman Robert Owen was much impressed by the Diggers and Levelers. Chiliasm's dialect also prepared the way for Marxism, and for the various forms of collectivism and anarchism that have been labeled secularized chiliasm.

This same religious chiliasm through Joachim, via Paracelsus and Leibniz, to Lessing and German idealism, also laid the foundation for philosophic chiliasm. As an image of the future this form of chiliasm exercised a profound influence on the future of Western culture.

Chapter 9. The Renaissance as a Renaissance of Utopism

The Renaissance stands out as a world apart between two worlds, for it is in this age that images of the future found their purest expression. But why should the Utopia, two thousand years after antiquity, reappear on the scene in a Renaissance setting, with Renaissance cast and costuming?' And what is the inner relationship between the spirit of the Renaissance and the spirit of utopism? The usual explanation is that with the coming of the Renaissance and its discoveries in space and time, new worlds were presenting themselves, in contrast to the only known and conceivable world of the Middle Ages, thereby stimulating newly enlarged minds to visions of other imagined worlds.

Only because man had developed the capacity to open up new real worlds, however, was he so successful in creating new unreal worlds. These new worlds of matter and mind are the two aspects of the same process, and globe-circling and mind-circling both stem from a common root, man's struggle for his future. The struggle presents a paradox in that it involves both liberation from and a return to the past. Here the past has two meanings: the Middle Ages, and antiquity. There are thus currents and countercurrents. An understanding of the reversals that took place in this intermediate period of the Renaissance, literally split between antiquity and modern times, is indispensable for an understanding of the reversal in our own times. This treatment of the Renaissance is adapted perfectly to our design of throwing light on history from the future, through the medium of man's image of the future.

The Other Man

The battle of historians over the Renaissance rages over the problem of the image of man. One faction maintains that there is no real difference between the Middle Ages and the Renaissance. An opposing faction maintains that Renaissance man is already typically modern man. Behind these opposing positions lurks another conflict: that between the Christian and the humanistic point of view.

The first position is simultaneously fought on two fronts, the Catholic and the Protestant. This has led in its turn to controversy in the realm of philosophy. On the one side stands Hegel, who would substitute Reformation man for Renaissance man, the Prussian Junker for the Florentine artist and scholar, Wittenberg for Rome, and the Teutonic for the Latin spirit. On the other side stands Nietzsche, who would elevate and blend the Renaissance man with his ideal type of the anti-Christian barbarian. Hegel attracts fierce resistance from both the Catholic and the anti-German camps; Nietzsche draws violent fire from the united Christian front. In this war of all against all so much dust was raised that it was no longer possible to make out the image of man. Leaving the field of battle we can perhaps reconstruct the main features of the image.

Christian Man

Many have claimed a monopoly of humanism and individualism for the Renaissance. Others have said these traits were already characteristic of the Middle Ages. This is chiefly a semantic battle. The Middle Ages certainly produced many exceptionally gifted "individuals." And in what period of history can one find a greater emphasis on "individual" salvation? To prove that humanity which found its most perfect expression in the Sermon on the Mount received a powerful impetus to growth in the later Middle Ages, one need only think of St. Francis, the friars minor, the voluntary poverty movements, and the "imitation of Christ."

There can be no argument with the view that this humanity is an advance guard of the biblical humanism which, still within the Catholic fold, fed the Renaissance and was in turn fed by it. Seen in this light, Erasmus, Colet, and Cusanus become transition figures. Nevertheless, to completely Christianize the Renaissance does violence to the reality, particularly from the point of view of man's images of the future. While the Renaissance is also a Christian Renaissance, it is not only or even for the most part Christian.

80

The Medieval Image of Man and Image of the Future: Medieval man, with respect to the future, kept his eyes fastened on life after death and on salvation in a hereafter. But a transition was already in process, in the form of the peasant insurrections. These insurrections, undertaken in the conviction that the end of time was at hand, were strongly opposed both by the Catholic Church and by Luther. This spirit of rebellion, which burst through the world-order of the Middle Ages, represents a transition in that it was considered both by the authorities and by the masses to be an unlawful rebellion of man against God. It is typical of Renaissance man, however, that he no longer accepted this position as axiomatic. This new man was ready to undertake the re-creation of the world himself.

The Reformation Image of Man and Image of the Future: While Luther in many respects represented a continuation of medieval patterns and a conformism which bordered on conservatism, Protestantism was after all basically a protest movement.[1] Even though the reformers kept insisting that they were only trying to restore primitive Christianity, their efforts nevertheless represented open rebellion against the established authorities.

While Luther called people to rebel, saying "Here I stand, I can do no other," he neither foresaw nor desired the Reformation and its accompanying break with the pope. He allied himself all too soon with antirevolutionary elements. Like every rebel, Luther felt the need of restoring discipline and authority. The authority was to be that of the Bible, as interpreted by himself, and of his church. Good works—the active efforts of man—fall away in the face of a belief in salvation arbitrarily bestowed by the grace of God. Lutheranism left the ordering of society entirely in the hands of the traditional authorities and, in effect, promoted social quietism by demanding submissiveness from its followers. The new emphasis on the ethics of industriousness and the concept of an earthly calling in the service of God did little to counterbalance this.

These tendencies toward social quietism were furthered by Calvinism. Pessimism regarding man, the inheritor of original sin, reverberated even more somberly in Calvin. The Calvinist's actions were

---

[1] See Crane Brinton, *Ideas and Men, the Story of Western Thought* (New York: Prentice-Hall, 1950), pp. 298 ff. Also Christopher Dawson, *Progress and Religion* (London: Sheed and Ward, 1945). For a discussion of the socio-psychological aspects of the opposing forces in this rebellion, see Erich Fromm, *Escape from Freedom* (New York: Farrar and Rinehart, 1941), Ch. 2.

determined either by God or by Satan, but scarcely at all by himself, except insofar as he dared to give a thoughtful hearing to the voice of the rebel Calvin, through whom, after all, God was speaking.

Calvin's effect on the social order was due to the indirect influence of Calvin's view of work and its stress on economic individualism. The social ethics and humanity of man's economic activity appear no more challenging in themselves, however, than those of the Middle Ages.[2] Salvation is still, as it was then, in the afterlife. One can scarcely speak of a general change in social awareness with the coming of Protestantism.

Humanistic Man

The establishment of the Platonic Academy in Florence by the Medicis, with the assistance of refugee scholars from Byzantium, brought the spiritual treasures of antiquity out of their hiding places in the storehouses of the East and spread them all over Europe. Socrates as well as Protagoras, Plato as well as Aristotle, Homer, Virgil, Cicero, Seneca, and all their company were made to live again. Through them, Greek-Hellenic thought came to life once more. Character traits of humanity and individual personality that had not been represented in the medieval image of man claimed precedence again.

Approximately halfway through the fifteenth century, Giannozzo Manetti wrote his *De dignitate et excellentia hominis*. Pico della Mirandola followed soon after. Pico was a courageous scholar who was initiated into neoplatonism by Marsilio Ficino, the orientalist leader of the Florentine Academy. Ficino, steeped in the lore of the Cabala, astrology, gnosis, and Pythagorean mysticism, was imprisoned as a heretic, acquitted and released, and attracted to the asceticism of Savonarola. Pico attempted to go beyond the scholastic-Aristotelian system of thought while still preserving the basic Socratic and evangelistic values. He stood out both against Christian determinism and astrological predestination, making a fervent plea for free will. His *De hominis dignitate* (1486) is the Magna Carta of this brand of humanism.

In this discourse Pico has God address man thus: "For you alone

---

[2] At the most, there were greater prospects for one special class, the bourgeoisie. Calvin unconsciously released the trigger for the bourgeoisie as Marx did later for the proletariat. Protestantism in general equated salvation with material economic blessings.

among all creatures there are no limits, except those you impose on yourself. You can degrade yourselves to the animal or elevate yourselves to the divine through the conquest of self, according to your own choice. You are your own unhindered creator. Born a citizen of this earth, you can become a citizen of heaven and a child of God."

The principle of "human dignity" is now clearly formulated. Man is not crippled by innate sinfulness, and he is dependent neither on blind faith nor on divine grace. He is free to apply his own reason to fulfilling his divine task. This idea had its effect on brothers in the spirit among the Catholic humanists, on the Christian Renaissance, and indirectly on the Protestant reformers.

The Drive Toward Freedom: The concept of human dignity presupposes a process of free human development, which must involve a struggle for emancipation from the countless chains that bind the human spirit. Imprisoned in sin and reaching for salvation, man had become estranged from this devalued world. The new concept of human dignity cannot be realized without man's coming to feel more at home in this world, but this humanizing process contains the seeds of secularization. The revaluing of this world is accompanied by a profound appreciation for the beauty of nature and the joys of earthly life, further supported by the rediscovery of Greek ideals of beauty. It is in the struggle for spiritual autonomy, however, that the old chains weigh most heavily. The trappings of scholasticism, Thomism, feudalism, dogma, and theocracy are thrown off in a rebellion only in part taken up into the Reformation.

Manliness: Another quality firmly embedded in Italian humanism—*virtù*, "manliness"—invites divergent interpretations. We treat it here as a blend of the Greek hero and the medieval knight (Roland, Le Cid). It encompasses a range of behavior from that of people's tribune (Rienzi) to condottiere (Giacomuzzo Sforza), from patriot to chauvinist. The overtones are predominantly aristocratic; there is a manly readiness for combat of every kind. *Virtù* is dynamic, Faustian, and engaging.

Virtù, however, also encompasses a degeneration and overstepping of bounds. The thinnest of walls separate its exuberance from excess. Not only the Greek hero, but the Greek *hubris* has returned. Boccaccio, Benvenuto Cellini, and Rabelais still stand on this side of the boundary; the legendary Don Juan, the wily Machiavelli, and the inhuman Borgias have already left it behind, extending a hand to the amoral *Übermensch*.

Creative Power: Nevertheless, it is not a negative freedom *from* that predominates in this age, but a positive freedom *to*. The other attributes of Renaissance man are almost covered by the luxuriant growth of his creative powers. It springs up everywhere: in art, in language, is philosophy, and in science. Adventurers explore the earth, and a new kind of adventurer explores the starry heavens. The pioneering Italian genius has come into its own: Dante, Leonardo, Pico, Leon Battista, Alberti, Michelangelo . . . *Dignitas* and *virtù* become one, in this drive toward Godlike creativity.

Human Self-Determination: The outstanding feature of the Renaissance is not, however, the flowering of culture, but the new faith of man in himself. There is an entirely new feeling abroad, an increasing awareness of human power, of the rights and duties of man. Even Savonarola and Machiavelli, the great counterweights of humanism, demonstrate this new awareness of man's own powers. They endeavor to persuade man to place this resource at the disposal of a higher power, in order to save himself.

The Split Man

The portrait of Renaissance man has been idealized. According to the pessimists, the Renaissance was a false dawn followed by no morning. For the optimists, it was the prologue to the world-drama staged and directed by man. We hold with the latter view. The emancipation sought was indeed not entirely successful, in part because it was characterized from the very beginning by a kind of ambiguity. The bonds of medievalism were not burst by men whose eyes were fastened on the future, but by men who were fondly gazing at the *via antique* of their distant past. Dante, following Boethius, pleaded for a *ritornar al principio*, which for the one meant Hellenic antiquity, for the other primitive Christianity.

The authority of classicism became as compelling as that of Thomism ever was; the truths formerly revealed by the church fathers were now revealed by the philosophers of antiquity. Suprahuman authority was undermined but not abolished; in some respects it was even more firmly entrenched, particularly when the backward look turned into a clamor for a *renovatio Romae*, a restoration of the eternal city and a revival of the Latin world-empire. Nationalistic and imperialistic strivings then came to dominate the humanistic idealism of the Renaissance, at last to find expression in pure tyranny. Nevertheless, the aristocratic ideal of *virtù* was not dead. While a creative minority of artists and scholars, poets and thinkers preoccupied themselves with an alluring past, another and ever-larger group looked steadily forward. This was the

84

emerging bourgeoisie, the industrious bankers and merchants. Chains of gold replaced the chains minted from a more spiritual coinage.[3]

This development implies a dialectic reversal for the image of the future. As long as the new class was upward-striving, man's budding self-awareness was encouraged from this quarter too. Its representatives were dynamic, forward-looking, and not afraid to take risks. Later changes in the bourgeois ideology as it shrank from the ideals of the great entrepreneurs to the petty self-interest of the small burgher, however, placed new limitations on freedom. As soon as members of the middle class became men of property, their chief concern came to be the consolidation of their newly-won status. Manly *virtù* toppled quietly from its place at the peak of the value hierarchy, making way for tranquility and security.

Did the waters of the Renaissance then run dry? No, it is just in this uncertain wavering between the breaking of existing bonds and the reforging of older ones that something of basic importance occurred. A breach had been made in time, cutting straight across both Christianity and humanism, through society and the state. In this process we find the Renaissance man no longer an ideal type, but a split man: split between individuality and submission, between the forward and the backward look. One leg is lifted to move forward, but the other drags back. Amazingly enough, man is able to live in such a precarious state of balance, and to live creatively. The shattering of that which was once whole drives him to reconstruction, and the dividedness of his life compels him to synthesis. Psychically torn apart, he finds himself spurred on to find a constructive compensation through a stable stylistic unity in his many-faceted life. His inward disunity, instead of blocking his further development, unleashes great strength.

There is a close relationship between this dividedness and man's creative struggle. One may think of Petrarch, with his heartrending religious doubts; of the Promethean heroism of Michelangelo;[4] of

---

[3] Sombart and Max Weber began the description of this process, the latter especially in his *The Protestant Ethic and the Rise of Capitalism* (Tübingen: in Ges. Aufs. z. Rel. soz., 1921). Von Martin penetratingly completed the analysis in *Soziologie der Renaissance* (Stuttgart: Enke, 1932), included by Karl Mannheim in The International Library of Sociology and Social Reconstruction as *Sociology of the Renaissance* (London: Int. Lib. of Sociology and Soc. Rec., 1945).

[4] Michelangelo alone, that much-described and little-understood man, the great mystery of the Renaissance, encompasses the whole spirit of the age in himself. George Simmel was the first to gain some inkling of the true nature of his tragic

Leonardo da Vinci; even of the split personality of the Medici and the broken life and thought of a Giordano Bruno or a Tommaso Campanella. The Renaissance man is indeed the Other man.

The image of the future lives in and on such a mental dividedness. It is these tortured split souls, tossed about by the currents of the age, seeking, liberating, binding, self-propelled and yet driven, who create the images. Split inwardly, it is they who generate the strength to split the outward world of space and time. Because of their own profound experience of the ambiguity and double meaning of life and their awareness of the split between this and the Other, they are uniquely equipped to create an image of the Other, to mirror the realm of the future.

The Other World

The inwardly split Renaissance man, torn loose from the cohesion of the hereafter-oriented Middle Ages, is driven by inner necessity to reshape this world and to shape new Other worlds in space and time.

Renaissance man added impetus to the horizontal movement that began with the Crusades. The world grew steadily larger at the hands of Vasco da Gama, Columbus, Amerigo Vespucci, and others. At the same time Europe was bombarded with strange new tales, from Marco Polo's accounts of his journeys to China to Montesquieu's *Persian Letters;* these stories of other lands and peoples with entirely different morals and customs were effective in introducing a note of relativity into the world-image of their readers and hearers. These new representations of space changed the people's own representations of time—their own future time.

Simultaneously, the world was enlarged and made anew in another sense, through a vertical movement. Through the happy double coincidence of the discovery of printing ca. 1450, and the fall of

---

dividedness, and Walter Nigg makes it central to his exposition in *Maler des Ewigen.* He builds on the discovery in 1925 of the only self-portrait of Michelangelo, concealed in the flayed skin of the martyr Bartholomew, whose story is the subject of the painting. In this picture Bartholomew (though still sound of body and very much alive) holds in his hand his own flayed skin. In this way Bartholomew is made to give a prophetic foreshadowing and symbolic representation of his own fate: to be flayed alive. In painting his own portrait in this manner, Michelangelo is announcing to the world that he identifies himself with Bartholomew and feels as if he is being flayed alive himself. (The picture in question is part of the mural of the Last Judgment in the Sistine Chapel.)

Byzantium in 1453, two doors were opened for the human spirit. One was to the world of books, the other to a community of scholars who streamed into Italy from the East with an unbroken tradition of Byzantine-Hellenic contact. They opened up for Europe that other, long-forgotten portal leading to the world of antiquity. Once again a new world was laid before man: Hellas, Persia, Israel, and the ancient glory of Rome.

Not only were new worlds opened up, but the very ground under Renaissance man's feet was made to tremble. The established social order and the existing political institutions were no longer considered to have been unalterably given, but rather tentative human creations in response to the varying demands of history. "When Adam delved, and Eve span,/Who was then the gentleman?"

The Renaissance thus gradually shaped another human society, one which offered daily bread in place of the Holy Grail. While the religious peasant insurrections were being forcefully put down, the worldly upward-striving middle classes came to power. Another process of change had begun which was to be continued centuries later by a new working class that had nothing to lose but its chains. But first this process of change had to direct itself toward the reformation of the Church and the institutions of government. Rediscoveries out of antiquity helped to feed the process of change in this latter area.

Is the *res publica Romana* the necessary model for a republic directed to the common welfare, a commonwealth? Can the Roman world-empire be restored? Or should philosopher-kings rule over city-states, as Plato taught? Dante, in *De monarchia*, Jean Bodin, in *La République*, and Machiavelli, in *The Prince*, all dealt with these problems.

In the meantime, man's own experienceable world, his spatial surroundings, were also being recreated. Landscapes, plants, animals, and even man himself were rediscovered. Admiration of nature led to wondering and pondering. As a result, still another world was opened, as man applied new methods of observing nature (the empirical) and new models of thinking (the mathematical). Machiavelli's attempt to consider human nature realistically was praised by Francis Bacon, who applied his approach to other areas.

The process of separation of the natural sciences from morality and metaphysics was a slow one. Renaissance man did not complete it, but he did accelerate it. The *De revolutionibus orbium caelestium* of Copernicus got the revolution under way, and it rebounded to earthly spheres. Bruno, Galileo, and Descartes continued it, each in his own manner. The spiritual revolution in regard to the biblical image of the world was closely related to the discovery of the astronomical image of the universe.

Michelangelo, one of the few men who defied the prohibition against making an image of God, depicted God the Creator on the ceiling of the Sistine Chapel, thereby changing both the act of Creation and the relationship between the Creator and man. Here was the Christian Renaissance, blended with the heritage of pagan thought.

The Reformation, on the other hand, both narrowed and widened the gulf between God and man. Further, the relationships between Italian humanism and biblical humanism, between the platonizing of Christianity and the movements for the "imitation of Christ," complicated the changing scene.

As the idea of a general rebirth gathered momentum, the capital of the Renaissance moved from Florence to a reborn Rome, once more the center of the world, and the capital of the realm of the future. Inevitably, man now paid more attention to the rediscovered images of the future of antiquity, particularly Plato's *Politeia* and the Dante-cum-Virgil poetic vision of an earthly Golden Age.

Two other diverging lines emanate from this point. One moves toward a systematic philosophy of history: the new science of the post-Renaissance Giovanni Vico. The other moves toward a systematic image of the future: Campanella's *The City of the Sun.*

From Backward Glance to Image of the Future

The Other worlds created by the split Renaissance man are the products of a futuristic exercise of the imagination and vary widely according to differences in world-view of their creators. We will discuss and compare three different types of Renaissance utopias and their offshoots: those of Thomas More, Francis Bacon, and Tommaso Campanella. More's literary image of the future has conferred its name of "Utopia" on all prior and subsequent images of the future. Today it is not only a term of mockery, but almost an epithet of abuse. Does Utopia itself contain in potential this dialectical reversal, or does the change simply mirror a change in the *Zeitgeist*? Do we have hidden here the essence of the contrast between Renaissance optimism and twentieth century pessimism? We cannot answer this question yet. We can, however, affirm the correlation between the new burst of life springing up from rediscovered antiquity and the revival of the largely lost belief in a human power available for human welfare.

Each of the three images of the future mentioned here reveals man as the architect of a newly ordered world. The travel and adventure tales of the time helped draw a picture of other possible ways of living based on other postulates concerning man and society. So did the revival of memories of the social aspirations of antiquity and the manner of life of the early Christian communities. To visualize a different future for one's own society was neither unrealistic nor irreligious.

It was not irreligious. Both More and Campanella were fervent Catholics. More gave up his life for his faith, and Campanella fought all his life for a messianic pope, wandering from land to land and from prison to prison.[5] Nor was it unrealistic. More stood by the position he had taken in his Utopia at the beginning of a political career that ultimately led him to the highest office in England, that of chancellor to the king. Bacon's Utopia came as the closing volume of a full life's work, after he had been dismissed from the selfsame post of chancellor after years of service. Both men were thus practical politicians.

We will now examine the concrete images of the future that these men delineated.

Utopia

More's *Utopia* preceded Bacon's *The New Atlantis* and Campanella's *The City of the Sun* by nearly a century, and served as a model for both. Nevertheless, each represented different worlds.

In More's world man stands at the center. The form of government is democratic, and every kind of tyranny is abhorred. The king, who is but the first among equals, is with his councilors entirely devoted to the tasks of promoting agriculture and the general welfare. Private property, the source of all distress and evil, is abolished. The document portrays the Arcadian existence of a peaceful farming people on an island totally isolated from the evil larger world, an *isola bella*.

The New Atlantis

Bacon's Atlantis is also an island, for how else should an English-

---

[5] Once he saw himself as this emperor, then it was to be the King of Spain, the Cardinal Richelieu, and finally, just before his death, he thought it was to be the newborn Dauphin of France, later Louis XIV.

man conceive of an ideal society? The image of Atlantis derives from Plato; this work, like its prototype, is philosophic in nature. Science stands at the center of this world, where the House of Solomon rules. The name refers both to the Old Testament king noted for his wisdom and to the philosopher-king described by Plato. The form of government is technocratic. The scholars are the ruling class, having dominion over both nature and man. The study halls and laboratories of the House of Solomon, which are to produce a whole new world of unbounded human power, foreshadow the world of Doctor Faust and the "brave new world" of our own times.

The City of the Sun

In the City of the Sun, it is God who stands at the center. The city is a sternly disciplined community of believers dedicated to the service of God. The government is theocratic, and the city is under the rule of an ecclesiastical hierarchy with a royal pope at its head. All men live like monks, cut off from the world in their walled city, living a life of strict, if voluntary, obedience.

The Creators of the Image of the Future

Thomas More owes his choice of an island-form for his never-never land to very old sources. The Greeks were familiar with mythological descriptions, as in Hesiod and Homer, of the Isles of the Blessed on the outer rim of the earth. The Elysian Fields, home of the heroes, were also to be found there. Plato described the legendary island of Atlantis in his *Dialogues*, in the *Critias* and the *Timaeus*. Ideas of an island-paradise lived on in the Middle Ages in innumerable folk sagas. In addition to Atlantis there were St. Brandon, Antilia, Avalon, and others—some also submerged and some even included in the maps of the day. More's genius knew how to describe his imaginary island in such a way that it would appear now as an image which was the antipode of the British Isles, now as a picture of the British Isles. Separated from the here and now by space, the gap is bridged by time: the future.

More's debt to antiquity goes beyond the borrowing of this ingenious device, however. One of the foremost classical scholars of his country, he wrote *Utopia* in Latin and the names are for the most part Greek inventions. Plato's *Politeia* has been seriously studied as a model. Raphael Hythlody, the garrulous narrator of *Utopia* is more than once compared to Socrates. More was familiar with Greek philosophy and acquainted with scholasticism, and traces of Augustine's *The City of God* can be found in *Utopia*.

More had strong ties with the Italian Renaissance and the work of the Florentine Academy. As a young man he translated a biography of Pico della Mirandola and had an important place in the circle of the biblical humanists. He was a close friend of Erasmus and corresponded with him voluminously,[6] following closely the progress of the latter's translation of the New Testament.

There is no doubt that *Utopia* achieves a blending of the apostolic community of believers and the platonic community. Together with Colet and Erasmus, More forms the humanistic wing of the so-called Oxford Reformers. He and Luther mutually detested each other, Luther calling him "Thomas Morus Tyrannus." His "back to" is back to antiquity and, above all, back to the Bible. Nevertheless there is also, as with Pico, an "onward": onward to the full unfolding of man's capacities for the building of a better world, onward also with the explorers who have demonstrated the existence of other worlds on the earth. The Florentine Amerigo Vespucci's account, *Quattuor navigationes*, unmistakably exercises its influence on both the form and the content of *Utopia*.

Is there also an "onward" in the sense that More meant his book to be a contribution to the realization of the ideal society he described? Opinions differ on this. Many have relished More chiefly as a humorist and have regarded his book as a whimsical play of the imagination. His statement at the end of Raphael's tale seems to support this: "There is much in this society," he writes, "for which one may wish rather than hope *(optarim verius quam sperarim)*." It is an unexceptionable remark for a realistic statesman, with just the right touch of skepticism, but the wish cannot thus be brushed aside. Besides, arguments can be adduced to support the position that behind the facade of wit, which never deserted More even in prison or on the scaffold; he was a profoundly serious man, and his book a profoundly serious work.

First, More completed the second part of his book, containing the description of the island Utopia, during a stay in Holland. Only after his return to England did he write the first part, a sharp criticism of English government and the misery of the masses. The first part is one of the best mirrors held up to the times, as the second part remains one of the finest mirrors of the future in existence. Some

---

[6] Erasmus is supposed to have arranged the original publication of *Utopia* at Louvain, and he dedicated his *In Praise of Folly* to More.

have even thought that the two parts were written by different authors. If the work was intended only as fantasy, why then should the tranquil atmosphere of the whole be destroyed by the biting satire on king and church?

Second, it is in the last part that the foreign policy of Utopia is extensively discussed. It so precisely foreshadows the actual foreign policy pursued by England in the following centuries that it has been described as the program of a future prime minister of the British Empire. The diplomatic gifts and statesmanlike abilities that More later demonstrated have never been questioned. Pure fantasy? It seems improbable.

If *Utopia* is an ideal human society, new difficulties open up before us. Does the objectionable foreign policy described fit into the picture? Other contradictions also appear. More, who decided against becoming a priest only after years of wavering, always leaned toward an ascetic way of life, even to the point of self-castigation. The Utopians, on the contrary, seek happiness. The way of life so alluringly described in *Utopia* is Epicurean. Further, a kind of natural religion akin to the humanistic outlook of the Platonic Academy prevails in Utopia, and there is complete tolerance of other ways of thinking. It is not sufficient to say that the first edition of *Utopia* is dated 1516 and that the Reformation did not really get under way until 1517, for More was always a faithful Catholic in his classical and biblical humanism, not just in his later years. He had a horror of any form of dissent. From his *Apology* it is clear that as a public servant he was merciless in his persuit of heretics.

Although these contradictions cannot be reconciled, they can be explained. More represents the purest form of the typical spiritually split man of the Renaissance. He *is* the Renaissance in his dividedness, pioneering the way into modern times. His image of the future, called the "golden booklet" of the ideal social order, is the fruit of this dividedness, and could not be otherwise.

Francis Bacon is also a split personality, and to the highest degree.[7] Seldom has one man been so praised ("the mightiest spirit of modern times, bringing Europe to its majority") and so reviled ("muddleheaded," "power-mad," "ignorant of the science of his own time").

Despite the title that Bacon gave to his new Atlantis, *Instauratio magna*, there is little of the backward glance; everything points to an

---

[7] This aspect of Bacon is well brought out in Will Durant's *The Story of Philosophy* (New York: Simon and Schuster, 1926).

entirely new future. He campaigns with the fervor of an armored knight against medieval scholasticism and its interpretation of Aristotle.

The new optimistic spirit of the Renaissance breathes through all Bacon's work. The spirit of self-confidence now threatens to swing to overconfidence and lust for power. All the misery of this world is caused by the darkness of ignorance and prejudice. Knowledge is power, breaking through the mists of obscurantism, to create a new and better world. Social and political reform are subordinated to scientific investigation, the condition of all progress.

Bacon predicted many scientific developments, and foreshadowed many later discoveries in the realm of the physical sciences and technology. These will bring the universe under man's rule (the *Instauratio magna* has as its subtitle *de regno hominis*) and provide a panacea for all the evils of the world. A communism not of material but of intellectual products will be established for the good of mankind. Bacon in effect has written a new page in the epic of man.

We find the same restless activity in our third Renaissance type, Campanella. Conspirator, freethinker, adventurer, poet, preacher, and declared heretic, continually hunted by the Spaniards, this complex figure was finally martyred as a traitor. The dividedness is there. An orthodox Catholic monk, he describes in *The City of the Sun* a naturalistic, pantheistic religion with a trinity of power, wisdom, and love. It includes worship of the sun and the stars, determiners of human destiny in God's name. The Dominican spent nearly thirty years of his life in prison and conceived *The City of the Sun* there. Campanella managed to combine the cloister, the prison, and the fortress into one institution, which was to achieve the liberation of man. In this unresolved contrast between freedom and chains, Campanella is indeed the most characteristic transition-phenomenon of the Renaissance. In the medieval image of the world that he accepted, human destiny is predetermined; nevertheless Campanella would influence man's future anew.[8]

The title of Campanella's Utopia is taken from a Greek travel tale of the same name by Jambulos. Plato's *Politeia* and More's *Utopia* provide the framework and also contribute to the contents of *The City of the Sun*. The education of the youth is Spartan, the physical

---

[8] Campanella wrote a great deal, perhaps as many as one hundred volumes. The subjects included politics, astrology, religion, science, and metaphysics. *The City of the Sun* was originally an appendix to an extensive philosophical work. As with Bacon, his Utopia must be regarded as the device which locks the whole mechanism of his philosophical system into position.

culture Greek. He takes the contrast between the warring powers of light and darkness from the gnosis. In *The City of the Sun* the power of light wins in the end. Astrologists play an important role in the administration of the city. They decide, among other things, who shall mate with whom and when, in order to breed the best possible children. Augustine's *The City of God* is also incorporated with a more worldly orientation, as regards the fusing of church and state. Confession proceeds hierarchically, so that the sins of the total population finally pour as one into the ear of the high priest.

Campanella's entire conception is based on a mixture of apocalyptic, prophetic, and messianic elements. Writing at the close of the sixteenth century, he calculated that a great change was to take place precisely in the year 1600. He therefore stood on the boundary between two worlds. On the one hand he represents a vigorous continuation of medieval chiliasm; on the other, he carries out and completes the Renaissance in his images of a universal pantheistic religion and a communistically organized brotherhood.

Thus, More, Bacon, and Campanella create their Other worlds in this world. More creates an Other set of social relationships between man and the universe, and Campanella an Other master-servant relationship between man and God. Each one glorifies creation in its own way: Mother Earth, the human spirit, the Heavenly Father.

The most unreal image of the future—that of Campanella—is in some ways the most real. It already existed in the empire of the Incas. The future Jesuit state of Paraguay was also modeled on this pattern. It exercised an enormous influence on all anti-ecclesiastical movements because of its chiliastic ties with the popular conceptions of a future reign of peace on earth. Both Comenius and Leibniz were powerfully influenced by Campanella.

Campanella found a follower within the Protestant fold in the Schwabian preacher Jakob Andreä, who produced a companion volume to *The City of the Sun* a few years later on the state of *Christianopolis*. The specifically Catholic traits and more daring characteristics of the earlier book are toned down in this version. The works of Bacon, Campanella, and Andreä had a great influence on the English utopists Samuel Gott and Samuel Hartlib. Gott wrote the *Nova Solyma* (1648), a description of the theocracy of the New Jerusalem; after the Reformation the ancient tribes of Israel once more came to the foreground, with their ancient image of the future drawn from the Covenant. The *New Jerusalem* presents a return to the Holy City, now modernized under the influences of the Renaissance, humanism, and the Reformation.

If we unfurl the scroll of history back to the Renaissance, we feel that we are being flung back and forth between two worlds. A threshold is crossed, and then it reappears. The Renaissance has a true Janus-head, facing both backward and forward.

The idea of rebirth includes both the backward and the forward elements: revival and new life. It is the secular form of the religious expectation concerning the return of Christ. The Renaissance Utopia became a transitional stage, fulfilling a dual role. On the one hand it provided for transmission to coming generations of older images of the future, embodied in myths, sagas, and legends. On the other hand, its keen forward vision opened up unique and stirring vistas.

Why should an entirely new perspective be needed at this time? The need arose from Renaissance man's vital new feeling about life. Nothing less than the entire relationship between human and superhuman power was at issue. The boundary between the two had shifted in the transition toward direct influence-optimism concerning self-determination of destiny. The purely eschatological image of the future with its elements of transcendence and determinism moved into the background. A predominantly utopian image of the future focused on man's role now made its appearance. The shift was most pronounced in Bacon and least pronounced in Campanella.

Nevertheless, through a combination of circumstances the Renaissance did not succeed in its great revolution. Only later would the new ideas embodied in its images of the future bear fruit, in the atmosphere of evolutionary optimism that prevailed in the eighteenth and nineteenth centuries. There are connecting links between More's *Utopia* and these later streams of thought, particularly with utopian socialism. A line of development can be traced from Bacon's Utopia to the Industrial Revolution and scientific socialism. Developments from Campanella's Utopia branched off toward religious socialism, in a mixture of eschatological and utopian ideas.

In retrospect, the Renaissance appears as much more than a rebirth: in the end the accent falls on its role as renewer of the future.

Chapter 10. The Image of the Future: Guiding Star of the Age of Enlightenment

This chapter compresses an extensive and rich period of Western history, from the end of the seventeenth to the beginning of the nineteenth century, a period which flows out of the decline of the Renaissance to emerge in the diverse styles of the baroque, rococo, and classicism. It represents a period of new faith, new world-outlook, and vigorous renewal of activity in all areas of culture.

The high points of the period are to be found in the natural sciences, with the social sciences in their train. In England we see the flowering of empiricism, positivism, and deism. In France the Encyclopaedists flourish, and Germany is bursting with its *Aufklärung*, *Sturm und Drang*, and philosophical idealism. Cutting across all these are the political movements of enlightened despotism, the American struggle for independence, the French Revolution, and Marxism. Another kind of revolution, the Industrial Revolution, leaves no aspect of life untouched.

As we plunge into the confusion of movements to seek out the reigning image of the future, we must inevitably abstract from and systematize the almost overpowering social reality. This historical overview will give central place to the image of the future as the guiding star of the Enlightenment.

From Essence-Optimism to Influence-Optimism

One outstanding chain of events that carries through from the Renaissance to the Enlightenment ultimately leads to a new precise image of a world conforming to natural law. This new image, largely derived from the work of Newton, makes possible a new conception

96

of God as a creator, at work shaping the world as a rational human being would have done. If this is so, man can analyze and master the divine plan through the processes of reason. What was formerly ascribed to supernatural power is now simply treated as the not yet known.

This new world of the Enlightenment which conforms to natural law is the Other world. The new type of human being who can systematically study this world, the scientist, is the Other man. Having made the discovery that the universe is essentially rational, man sees that Homo sapiens, himself, and all his social institutions, must be equally rational. Therefore human behavior and culture can be subjected to the same systematic analysis as the natural world.

The parallels between the social and the natural order are sometimes carried to a *reductio ad absurdum*. We see this especially in the works of the French philosophers, as for example Claude Helvetius and Baron d'Holbach, author of *Système de la Nature ou des Lois du Monde Physique et du Monde Moral* (1770). Holbach's ideas stem directly from Denis Diderot and his Encyclopaedists. These men awaited a second Newton who would discover the laws of social gravity and reduce all human events to one common denominator. If the macrocosmos was an enormous machine whose behavior could be predicted, then man, the microcosmos, was equally predictable. This is the theme of Julien de La Mettrie's *L'Homme Machine* (ca. 1750).

Francois Quesnay, founder of physiocracy, maintains that there are natural laws that would automatically govern the social order if nothing interfered with them. Adam Smith describes a natural economic order guided by a "hidden hand," in which self-interest and the common good are naturally united. Certain contradictions emerge from the work of both Quesnay and Adam Smith. Although there may be a law of harmony built into all social structures, it is all too evident that the actual operations of human society reveal disharmony, arbitrary exercise of power, and mass misery.

The contrasting approaches to thinking about and building for the future arise out of this conflict between the ideal and the real. An element common to both is the conviction that man himself has temporarily destroyed the natural divine harmony of the social order. The approaches diverge, however, in the solutions they offer to the problem. In one view the world's evil will turn to good of itself in the course of history. In the other view, man must himself undo the evil he has wrought and re-create the social order. The two images of the future of essence-optimism and influence-optimism are here in conflict.

The first view is actually a theodicy, a justification of the ways of God to man. From Descartes to Spinoza a line of thought is developed in which God himself takes on the form of a mathematical formula for the ethical *summum bonum*. This lays the foundation for the Leibnitzian best of all possible worlds and for the God of Hegel, world-reason. Man must thus refrain from attempting to intervene in the divinely rational order, as the philosophy of laissez-faire makes explicit.

Neither Quesnay nor Adam Smith were ready to subscribe to this plea for automatism. Quesnay was a defender of enlightened despotism, and Smith was no dogmatic opponent of state intervention. There is, however, quite another line of thought concealed in the same reasoning. If God has created and set in motion the machinery of the universe, this machinery now goes of itself. God has stepped aside. Man has taken up the task that God laid down, but without paying proper attention to the laws. The result is the manmade mess of history called civilization.

Voltaire attacked in countless writings the belief in the best of all possible worlds, particularly in *Candide* (1759), and most systematically in the *Essai sur les Moeurs* (ca. 1743). He is a destroyer of the old, not a builder of the new.[1] Only as rationalism connects with a certain type of naturalism does the reforming zeal of influence-optimism develop. Rousseau, spiritual father of later romanticism, is the intellectual father of the development in which reason is paired with emotion. Society is not only rational, but good. A once ideal state of nature, later corrupted by civilization, may prevail again in the future.

The opposition between rationalism and romanticism tends to be somewhat overemphasized, at least with respect to the image of the future. Already in Pascal we find a synthesis of reason and emotion, even predating the higher mathematics through which the heart generates its own enlightenment. For Pascal this synthesis was the basis for faith beyond reason, *credo quia absurdum est*.[2] On the

---

[1] Consider, for example, his cynically resigned novel, *Le Monde Comme Il Va*. Because of this one-sidedness it is not accurate to say, as has been said, that to understand the Enlightenment one need only understand Voltaire.

[2] In the split personality of the genius Pascal, born too soon and departed too young, the world lost a great utopian thinker. He lived in the two worlds of science and faith, sometimes in each by turn, sometimes in both simultaneously. Able to move in an Other world of roulette and mathematical probability, yet not ready to accept the world-view of Copernicus, he nevertheless was convinced of a cosmic, if incomprehensible, infinity. Pascal's "abyss" is well known. He

whole, in spite of certain conflicts, rationalism and romanticism stand together at this turning point in human thought. Both are directed against the influence-pessimism inherent in the concept of original sin. They are concerned not with the fall of man but with the fall of culture, and consequently focus on social reform.

Rousseau's teaching on the Social Contract is the great stimulus for active influence-optimism, building on Locke's doctrine of *tabula rasa*, which helped to free man from a preoccupation with original sin, and Locke's teaching regarding the sovereignty of the people. Rousseau's image of the future[3] leads straight back to the supposed original state of man, in which naturally good men lived together in liberty, equality, and fraternity. Today this phenomenon is only to be found where *le bon sauvage* still exists, unspoiled by civilization.

There is a twofold reversal here: first, regarding ideas of good and bad; second, a reversal to active influence-optimism, even though the will is directed to a return to a state of nature. Rousseau's romantic prescription for perfection involves a Renaissance theme, "Turn back." But there is an activist theme of building the Other world. Reason offers the necessary values, standards, and tools. Man knows how good things once were, so he alone is responsible for his own misery. This enthusiastic belief in man's self-liberation was opposed to the Christian Church as a threat to its doctrine of salvation. But the flood tide of this deistic (rarely atheistic) faith in the human spirit could not be stemmed by the cloistered walls of the Church. In the end, it transformed Christian thought.

That the attempted breakthrough to an Other world which failed in the Renaissance succeeded so remarkably in the Enlightenment, is due to the vistas opened by scientific discoveries. The minds of men were thereby prepared for other discoveries and different views of the world.

---

was certainly responsible for establishing the concept of historical relativity: "Truth on this side of the Pyrenees is error beyond." Alternately worldling and ascetic, Pascal is typically the Other man, and as such a source of endless dispute among his biographers. His utopian thought, partly expressed in the polemical *Lettres Provinciales* and the random *Pensées,* would probably have found a more complete expression in his unfortunately unwritten *Apologie,* intended to be about "the faithful believer" who as a "fallen angel remembers the heaven whence he came."

[3] Emilie Schomann, who has made a special study of French utopian thought in the eighteenth century, "Französische Utopisten des 18. Jahrhunderts und ihr Frauenideal" (Berlin: E. Felber, 1911), considers Rousseau the greatest of the French utopians. Rousseau himself greatly admired the Utopias of his predecessors, including More, Fenelon, and Vairasse.

Reason and Utopism

As the classical natural sciences sought emancipation from religion and metaphysics, so reason sought a basis in natural law for religion and the social order, and found that utopists had already worked on this problem, in their search for the ideal social structure. The utopist uses the scientific method as he works at the construction of an Other world, not perceivable by the untrained senses.

Utopia is a model thought-experiment, setting the stage for all ensuing thought-experiments such as those of Copernicus, Newton, Georg Riemann, and Einstein. In another sphere it sets the stage for the appearance of Rousseau's natural state, Kant's moral conscious-ness, Freud's unconscious, Bergson's time-consciousness, Darwin's theory of evolution, and Marx's dialectical materialism. Utopias have paved the way for all radical departures from accepted modes of systematic thought. One might say that the imaginary numbers of mathematics have their origin in the imaginary island of Utopia. The discovery of multi-dimensional geometry is a natural offshoot of the discovery of new dimensions in time: the image of the future. The space-time continuum is not a strange concept to those who have already dealt with the spatio-temporal qualities of the realm of the future. The fiction of the utopia becomes the philosophy of as-if[4] and animates philosophical systems from Plato to Bergson, as well as providing methodological tools such as Max Weber's ideal types.

The utopia of the Enlightenment bridges the gap between the old and the new in two ways. First, it provides a fairly detailed critique of the contemporary scene, attacking conservatism and corruption; second, it offers a careful plan for a new social order. The Age of Enlightenment and its utopias produced a new outlook on the present and a new vision of the future. By unmasking learned ignorance, the Englightenment cleared the way for the exercise of human reason in areas beyond the scope of previous scholastic knowledge. This is what Erasmus had already tried to do, too far in advance of his time, in the utopian world of *In Praise of Folly*.

Types of Enlightenment Utopias

The utopias of the Enlightenment are characterized by both con-

---

[4] H. Vaihinger, *Die Philosophie des Als-Ob* (Leipzig: Felix Meiner, 1922). First printed in 1911.

tinuity and innovation. They continue the rational approach exemplified by Plato and More, but innovation enters at the point of fusion between the rational and the romantic that is so typical of the Enlightenment spirit.

The Platonic Utopia

The unfortunately labeled *Staatsroman* is concerned not so much with a particular nation-state as with social and political institutions in general. It is an essay on a desirable social order rather than a novel. James Harrington's *Oceana*[5] is the best example of a utopia in the Platonic style. Harrington was a follower of Machiavelli and a forerunner of Marxian dialectical materialism. He himself was followed by Louis de Saint-Just with his *Institutions Républicaines* (1800) and by Abbé André Morellet with his revealingly titled *Code de la Nature, ou le véritable esprit de ses lois, de tout temps négligé ou méconnu* (1755).

Many others could be named. Hartlib has been mentioned previously. Gerard Winstanley, a leader of the Digger movement in England, and author of *The Law of Freedom or True Magistracie Restored* (1652), is of some interest as the representative of a type of "natural" communism inspired by the very highest religious ideals. There were many imitators and also-rans among utopian writers, and there were some reactionaries, too, as for example Sir Robert Filmer, who wrote *Patriarcha or the Natural Power of Kings* (1680). Other writers moved in the direction of political treatises, as Montequieu in his *L'Ésprit des Lois; ou du rapport que les lois doivent avoir avec la constitution de chacque gouvernement, les moeurs, le climat, la réligion, le commerce, etc.* (1748). Others dealt with comparative forms of government on the international level.[6]

A gradual fusion of rationalistic and nationalistic thinking took

---

[5] *Oceana* (1656) is a mixed product of Renaissance rationalism. Obviously referring to England, it nevertheless draws on many sources—from Jewish, Greek, and Roman history as well as from the current scene in Holland, Switzerland, and Italy—for its materials.

[6] It is somewhat difficult to make a sharp distinction between utopism and that political idealism which is nourished by utopism. No such doubt exists concerning the last links in the chain of platonic utopias at the turn of the century, such as Fichte's *Der geschlossene Handelsstaat* and Othmor Spann's *Der wahre Staat*, which will be discussed in Chapter 12. Formally, they fall outside the historical period under discussion, but they are philosophically unintelligible except as a continuation of the Enlightenment.

place in utopism. English writers had an island to work with, so the necessary characteristics of isolation and self-containment were already present. Continental utopian writers sought to achieve this same self-containment through postulation of rigid autocratic rule or by using imaginary space or time barriers that prevent ordinary mortals from reaching the utopia, thus also introducing a romantic element into utopism. For this reason, works like Fénelon's *Voyages de Télémaque* (1699) and Bernard de Fontenelle's *République des Philosophes ou l'Histoire des Ajoiens* (1768), which have a highly narrative style in spite of socio-political orientations, do not present the purely platonic form, and are on the borderline of the romantic utopia.

The Romantic Utopia

The blending of rationalism and romanticism characteristic of the inward spirit of the Enlightenment, also influenced the outward form of the utopia. By creating more romantic settings, utopian writers of this school made room for love, even to the frank eroticism of the French utopias, as in Rabelais, Vairasse, Morellet, and Étienne Cabet. Readability as a novel came to take precedence over acceptability as a social model. This shift was also furthered by the need of the utopist writing in a despotic age to clothe his criticism of the contemporary scene with literary diversions that would fool the censors. The French writers were the worst offenders in being carried away by their own clever devices; however, it would be shortsighted not to see the images of the future that the devices shielded.

Once we leave the classical platonic utopia and its variant, the romantic utopia, we enter an area where fantasy reigns and holds up many ingeniously contrived mirrors for man. Each mirror expresses a different facet of the Enlightenment, and we have named four types: folk mirrors, comic mirrors, mirrors for monarchs, and contrasting mirrors. The term mirror is meant to convey the idea of reflection in both its meanings: philosophical reflection and image-reflection.

Folk Mirrors

This type of mirror focuses on travel tales. Accounts of travelers in other lands are an excellent device for describing a more attractive society than the writer's own, and provide an innocent opportunity for holding up one's own society to the glass. The real-life voyages of discovery so dear to the Renaissance are now replaced by imaginary overseas journeys. Often there is a shipwreck incident preceding the discovery of the ideal society, and then it is sometimes difficult to distinguish real utopias from romantic "robinsonades." The author of *Robinson Crusoe*, for example, also wrote an authentic utopia.[7] Whether or not a work should be classified as a utopia depends chiefly on the author's intention, although the reader's judgment also enters in.

The tales of Rabelais belong to this genre of utopian-fantasy travel tales, but will be discussed later. In England we find the simultaneous appearance in one year of Francis Godwin's *The Man in the Moon* and John Wilkins's *The Discovery of a World in the Moon* (1638). From this point on we find the voyage-to-the-moon theme and the related idea of another world as dominating themes in the literature.[8] Savinien Cyrano de Bergarac also uses the voyage-to-the-moon theme in his remarkable literary productions combining heroism, libertinism, burlesque, science, and a vision of the future, especially in *L'Histoire Comique des États du Soleil* (1652), *L'Histoire Comique des États de la Lune* (1656?), and *L'Autre Monde*. On one of his "trips to the moon" Cyrano "discovers" the lost earthly paradise, the prophet Elias, and the good daemon of Socrates.

Of the innumerable travel fantasies written in this period there are perhaps fifty that are still known. Among the outstanding ones are Vairasse's *L'Histoire des Sévérambes* (ca. 1675); Gabriel de Foigny's *Les Aventures de Jacques Sadeur* and *La Terre Australe Connue* (ca. 1675), and Morellet's *Le Naufrage des Îles Flottantes ou Basiliade* (a romanticized early version, published in 1735, of his already mentioned *Code de la Nature*, which appeared two years later). During this period Voltaire was writing his utopian-style novel, *Micromegas*. Nicholas Edme Restif de la Brétonne was a prolific writer of utopias, among them *Les Megapatagons ou la découverte Australe par un homme volant* (1782). The Danish metaphysician and humorist Baron Ludvig Holberg had already written *Nicolai Klimii iter subterraneum (Nicholas Klim's Underground Journey)* as far back as 1741. We will discuss the famous travels of Swift's *Gulliver* (1762) in another connection, as well as the later utopian journey of Cabet (1840).

Bunyan's allegorical journey, *The Pilgrim's Progress from This*

---

[7] Daniel Defoe, "Essay of Projects," (1697). Even in *Robinson Crusoe* we find a distinctly utopian "back to nature" trend.

[8] One interesting aspect of the moon-theme is the identification of the insane with the moon-dwellers: "lunatic," *lunatique*.

103

World to That Which Is to Come (1678), is in a class by itself. This earthly journey has a strictly transcendental goal and is eschatological in character. The utopian element, however, is not entirely absent.[9] In a way *The Pilgrim's Progress* does not belong to the Age of Enlightenment. Strongly characterized by influence-pessimism, it might have been written before the Renaissance. Still, it contains elements of "back-to" romanticism and the basic theme of the imagined journey to bind it to its own age. The figure of Bunyan towers above this environment. Belonging to a little band of Puritan nonconformists and hemmed in by prison walls for much of his life, he emerged from a compulsive obsession with his personal sins in order to sound a call to reform—not of human institutions but of humanity itself.

Comic Mirrors

Humor is the oldest weapon in man's arsenal for attacking the social order and appears in many forms. In Thomas More it speaks softly, as subtle irony. But the true comic mirror uses biting satire and naked parody. It makes fun of what it sees. The main goal of the comic mirror is not amusement but annihilation and, afterwards, reconstruction (though this may not be easily discerned).

Among the oldest examples of this kind of utopia are the adventures of *Gargantua and Pantagruel* (1530—1540) by Rabelais.[10] In Rabelais we see the typical, many-sided divided personality so prevalent among utopians: Benedictine monk, medical man, scholar, Epicurean, virtuoso of the written word. This fierce critic of social evil was often accused of heresy but never officially condemned.

The travel tales of Cyrano de Bergerac and Holberg, already mentioned, might also be classified with the satirical utopias; so too might Voltaire's *Candide*, with its devastating criticism of the age and the famous if hardly soul-stirring conclusion, *Il faut cultiver notre jardin.*

The place of honor among utopian comic mirrors goes to *Gulliver's Travels* (1726) by Jonathan Swift. All the foibles of the age are mirrored in the lands visited by Lemuel Gulliver: the land of

---

[9] This work is not ordinarily regarded as part of the utopian literature. For an extensive, if one-sided, treatment of *The Pilgrim's Progress*, see Aalders in his *Toekomstbeelden uit vijf eeuwen.*

[10] These adventures are directly connected with those of More's *Utopia*. The wife of Gargantua and mother of Pantagruel is a daughter of the king of Utopia.

giants (Brobdingnag), the land of dwarfs (Lilliput), the flying island (Laputa), and the great academy (Lagado). Swift, a dean, poet, politician, theologian, misanthrope, and split personality, ended his years in a state of mental unbalance. He was a high church dignitary, Anglican apologist, and cutting critic of both Catholicism and Protestantism *(Tale of a Tub)*. Full of contradictions, he was a woman-hater and yet caught in tragic liaisons with two women; he was first Whig, then Tory; at once a grim pessimist and an untiring fighter for changing causes; an exile in the flesh, a world-traveler in the spirit. He was small in small things and great in great things. Destroyer of this world, he saw himself as a builder of a better one.

It is this last element that is definitive for this type of mirror-utopia. Horace, the gentle satirist of Rome; Juvenal, the grim one; Boileau, the iconoclast; La Fontaine, the subtle commentator on the foibles of French society; and Fontenelle, the attacker of the rule of the classics of antiquity over his contemporaries, were all satirists, but none of them were utopians. The comic mirror of the Enlightenment, like Alice's mirror several centuries later, has two dimensions. It not only mirrors (and distorts) the contemporary scene; beyond the surface distortion lies the vision of an Other, beckoning time. The freakish travel adventures are only means to a higher goal: the description of human existence in an ideal setting.

Mirrors for Monarchs

The monarch-centered utopias go one step further than Plato's *Politeia*. Would it not be possible to transform the legitimate heir to a throne into a philosopher-king through a purposeful design of rational education? To the critique of the times and of the monarch is now added expectation for the immediate future, concentrated on the dauphin or on a younger descendant in the direct line of succession to the throne. This note had already been sounded by Campanella in *The City of the Sun*. While this is in one sense a step forward, it is also a considerable step backward. The time-horizon has shrunk to the immediate future, and the space-horizon is nothing but a national boundary. Fénelon's *Télémaque* (1699) is the classic example of this type of mirror-utopia. Here we have a description of the kingdom, Salente, whose enlightened despot is concerned only for the happiness of his people.

Fénelon's mirror was reflected again by many imitators. Many of these built their ideal around the figure of Cyrus,[11] founder of the

---

[11] This literature is so extensive that it is referred to as the cyropaedia.

105

Persian Empire around 500 B.C. Others fused their image of an ideal monarch with the conception of an ideal state or an ideal religion. Jean Terrasson's *Sethos* (1731) is a utopia of the travel-romance type, filled with both heroism and mysticism, and takes for its setting the courts of an idealized dynasty of ancient Egypt and Atlantis. This book is supposed to have been a great favorite of Frederick the Great. In Vairasse's *Sévérambes*, already mentioned among the folk-mirror utopias, we find a theocracy under the rule of the sun god, who is represented on earth by a sun king *(Le Roi Soleil)*.

Finally, we find Quesnay and the physiocrats pleading for an enlightened despotism following the Chinese model, in which the natural order is incarnated in the imperial son of heaven, founder of the earthly Celestial Empire. Quesnay's philosophy is best expounded in "Le Droit Naturel," published in the *Journal d'Agriculture* (1765) and in *Essai physique sur l'économie animale* (1746).

In effect, the utopia was now being used to propagate the idea of enlightened despotism, of ecclesiastical hierarchy, and of world-empire. As long as they also incorporated a genuine critique of the times and the concept of an ideal society, the label of utopia may still be applied. A gradual secularization of the idea of the Kingdom of God on earth is involved as a deified earthly king is substituted for the King of Kings. There is still an element of the old idea of *l'état, c'est moi*, but the concept of kingship is on a much higher plane.

Contrasting Mirrors

Contrasting mirrors are closely akin to comic mirrors, and many utopias are both. Both use queer beings and unfamiliar situations to clothe their critique of the times. The stories are frequently rambling and disjointed, borrowing at random from ancient sagas and fairy tales.

The unique element in the utopia of the contrasting mirrors is the axiomatic reversal of all existing postulates, in purposeful thought-experiment. Another upside-down world is constructed with great precision and attention to detail. The social criticism of these contrasting-mirror-utopias is a distillate of the chemistry of revolution.

The upside-down quality of these utopias comes out in many ways. In *Nicholas Klim's Underground Journey*, Holberg describes headless wise men, full of excellent advice, and contrabass men who speak by plucking their own strings. In one of the countries visited by Gulliver the dead function as servants for the living. In the French

106

utopias of this contrasting type, we find reversals and scramblings of names: Sirap (Paris), Mreo (Rome), Enegu (Genève), Yrneh (Henry IV), Eriatlov (Voltaire), and Noffub (Buffon). This was the precedent for Samuel Butler's *Erewhon*. A reversal of reality does not in itself make a Utopia of contrast, however. The reversal of sexual morality in Marquis de Sade is not utopian; among other things, the element of systematic thought-experiment is lacking. A few of the Enlightenment utopias which do fall in this category of contrasting mirrors will be mentioned here.

The change of outlook following from a change in position is well illustrated in one of Cyrano's many heroic adventures, in which the relative positions of the earth and the moon are reversed. In Godwin's *Man in the Moon*, the moon is a paradise reserved for the blessed, while evildoers are deported to the earth. Cyrano's moondwellers refuse to recognize the possibility that the earth is inhabited by living beings. It is only a moon, they say. They walk on hands and feet, and their priests make fun of the creatures who can only walk on two legs and look about from an erect position.

The oldest and most famous of this type of reversal is in Rabelais's utopian romance, *L'Abbaye de Thélème* (1534). This monastery is in every respect the opposite of the monasteries of the time. Standing in open country, without the walls and clocks that form the boundaries of human existence, it has engraved over the door *Fay ce que vouldras*, "Do what you will." Only handsome men and beautiful women are admitted. Instead of "Chastity, poverty, and obedience," the motto is "sex, wealth, and liberty." There are no regulations, and everyone is free to come and go as he wishes. Every inhabitant has his own spacious and well-appointed apartment. Every imaginable cultural resource, comfort, and luxury is provided. It is a community of emancipated humanists living together in mutual understanding, entertaining each other with learned conversations, song, and music. It is a refutation in advance of the utopia to be conceived a century later by the other monk, Campanella.

Swift demonstrates how we may see ourselves through the eyes of other species possessing human intelligence. The most significant of his portrayals is his genuine utopia, the land of the Houyhnms. This race of wise and noble horses uses a bestial species of human beings as its beasts of burden. Foigny, whose work was mentioned under folk utopias, provides a unique way of viewing man and his problems. He paints the ideal man as a hermaphrodite, man and woman in one person. These people have an ideal problem-free society. They are aggressive in only one respect: they cannot tolerate stray human beings of one sex. These are labeled *demi-hommes* and exterminated.

The genre of the contrasting-mirror utopia arises through a sharpening of the outlines of the folk-utopia to the point where a structurally complete counterimage of the existing world emerges. The restless and enterprising "geometric" man succeeds the decrepit *homme dévot* of quietism, as men learn to rethink in a relativistic way.

In the beginning the utopist's problem is simply to find a suitable geographic contrast to the contemporary scene somewhere on the face of the earth. The Other world is then often no further away than the other hemisphere. The new world is not America, already too well known. Often it is the still unexplored continent of Australia. This land is at once the Mecca and Eldorado of the utopia of the Enlightenment.[12] The novels of Vairasse, Foigny, and Restif de la Brétonne are all placed here. The moon or other heavenly bodies also provide a convenient counterworld. In *Micromegas*, Voltaire brings inhabitants of Sirius and Saturn in contact with the earth.

In the realm of customs and manners every conceivable trick of variety and contrast is offered. There are children who punish their parents in a land where youth, not age, is respected. Sometimes courting procedures are reversed and the women pursue the men (not such an unfamiliar reversal in the eyes of the modern American man), or perhaps the armies are composed of female combatant soldiers, or the women possess the men communally. Free love is naturally a fairly frequent phenomenon. Sometimes even incest is permitted, especially in the form of brother-sister marriages.[13] In general, there are no checks applied to eroticism, and Freudian complexes would not flower in this free soil. Man wanders in the innocent and happy nakedness of Eden.

Here are examples of other types of deviant attitudes: gold is frequently a despised metal in these utopias, private property is

---

[12] Australia was the setting for an early travel-romance, concerning an uninhabited island, written by the Dutch physician and surgeon, Hendrik Smeeks, under the pseudonym of Exquemelin, and entitled *Beschrijvinge van het magtig Koninkrijk Krinke Kesmes (Account of the mighty Kingdom of Krinke Kesmes)* (Amsterdam: Nicolaas Ten Hoorn, boekverkoper, 1708). This work is supposed to have been the inspiration for Defoe's *Robinson Crusoe*.

[13] According to Raymond Ruyer's *L'Utopie et les Utopies* (Paris: Presses Universitaires, 1950), tolerance of incest was in the eighteenth century a test of the truly philosophical spirit. Even in the nineteenth century, we find traces of this tendency in Byron, Chateaubriand, and Baudelaire.

replaced by communal ownership, class and position are abolished, private enterprise is frequently replaced by collectivist systems and state control of economic institutions. Often working hours and leisure stand in reverse relationship to each other from the workday norm. These and many other common usages are turned inside out or upside down.

The most noticeable characteristic in these utopias is that of movement. Utopias are only found by journeying either on the globe or in space. Closer to home, they are also found in the bowels of Mother Earth. One traveler reaches Eden by falling into Vesuvius.[14]

In a certain sense the spatial characteristics determine the contents. The utopia offers a self-contained image of the Other, situated somewhere else, but does not as a rule suggest ways of achieving the utopian existence described. The chiliastic element of apocalyptic time-calculation is also, in general, absent.[15]

A second characteristic of these utopias is an overwhelmingly this-wordly orientation. (Bunyan's pilgrimage is a notable exception.) As a rule the focus is on human happiness and the general human welfare. Religion usually appears as deism, an undogmatic blending of the City of God and the City of Man. The monarchic utopias strengthen the worldly element in their identification of the ideal prince and the ideal society.

Sometimes fantasy takes over and leaves utopian reconstruction behind. The fantastic utopias are not to be too lightly dismissed, however. Through all the absurd adventures, there runs the golden thread of the Other, an ever-present core of all the varied utopian tales. Enlightened despotism may be upheld, or all differences in rank abolished; the government may be absolutistic or anarchistic, aristocratic or democratic, communistic or cooperative. Family patterns may be traditional, or communal possession of women and children may be advocated. It is surely not without significance that so many of these utopias have partial or completely communistic forms of social organization. These forms are not a goal in themselves, but means to a goal, representing one choice out of the range of possibilities. Whatever the picture presented, the goal is always a human society organized according to reason and natural law.

---

[14] This genre of subterranean utopia continued until the end of the nineteenth century, when it appeared in the works of Bulwer-Lytton, among others. Gabriel Tarde, the French sociologist, also wrote a utopia of this type.
[15] One exception to this is in Fénelon's *Télémaque*, a monarchic utopia specifically alluding to his pupil, the prince of Burgundy, grandson of Louis XIV, and due to succeed to the French throne.

Chapter 11. The Image of the Future: Primary Source of Socialism and Marxism

The concentration of utopias appearing in France in the third quarter of the eighteenth century, and the revolution in 1789, are not unconnected events. Similarly, the revival of utopism in the first half of the nineteenth century and the revolutions of 1830 and 1848 are not unrelated. In fact, the connection between utopism and the revolutionary mentality is intimate. However, idealistic utopias have much wider horizons than revolutions, with their realistic boundaries in time and space. Revolutions can realize only a part of any utopian vision.

The French Revolution demonstrates how small a part of these visions a revolution can achieve. Spitefully labeled the bourgeois revolution, it was in fact more a citizen's revolution than an upper-middle-class revolution. But it is true that one of the most striking aspects of this revolution was that the institution of private property remained inviolable. Monarchy, nobility, and feudal privileges all fell in the battle for equality—even God was declared dethroned. But private property was protected.[1] Restif de la Brétonne published his utopian novel *L'Andrographie* in 1782, delineating a completely communistic ideal state, then produced a revised edition in 1789 allowing for private property. The French Revolution was, if anything, antisocialistic in its solutions to the social problems of the "equal" citizens of the state. Its leaders failed to understand that an

---

[1] Even Marat and Robespierre state this expressly, although Rousseau remained stubborn in his opposition to private ownership. The position taken was exactly that of the physiocrats, who use the phrase in Article 17 of the "Déclaration des Droits de l'Homme," *le propriété étant un droit inviolable et saint*. This is a far cry from Pierre Proudhon's later *La propriété c'est le vol*.

industrial revolution was already underway which would produce a new class, the proletariat, and an accompanying class conflict that would rip apart the legal fiction of equality which the political revolution had established.

If the short-run results of the revolution of 1789 seem negative, however, the long-run effects are much more positive. The revolution had profoundly impressed on the minds of the age the fact that men could take fate into their own hands, just as the utopias had claimed. It appeared that social institutions really did rest on a revocable contract, as Rousseau had said. In spite of immediate disillusionment, the utopian vision of the future came out of the battle strengthened rather than weakened.

If utopism has influenced history, however, history in its turn has reshaped utopia. It becomes increasingly clear that the problem of human equality, largely bypassed by the French Revolution, is the basic social problem, and its solution is the *conditio sine qua non* for the establishment of the ideal society. This idea is not new, but comes to play a more important role in the utopias as a result of the pressures of history and the advances of science.

Historical Continuity: The Theme of Revolution

There is an unbroken thread of historical continuity running from the communistic societies of primitive Christianity to the apostolic mendicant movements and heretical sects, from the communistic program of Plato's *Politeia* to More's *Utopia* and the work of his literary descendants. These ideas never lost their currency for each generation. The realm of the future had always been seen as a realm of peace, a concept which included social peace and justice. This idea was the unchanging backdrop for all revolutions; in the Netherlands it was the Kennemer rebellion and the conflict between Hoeksen and Kabeljauwsen; in France, the Jacquerie; in Germany, England, and elsewhere the peasant insurrections against oppression and exploitation. Medieval folk literature bore witness to this vision. Between the time of Plato and More they became the living medium for social-utopian images of the future.[2] The folk poets are the testators of the future.

---

[2] See G. Dudok, *Sir Thomas More and his Utopia*, a doctoral dissertation (Amsterdam: H. T. Paris, 1923), pp. 45 ff., for a discussion of folk songs as forerunners of utopism.

Jacob van Maerlant's Martin Songs, which because of their popularity were translated into many languages and found an audience far beyond the narrow circle of the Low Countries, are an excellent example of this.[3]

The same type of ideas can be found in the English folk poetry and political songs in vogue during the Middle Ages. William Langland's *Piers Plowman*[4] and Chaucer's *Canterbury Tales* contain the same kind of revolutionary ideas concerning an oppression-free social order. The satiric Chaucer and the sober Langland each move towards the utopia of social criticism.

One of the oldest English blueprints for social reconstruction is the previously mentioned work of Winstanley,[5] which came out of the sectarian movement of the Diggers and Levelers. Robert Wallace, author of a utopian model for a society without private property (*Various Prospects*, 1761), follows in Winstanley's footsteps. He already sees that such a plan cannot be realized except through a successful experiment by a well-to-do élite or through revolution.

In France, the scene of the revolution, nearly all the pre-revolutionary utopian writings of the seventeenth and eighteenth centuries made use of a more or less drastic communism as the point of departure. We see this in the works of Vairasse and Foigny, in both of Abbé Morellet's books, in that of his follower, the Abbé Mably—*Doutes proposés aux philosophes économistes sur l'ordre naturel et essentiel des sociétés politiques* (1768), an attack on the physiocrats—in Curé Meslier's *Testament,* and in the utopias of Fontenelle, Brétonne, Saint-Just, and others.

These ideas continued after the revolution, although every attempt at realization was smothered in blood. Jean Pierre Brissot de Warville was beheaded in 1793 as a Girondist. Saint-Just followed him to the guillotine in 1794. François Babeuf (who took the Christian name of Gracchus), admirer of Rousseau and Morellet, gave out his communistic "Manifeste des Egaux" in 1796, after the founding of a secret conspiratorial club, the Société du Panthéon. Morellet's *Code de la Nature* served as a basis for this manifesto, for which Babeuf too paid

---

[3] In one of these songs the poet speculated about how fine it would be if the words "mine" and "thine" were abolished from the language.

[4] In addition to a fervent plea on behalf of the peasant land-laborers, this contains a reference to Robin Hood, the robber-knight who took from the rich to give to the poor.

[5] See J. K. Fuz, *Welfare Economics in Some English Utopias from Francis Bacon to Adam Smith* (Den Haag: Martinus Nijhoff, 1951), which on the whole contains a complete misunderstanding of utopism, in our opinion.

the price of his head in the same year. This radical and revolutionary socialism, and the appearance of a bold minority in the face of the rising power of the forces of reaction, came about too soon: "Babeuvism" miscarried. But neither the idea nor the will to action were permanently lost.

Utopism now entered its second stage, that of adaptation to both historical and scientific developments. It is the state commonly known as utopian socialism. This development is of exceptional importance. Some writers, including Hertzler, make this the link between the Renaissance and modern times. Others, particularly the later "scientific" socialists, are inclined to consider this stage simply a primitive attempt at socialism before Marx. Both points of view are equally incorrect. Although much has been written about utopian socialism by historians of thought, it must nevertheless be emphasized here that socialism, of whatever variety, can neither exist nor be understood apart from utopism and utopian socialism.

Utopian Socialism

Utopian socialism's prime virtue is that it has attempted to link the Industrial Revolution and the image of the future. It has also tried to provide a scientific foundation for rational-romantic utopism, incorporating the necessary conditions for economic efficiency.

Robert Owen and Claude de Saint-Simon are the most interesting representatives of utopian socialism. The Englishman and the Frenchman were both very much aware of living in a new time.[6] The word "new" appears in almost all the titles of Owen's numerous works, as does the word "industrial" in almost all of Saint-Simon's works. Owen was an industrialist and "discovered" society. Saint-Simon was a *grand seigneur*, an adventurer, and a philosopher, and he "discovered" industry. Both strove to find the ideal relationship between economics and ethics, and found it in socialism. As a result, both came into conflict with dogmatic Christianity and wished to replace it by a new religion. For Owen the development was from the *New View of Society* to *The New Religion*. For Saint-Simon it was from the *Système Industriel* to the *Nouveau Chrétienisme*.

---

[6] Characteristic of Owen is his *The Signs of the Times*, or the *Approach of the Millenium*, which appeared in 1841 while his major work, *Book of the New Moral World* (1836—44) was still in process. Saint-Simon's first characteristic publication was *De Réorganisation de la Société Européenne* (1814).

Owen's own experiments, especially his factory at New Lanark and his cooperative "Villages of Union," had great success for a time, and then later fell apart. Many of his ideas were rediscovered in the twentieth century and applied in the fields of industrial sociology and psychology. Saint-Simon himself had little success, but his spirit lived on in Saint-Simonianism; for once, the disciples far surpass the master. They are predominantly men of action, pioneers of great world-wide undertakings; the Panama and Suez canals, public works, railroads, water works, credit banks, trade organizations, and other activities are all to their credit. Although with Saint-Simon the socialistic utopia ended in religious mysticism,[7] his disciples combined this with a strong sense of practical reality.

Saint-Simon's outstanding disciple, Auguste Comte, gave utopism a new impetus, however. If the divided genius typical of so many front-rank utopists is in itself sufficient to insure fame, Comte certainly deserves a place at the very top. The founder of the philosophy of positivism and the science of sociology, Comte proposed a new social order based on these principles. In the end he established his own religion and his own dogmatics, with himself as the high priest. Thus a utopia which began in mathematics ended once again in mysticism.

Comte saw social development as occurring in three stages. The metaphysical stage was to succeed the theological stage and in turn be replaced by a final positivist scientific stage. He himself, however, fell back into a mixture of the first two stages. But in spite of the fact that Comte's work falls apart through its own logical contradictions, he attached to utopism the idea of a scientific structure of rational prognosis of the future.

The brilliance of Comte overshadowed a remarkable contemporary, Charles Fourier. This contemporary of Owen died while Comte's many-volumed *Positive Philosophy* was still in process of appearing. The contrast between the two is great, as are the similarities. The one was a great entrepreneur, widely honored, the other an insignificant traveling salesman, repeatedly declared insane. Both were inspired by the Industrial Revolution, however.[8]

The similarities go further. Both Owen and Fourier expected everything from a new environment, in which man could develop his potentialities to the fullest. Owen's Villages of Union have been

---

[7] Saint-Simonianism as a religious sect fell to pieces.
[8] One of Fourier's last works was *Le Nouveau Monde Industriel* (1829). In *Oeuvres Complètes, Aux Bureaux de la Phalange,* (Paris: 1841—1846).

called parallelograms, and Fourier labeled his voluntary associations *phalanstères*. Both taught the "back-to-nature" doctrine. In addition to their creative role in furthering the cooperative movement, they are the spiritual fathers of the modern garden cities.[9]

The development of Fourier's ideas and the way in which he announced them [10] were so bizarre that the scientific community could find no good word to speak for this self-taught man. Instead they sanctioned the association of the words *Fourier* and *fou*, "crazy." Hypnotized by Newton's natural science, Fourier thought he had discovered a "law of gravity" operating in the life of the body social. In this same tradition Comte and Lambert Quételet were later to speak of the *physique sociale*, "the social organism." Fourier's fundamental Newtonian principle of social relationships is that of *l'attraction passionelle*. This must not be regarded as erotic passion alone, although that element is present. Fourier's philosophy of giving free vent to the passions, as *voulus de Dieu*, goes hand in hand with an anticipation of feminism and ideas concerning the emancipation of woman in society. The application of his basic principle to labor is even more interesting. His demand for *le travail attrayant*, "attractive labor," establishes him as a forerunner of the modern concept of taking pleasure and pride in one's work. But unfortunately his ideas concerning sexual attraction came to overshadow his ideas concerning the attractiveness of labor, and so the real value of his general concepts was compromised.

It is in connection with the concept of "attractive labor" that Fourier's most interesting utopian constructions are to be found. Work is to be organized on the basis of voluntary association into special groupings.[11] Fourier not only recognized the characteristic differences between the integrated *Gemeinschaft* and the disintegrated *Gesellschaft* long before the advent of the sociologist Tönnies, but he concentrated more systematically than his predecessor utopists on the solution of the social question through the group—the

---

[9] Friedrich Froebel, originator of the kindergarten, was a disciple of Fourier.

[10] Main works: *Théorie des Quatre Mouvements ou des Destinées Générales* (1808) (translated as *The Social Destiny of Man, Theory of the Four Movements* (Philadelphia: C. F. Stollmeyer, 1840), and *Théorie de l'unité Universelle. Oeuvres Complètes.* (Paris: 1822) (translated as *The Passions of the Human Soul*, 1851).

[11] See *Traité de l'Association Domestique et Agricole* (London: Bossange and Mongie, 1822). By his plea for voluntary associations of workers, Fourier took a point of view diametrically opposed to that of the revolution of 1789, which forbade such organizations in the name of liberty.

work group, the neighborhood group, the village group. Both Fourier and Owen addressed themselves to many of our contemporary problems, such as wage systems, participation of workers in management, profit-sharing, and so on.

Fourier did not escape the pattern of his contemporaries in shaping a kind of theodicy. He depicted a most alluring climatological and cosmological image of the future, allied to utopian chiliasm, and also not un related to Saint-Simonianism: the salt of the seas shall become sweet, the polar ice will melt (he obviously did not foresee what havoc this might wreack on the continents with the resulting rise in the water level), the deserts shall be watered. Man will come into contact with life on other planets. An earthly realm of peace, with Constantinople as its capital, will climax these developments. Fourierism failed, but his seminal ideas lived on.

There is still disagreement as to whether Proudhon belongs in the ranks of the utopists. He himself did not wish to be considered one. Marx, however, degraded every non-Marxian socialist to utopist. At first he distinguished between the good utopists, his predecessors, who could not know better, and the bad utopists, his contemporaries and adversaries, who should know better. Buber,[12] who certainly sees through the Marxian tactics at this point, nevertheless reckons Proudhon among the French utopists on his own merits. We tend to hold with Rist,[13] who takes him out of the ranks of the utopists and places him instead with the scientists. We would definitely consider Proudhon as one of the founders of the modern trade-union movement and as a forerunner of revolutionary anarchism. The so-called scientific socialism of Marx himself, on the other hand, we would classify as utopism in the face of all the latter's protests to the contrary.

Before presenting the evidence in support of this bold assertion, we would like to mention the last utopist of the French school of economics, Louis Blanc. His little book, *L'Organisation du Travail* (translated as *The Organization of Work*, 1911), contains little that is original. Even the title is borrowed from Saint-Simonianism, and he makes use particularly of the ideas of one of its last representatives, Philip Buchez. He also used ideas of Philippe Buonarotti, one of the participants in Babeuf's conspiracy, who recorded some of its ac-

---

[12] Buber, *Paths in Utopia* (London: Routledge and Kegan Paul, 1949).
[13] See André Gide et Rist, *Histoire des Doctrines Economiques* (Paris: 1922). This excellent standard work on the history of economics has never been superseded.

116

tivities, of Fourier, and of others. It is nevertheless of interest as a milestone of socialism and also, in a certain sense, as the close of one phase of utopism.

Characteristic features of the book are the sharp condemnation of free competition, the recognition of the "right to work," and the proposal to replace individual enterprise by collective *ateliers sociaux*. Ideal systems of production and an ideal social organization would follow automatically from such measures. Unfortunately for utopia, Louis Blanc became a high-level practical politician after the appearance of this book, and the workers expected and demanded that he would carry out his proposals for social workshops. Suddenly the image of the future must be actualized. In this situation Blanc showed up as an inadequate leader. A reluctant government established *ateliers nationaux* by paper decree in order to pacify the popular mass movement, and a bitter opponent of Blanc was placed in charge of carrying out the decree with the express intention of demonstrating its impossibility. This plot succeeded so well that the entire idea was completely discredited for a long time to come.

In this same year of 1848, even before the February Revolution, and unnoticed at the time, the Communist Manifesto appeared. Karl Marx and his coworker Engels may be considered the editors-in-chief of this document, which sharply denounces "utopian" socialism. Marx's *Das Kapital*, the bible of "scientific" socialism, did not appear until nearly twenty years later. This work is probably second only to the Bible itself in the extent to which it has been quoted, criticized, and "commentaried." For the dogmatic Marxist, it is gospel. Streams of ink and blood have flowed forth from its exegesis. However, it is nowhere identified or recognized as an indispensable link in the chain of utopia-development.[14]

The Utopism of Anti-utopian Marxism

Marxism[15] has much for which to thank utopism. The antagonism

---

[14] One exception to this is Doren's essay (see Chapter 14); he makes some insightful comments on the relationship between Marxism and utopism. Fritz Gerlach demonstrated a systematic relationship between chiliasm and Marxism in his *Der Kommunismus als Lehre vom tausendjahrigen Reich* (Munich: H. Bruckmann, 1920). This position is taken over by Taubes and extended to the field of eschatology. The sociologist René König lends his support of the position of his student, Taubes, in *Soziologie Heute*.

[15] Marx himself said on one occasion that he was no Marxist. We use the term here to refer to the doctrines of Marx and their official interpretation by those fellow workers who were closest to him in spirit.

is the rebellion of the adolescent child who must learn to stand on his own feet. There were older competing communistic movements with reputation and authority behind them, which made themselves strongly felt in the first international congresses. Marx and his followers launched a powerful attack on these movements for reasons of political strategy, and condemned them as "utopian" or "bourgeois" socialism; all praise for them was henceforth revoked. This party line was pursued so strictly that the adherents, and perhaps even Marx and his associates themselves, actually came to believe that "utopian" and "scientific" socialism were two completely opposed entities.

Agreements and Differences with the Preceding Socialism

The postulated opposition between Marxism and utopism cannot be rooted in the idea of socialism as such, since this idea was always contained in utopism. All roads seem to lead to Marx: in England, from Owen and Francis Thompson; in France, from Jean de Sismondi, Saint-Simon, and the just-discussed utopian socialists of the first half of the nineteenth century. Marx had personal contact with most of these men. He studied their writings intensively. He knew the industrial system and the exploitation of the workers with and through Owen, the Saint-Simonists, and Fourier; he was familiar with the question of private ownership from utopian socialism to the much-maligned Proudhon. He knew the thinking concerning free competition of the utopists, including Louis Blanc. He was acquainted with the problem of how to have an ideal society without centralized government authority.

Thus the credit for the new turn of Marxism cannot be granted to its component socialism as such. The specific claim resides rather in the two attributes, "scientific" and "revolutionary," terms usually applied to Marxism. Both these modifying adjectives are, in our opinion, accurate. We maintain, however, not only that Marxism does not basically oppose utopism at these two points, but that it continues and strengthens the utopian tradition, for utopian socialism also strove in its own way to be scientific and revolutionary. In fact, it is precisely in its scientific and revolutionary aspects that Marxism is most strongly utopian.

First, a few remarks on the "scientific" element. Leaving out of consideration Marx's contributions in the field of economic theory, we are here concerned only with the question of whether Marxism was scientific and utopism contrastingly unscientific.

Marx postulated a new, "natural" order as a final goal, entirely in the spirit of enlightened utopism. Even the return to the natural, first state of man is not lacking. Marx writes in a famous passage in *Das Kapital*, "Accumulation plays the same role in the economic system that the fall of man plays in theology." This sin of accumulation will continue, he says, to the point where the entire system is ready to explode, with the ensuing expropriation of the expropriators. Then the lost paradise can be reconstituted by the freely united workers.

The analogy goes even deeper than can be expressed in such a passage. The idea of a natural three-stage law of social evolution was used by Saint-Simon and Comte, to say nothing of Vico and Joachim, before Marx. Comte sought to find laws underlying social processes; his search carried him on a long journey, via Quesnay and Morellet, but he did not find what he was looking for. Fourier sought, and found—at least to his own satisfaction—the law of social gravity. Marx found another law and based his entire system upon it. Whether it was right or wrong is here irrelevant, and does not determine whether it was more or less scientific.

It was, indeed, through his discovery of this law of social dynamics that Marx created a certain distance between his system and the enlightened utopia—not because of its content—for this law implied a change of view precisely in respect to the traditional twofold task of utopia, the destructive critique of the times and the systematic reconstruction. The logic of his system caused Marx to assign a different place to both functions. Seen in the light of the evolutionary laws of the social mechanism he postulated, the present with all its misery becomes a necessary phase of transition. Capitalism as such is thus for Marx indispensable. He has little use for social criticism; on the contrary, it is unavoidable that the existing state of affairs be further sharpened to a point of final crisis before the dialectic reversal can take place. Critique of the current scene, then, is superfluous for Marx.

Similarly, and on the same grounds, a detailed reconstruction of the society of the future is unnecessary. Social evolution will itself take care of this future. Not only is such a reconstruction unnecessary, but it is undesirable, if confusion is to be avoided. The predicted revolutionary change will come when the time is ripe, and it is sufficient to be aware of the main direction of its predetermined course. That which stands central in Marx's image of the future is not a precise and complete image of the future, but the fact of a coming.

Now we turn to the second, the "revolutionary" element in Marxism. Are its specific differences with utopism located here? On the contrary, the revolutionary element is inherent in utopism. Even if Marx really had achieved an entirely original creation, he would still be indebted to utopia for the technique of axiomatic reversal which we have learned to recognize as its hallmark.

Marx used this reversal again and again. Is his reversal of Proudhon's *Philosophie de la Misère* into the sharp *Misère de la Philosophie* only a coincidental play on words? Marx also makes use of the current romantic contrast in the utopia literature between the unnatural (this civilization) and the natural (that which existed once and will come again). Bourgeois economics, says Marx, state that the feudal system was artificial and that present-day institutions are the natural ones. Nothing could be less true. It is the present-day insitutions which are artificial, and they will be replaced in their turn by the true natural institutions of the working proletariat. Further, one of Marx's most widely-acclaimed reversals is the unmasking of absolutes of the existing order as nothing but historical relativities. But this is precisely the anvil at which the enlightened utopia had been hammering for a hundred years.

It is no different with his famous threefold dialectic: thesis, antithesis, and synthesis. We have encountered this repeatedly in the history of the images of the future, as an essential element in a tradition that continues unbroken to Hegel. The fact that Marx borrowed this concept from Hegel for his laws of social dynamics tells us nothing more (or less) than that he has chosen this image of the future for his own; the image of paradise, paradise lost, and paradise regained; the image held by Israel of ascendancy, collapse, and final resurrection. That he daringly stood the historical idealism of Hegel on its head and turned it into historical materialism also stamps him as a pure-blooded utopist, both because of his technique of reversal of historic cause and effect (with deliberate disregard of functional interaction) and because of his belief, also stemming from the Enlightenment, that man is exclusively the product of his social environment and that a new environment can produce a new man.

We have thus far been speaking only of parallel paper reversals. But what of the reversals in the actual deed? Here there is a significant difference. In the Marxian view of historical materialism, there is no place, as in previous utopism, for an independent awakening of intellectual revolutionary awareness into a final explosion. The revolution cannot start before the time is ripe. (This view stands in flat contradiction to the attitude held by Marx's followers.) According to Marxian doctrine, both the desire for and act of revolution are not made but born out of the dialectical process. Revolution in utopian

120

socialism, on the other hand, means to change the course of history by human power. The important difference between Marx and the utopian socialists does not revolve around the fact of being revolutionary or nonrevolutionary; rather, it stems from a difference in vision concerning the character and function of revolution. The classic model of utopism, and also of utopian socialism, involved an overturning on behalf of the entire human society, for mankind as such. The Marxian overturning, on the other hand, is thought of as the result of a class struggle, brought to foreordained completion by and for the workers. The utopists see the revolution as the external transformation of this world into an entirely Other and better world. The Marxists confine their contrasts to within this world. Their transformation is not a turning inside out, but a turning upside down; the class on top is pushed down, and the class underneath is elevated, resulting in the worker's paradise.

In the second place, and compellingly related to the first point, there is a difference of priority between utopia and revolution. The utopists consciously project their revolutionary images of the future so that the times may be moved in the direction of this ideal. The utopia is primary, and its fulfillment is brought about by man's activism. The Marxists, on the other hand, see the autonomous mechanism of natural law operating independently of man; the revolutionary class struggle is only a by-product which can hasten the inevitable. Once the dictatorship of the workers has come about, then the utopia will materialize of its own accord. The socialist's utopia is prerevolutionary, the Marxists' utopia is postrevolutionary. The one requires human effort from beginning to end, the other requires it only at the end.

The Transformation of Eschatology into Utopism

What are the contours of the anti-utopian Marxist's new order? Work stands central in the new socio-economic dispensation, and no differentiation is made between headwork and handwork. It is to be free, voluntary work, without compulsion, so joy in work comes of itself. This joy comes also because the means of production are held in common by the workers, as are its fruits. Through a rise in productivity, the fruits of production shall become increasingly abundant. There shall be no more unemployment and poverty; wage slavery will automatically cease. Since power will come to the community of workers, the state itself with its false authority will atrophy. A new natural man will flower in this new natural environment.

This is the dimly revealed core of the Marxian image of the future. This is what is disseminated, not as a compact presentation, but as a stringing together of widely scattered fragments. We challenge anyone to deny the utopian quality of the basic message of the Marxian image of the future.

The typically utopian elements of "scientific" Marxism go much deeper than this, however. All the characteristic features of older images of the future are to be found in Marx. One of these characteristics relates to emotions. Marxism itself rejects an atmosphere of tender feelings to replace it by realistic reasoning. Nevertheless, Karl Marx reveals his hope of paradise regained at every turn; in his compassion for the dehumanizing situation of the proletariat, with the long working hours even for women and children, the crowded city slums for shelter for the forcibly uprooted rural immigrant. The passion of these unscientific feelings is for the most part carefully hidden. But does not his very choice of terminology—"exploitation," *Verelendung*, and *Zusammenbruch*—bear witness to a basic pathos?

It is the eternal human utopian longing which arouses Marx to his discovery of the law of social dynamics and places him in the long tradition from Plato to Morellet of seeking the one way to the one end-state. The Marxian image of the future is not only utopian but also apocalyptic. The specifically Jewish apocalyptic character of the Marxian image of the future is easily recognizable in the doctrine of necessary suffering. The dispossessed and downtrodden workers are the chosen ones, predestined to be elevated. No one must ask for a softening of the hard lot the present imposes, for only when the abyss between the classes leads to climactic tension can the great upheaval take place. It is this consistently apocalyptic character of the image of the future which compels Marxism to oppose all attempts at reform on the part of bourgeois socialism. Orthodox Marxism is as dependent on revolutionary upheaval as is orthodox apocalypticism.

In general it can be said that Marxian thought contains a religious image of the future in secularized form. By opposing religious imagery, it contributes to the latter's decline. This decline of religious visions in turn later undermines the secular faith of Marxism itself, since eschatology and utopism are both rooted in the fundamental capacity of the human mind to split its perceptions and imagine the Other.

Like all utopists, Marx delineated a cleavage in time, as decisive as that of before and after Christ. The sharp pendulum-swings of change up to the time of the total revolution he categorizes as prehistory. The true course of history for human civilization begins after the great liberations of the proletariat. Marx comes into conflict at two points with the more realistic view of human events held by utopian socialism.

In the first place, he had insufficient insight into the significance of the Industrial Revolution and its accompanying technological changes. These changes had a direct effect on the modes of production, a concept on which he had based his whole theory, with resulting change in economic productivity, working hours, the development of new social classes, and so on. In the second place, his understanding of the development of party politics was inadequate: he did not comprehend the significance of the transition from majority power to a new kind of minority power, nor did he foresee the inevitable expansion of government powers as the consequence of collectivization.

How can these failures of insight be explained in one whose profound scholarship is not disputed by even his worst enemies? It is not so difficult to understand how Marx's unworldly teacher, Hegel, could have his idealistic dialectic of world-reason end in his own contemporary state. But how could the worldly wise Marx make a similar mistake? There is little doubt that the "scientific system" and the utopian image of the future come into direct conflict at both these points; the fight has been fixed in advance, so the predestined image of the future is bound to win.

Marx, like Buridan's ass, hesitates between two bales of hay: on the one side, continuing evolution; on the other side, the finality of the revolution. How can these mutually exclusive factors of dynamics and statics be forced into one and the same formula? His ingenious solution is to place them both under the heading of natural law. This takes care of both the dialectics of the antithesis and the lasting synthesis after the reversal. At a chosen moment the Greek device of metamorphosis is used to transform dynamics into statics. The law of nature thus eliminates future change, and itself, as source of change.

What price does Marx pay for this artificial freezing of his image of the future? That of the relative once again becoming absolute. In actual fact, Marx is only one step ahead of orthodox laissez-faire, which holds that a system of natural law maintaining social and economic equilibrium is already in operation in the existing order. Marx foresees this automatic equilibrium only after the revolution,

123

when the laissez-faire and nonintervention of classical economics becomes acceptable.

The Unmasking

For the Marxist utopia, the time of reckoning comes with the nonfulfillment of the historical predictions. Now the price must be paid for having abandoned the road of the prerevolutionary utopia: there is neither an up-to-date critique of the times nor a revised vision of reconstruction. Everything had been left to the automatism of natural law; now this bottom has dropped out, and the Marxist is suddenly left standing on his own feet, unsupported. With neither the mechanism of natural law nor a concrete image of the future at its disposal, the social movement toward collectivism threatens to degenerate into a purely political struggle for power.

Balancing the accounts for the utopian image of the future after the failure of the Marxist utopia, we see the following picture: the bitter opposition of Marxist socialism has dealt a blow to the pure utopia from which it has never recovered. In proportion as reality has increasingly given the lie to scientific Marxism, men have become dimly aware of its disguised utopism. Applying to Marx's doctrine the ingenious procedures which Marx himself used to unmask bourgeois ideology, it became possible to unmask the Marxian ideology. But in this process of debunking, no distinction was made between the explicit and the implicit utopia. The same comb was drawn over both threads, and both were condemned as "the utopia." Since then there has been an effort to build up a new scientific socialism apart from utopism.

Marx has thus had the ultimate victory in his battle with utopism, but it is a Pyrrhic one. For that which he attacked most bitterly as "utopian" socialism—bourgeois socialism—is the phenomenon which benefited most from the failure of Marxism. The new scientific socialism of Western society may not be utopian or visionary any longer, but even less is it revolutionary, rather being directed organizational consolidation. The bond between the image of the future and political power has been cut away, and now we have gotten ahead of ourselves, arriving at the one-dimensionality of our own time.

Chapter 12. The Image of the Future: Conductor of the Age of Progress

The jigsaw puzzle of the Age of Enlightenment is not yet complete; one piece is still missing. To find it we must return to the pre-Marxian and prerevolutionary phase of the Age of Enlightenment with its special blend of rationalism and romanticism.

The Utopia of Progress and the Regression of Utopism

The remaining odd piece of the puzzle could well be labeled progress, if we adequately recognize the complexity of this concept. Ideas concerning progress diverge widely; even more do judgments differ concerning progress in the world of thought.[1] We find the contradictions coexistent in the eighteenth-century and nineteenth-century concept of progress most sharply delineated if we consider them in terms of the image of the future.

The first and most pronounced contradiction is between an independent essence-optimism which is entirely sufficient to itself, and an essence-optimism which can only be justified by the supporting presence of influence-optimism. The trends of passivism and activism which Marx tried to combine in one system are now drifting apart. The entire problem-complex concerning the future once more pushes its way into the foreground.

The second contradiction revolves around a twofold shift, on the

---

[1] The reader is referred to my essay "Over de Vooruitgang van het Maatschappelijk Denken" ("On the Progress of Social Thought") in *Om het Behoud van ons Bestaan (On the Maintenance of our Existence)* (Leyden: H. E. Stenfert Kroese's U.M., 1951).

one hand from spatially-oriented images of the future to predominantly temporally-oriented ones, and on the other hand away from temporal images to a special localized kind of spatial image. The Renaissance gave the impetus to the first shift toward a temporal image. While standing with one foot still firmly planted in antiquity, it was crossing the boundaries of the future with the other. The Enlightenment gave an even more decisive push in this direction. Although Rousseau lingered in the Golden Age of the past, Comte and Marx faced towards an altogether new time.

Simultaneously, however, there was an uprush of interest in reforming the social order as a spatial entity. The result was two opposing tidal movements, one forward from spatial to temporal images of the future, the other back from temporal to spatial images. This clash of currents was no accident, but rather characteristic of the idea of progress as such, for this was just the point at which the two opposing forces in the service of progress—pure essence-optimism and conditional essence-optimism bound to influence-optimism—actually met. This phenomenon was highly symptomatic of the further course of events. Even at the height of progress, a retrogression was taking place which caused the decline of the images of the future of Western civilization.

Essence-Optimism

The philosophy of progress-optimism holds that any given course of historical development is the best that can exist, and moving toward the better. We will now consider the two diverging lines of thought concerning progress, the temporal and the spatial.

At a given moment in history, the effects of a long and gradual process become suddenly visible. The first evidence of a decisive change was already observable in the mid-eighteenth century *querelle des anciens et des modernes.* Fontenelle, secretary of the Académie des Sciences, and Swift, author of *The Battle of the Books,* both utopists, were both associated with this epochal literary struggle. The idea of progress even beyond the high points of Greek and Roman culture, was accepted at this time. Cultural progress was seen as related to technological progress. This meant that the apex of civilization need no longer be projected into the elsewhere; it could simply be projected in time.

The first genuine time-utopia, *L'An 2440,* was produced by Louis Mercier, admirer of Montesquieu and Rousseau and a friend of Restif de la Brétonne, in 1770. Mercier's image of the future is boldly

126

located in Paris and is the first anticipation of coming times. This utopia is full of prophecies, some accurate and some wide of the mark. (The accurate ones were for the most part realized long before the prophesied dates.) Here for the first time the dream-device is used, giving the hero an age of seven hundred years so that he may be present in the new time. Both this device, and the attention given to technological inventions, are symbolic of coming trends. This utopia is chiefly important because it represents a definite shift toward time-conscious representations. Simultaneously we find a counter movement which takes the pure concept of progress in time and forces it once more into a spatial framework.

Let us take as an example the treatment of history itself, which has alternated the temporal and spatial emphasis, and between the global and the nationalistic frame of reference. Voltaire is a typical transition-figure who struggled to escape from this ambiguity. History, says Voltaire, is nothing but a bag of tricks played on the dead. We change the past according to our present wishes for the future; history demonstrates that everything can be demonstrated through history.[2] His *Lettres sur les Anglais* was the cockcrow before the French Revolution. His famous "Essai sur les Moeurs," blamed for a lack of patriotism, considers Europe and the little piece of it labeled France as but a peninsula of a new Other world in the East.

Ultimately man's belief in himself and his own calling also led to a renewed belief in his own country, however, and again there was a revival of nationalistic and imperialistic aspirations. This degenerated into a look backward to the great past of one's nation instead of forward to the future of mankind.

In France a chain of events unfolded from man, discovering his own individuality, to the Third Estate, discovering itself as the core of the nation, to the citizenry, discovering itself as sovereign over king and aristocracy, and finally to the mobilized masses, discovering themselves as the French nation in the Assemblée Nationale in 1871. Thus, at the same time that the related ideals of freedom and progress had expanded to encompass a sense of world citizenship, the hard-won rights of man were being narrowed to support the principle of self-determination of national groups.

---

[2] His fiercely critical view of national and military history as a creation of despots and generals led him to try rewriting the past as a history of culture and *l'esprit de l'homme;* he wrote studies of Charles XII, Louis XIII, and Louis XIV in quite a different vein from the heroic saga of Henry of Navarre, written earlier in the Bastille.

Adam Smith's *The Wealth of Nations* appeared in the same year as the American Declaration of Independence. This work was based on the principle of the rational self-interest of the individual. It was not Adam Smith but his epigones who were responsible for the glorification of the doctrine of laissez-faire, inspired by the fact that economic man involuntarily acted in a way favorable to the general economy. Frédéric Bastiat sang of that beneficent system of natural law which results in the *harmonies économiques,* a state which can only be maintained as long as man is free to seek his own gain in every transaction. The state need only concern itself with protecting this economic liberty, and economic progress for the country is ensured. This new emphasis is best expressed by the Manchester School. National welfare and imperial interests are best served through free trade.

Since the development toward the economic optimum can only take place if the free movement of money, goods, and persons is not interrupted by government intervention, every attempt at regulation on behalf of the poor is pernicious. That same industrial flowering of England which provided Marx with the material for *Das Kapital,* appears from the point of view of liberal economics as a demonstration of how God helps those who respect his laws.

New evidence for this spatial image of the future seemed to result from new developments in biology. Darwin, working out the population theories of Malthus, discovered the struggle for existence and the survival of the fittest on the basis of natural selection. "This is it!" chorused the liberal economists, as they translated this doctrine to the milieu of social relationships. In free competition the strongest will win. The sociologist Herbert Spencer developed this doctrine to an extreme of quietism, actually condemning individual philanthropy as harmful to the course of progress. Even the threatened split of the English people into Disraeli's "two nations"—the small number of wealthy men and the great mass of paupers—did not shake this type of spatial essence-optimism, for the wealth of England was visibly increasing all the time.

The natural and applied sciences also contributed to the development of the spatial image of the future: indirectly through the discovery of regularities in the social system, directly in that the Industrial Revolution was an immediate result of scientific development and its accompanying technology. How much the Industrial Revolution was to contribute to this type of progress would only appear later in the New World.

Even theology was affected by the *vis vitalis* of the optimistic spirit, and the pessimistic doctrine of original sin could no longer be maintained in the orthodox form.

Philosophy was now headquartered in Germany. Here lay Archimedes's fixed point on which man could stand and move the world. The construction of philosophy *more geometrico*, begun by Descartes, Pascal, and Spinoza, was completed by Leibnitz. His doctrine of the Divine Architect who has pre-established an encompassing harmony was more maliciously expressed by Voltaire as *tout est pour le mieux dans le meilleur des mondes possibles.* According to this theodicy of the existing order, the actual conforms with the necessary. It is less well known that Leibnitz also had a vision of a German culture-state.[3]

Influence-Optimism

Pure essence-optimism resulted in unadulterated progress-optimism. An unbroken line of evolution was seen flowing from the protozoan to the philosopher. As Bertrand Russell later pointed out, we have only the word of the philosopher for this, and not that of the protozoan! The philosophy of progress-optimism is as deterministic in character as the earlier philosophy of regression. It is impossible for man to hold back the wheels of progress, nor can he deflect from the course on which the world is irrevocably set.

At the same time that the human spirit was riding high on the crest of the tidal wave of essence-optimism, we suddenly find influence-optimism at work as a powerful undercurrent, and influence-optimism in its most revolutionary form at that. Contrary to all logic, it had never really died out. This is a time of contrasts; the thriving of images of the future stemming from influence-optimism is also a thriving of temporal images of the future as such. But from the beginning there is a paradoxical and tragic conflict between temporal and spatial images of progress. Possibly the spatial forms have had a more destructive influence on man's destiny than the hubristic philosophy of endless evolution in time. Progress-optimism must after all face up to an Edenless present. But when spatial images begin to dominate, the regression of the image of the future as a category of human thought becomes an accomplished fact.

In 1840, just a few years before the appearance of the Communist

---

[3] His pupil, Christian Wolff, who systematized and germanized the work of the great master, also produced a political doctrine which contained a model of the German police-state and welfare-state.

Manifesto, Étienne Cabet's communistic utopia *Le Voyage en Icarie*[4] was published in France. In this work the element of the strange and faraway is rejected as the central theme of island-utopias. Cabet places his Icaria on an island in the Indian Ocean, where it can be easily reached by a young English lord traveling for pleasure. The ideal country is now made accessible to everyone.

Icar, the leader, is a postrevolutionary Napoleon, who goes to work, however, in quite another fashion to shape a new social order. The book's oft-repeated cry "Heureux pays! Malheureuse France!' is an appeal from Cabet to France to create for herself the conditions of a comparable happiness.

Cabet's morality is conventional and his literary talent slight, and yet here is a book that was read to pieces in edition after edition and translated into many languages. Cabet is one of the few men who attempted to realize his utopia in his own time. The Icarian colony he founded in America soon split apart, and Cabet himself was thrown out by the Icarians, who were converted to the communist ideal.

The basic principle which pervades *Le Voyage en Icarie* is that of complete equalitarianism, even at the cost of liberty if necessary. Uniformity takes precedence over individuality. A strong centralized communism is introduced to ensure this absolute, all-leveling equality. Domestic relationships are excluded from this communism, however; strict chastity is required of young people, and absolute fidelity in marriage. Every detail of the system is minutely described with dreary precision: child-rearing, education, public health, agriculture, economic institutions, the system of government, the courts, and so on. Nevertheless, behind the somewhat pedantic schoolmaster stands the visionary organizer who anticipated many later developments.

Three features typify this work as a time-Utopia. First, there is the fact that the work includes an analysis of the principles of communism and an extensive historical survey of the development of communism from antiquity to about 1840, with many citations from earlier writers, thus relating the future to history as the work of man.

Second, *Le Voyage en Icarie* introduces a new note in utopian literature by describing the dynamics of the developmental process leading to the utopian end-state. The development takes place in

---

[4] Although this book has not been translated, a study of it has appeared in English: Albert Shaw, *Icaria, a Chapter in the History of Communism* (New York: G. P. Putnam, 1884).

stages, with a fifty-year transition to a communist regime. Meanwhile the older generation may retain its bourgeois rights of property and liberty. Only the younger generation is to be subjected to a rigorous training in the new ways. To abolish the tyranny of a personal monarchy is child's play: it can be wiped out by revolution. But to abolish the impersonal tyranny of private property is more difficult and can only be accomplished by a carefully organized evolutionary process. Here is the first example of modern planning. It is also the first utopia which deals fully with the transition in time from present to future.

Third, Cabet is aware of the significance of the Industrial Revolution—more so than Marx. He even presents technological development as the driver towards communism. He foresees the inevitable standardization resulting from mass production, which both presupposes and institutes the homogeneity of consumers.

Cabet is highly optimistic about the effect of technology in liberating mankind from the sweat of slave labor. The hitherto intractable inequality will be abolished. In this respect, *Le Voyage en Icarie* forms an early point of departure for a long line of utopian works which center on future technological developments.

We will encounter these antipodes of evaluation of technology over and over again in ensuing utopias. It is first remarked in isolated writers, such as Wells, Butler, Bellamy, Morris, and Stapledon. Later schools of culture-pessimists and culture-optimists emerge, the pro-machinists and the antimachinists.

Returning to the temporal image of the future of the Enlightenment, we must trace another development of influence-optimism in the historical stream, that of chiliasm. After the violent sectarian movements of the Middle Ages, subsequent development took several different directions. Communistically oriented-chiliasm had its effect on many utopian socialists with a mystical-religious bent.

Another development is towards pietistic chiliasm and the beginnings of the related idealistic philosophy[5] of Lessing, Kant, Herder, and Fichte. Lessing undoubtedly provides the crucial meeting point between the old and the new spiritual outlook. The transition from sectarian chiliasm to philosophic chiliasm, so important for the image of the future, takes place in him. Here the narrow bonds of both nationalism and the Christian Church are burst to focus attention on

---

[5] In connection with the relation to chiliasm, see Taubes, *Abendlandisch Eschatologies* (Berne: A. Francke, 1947), Vol. II, p. 136, and Nigg, *Das ewige Reich* (Zürich: Reutsch, 1944).

the future of all mankind.

He borrows from Origen, for whom the one way of salvation laid down by God and available to free men consisted of *pronoia*, "foresight," and *paideusis*, "education." Lessing also equates true revelation and education.[6] Education must focus on the inward formation of a new man, who as a freemason recognizes none of the boundaries and walls of a bourgeois churchly society. Lessing's image of the future is that of a "utopia of men." The idea of a "utopia of measures," with new social and political institutions, he rejects completely.

This type of thinking leads directly to Kant, himself influenced by Rousseau, thus drawing on both the rationalism and the romanticism of the Enlightenment. It is Kant who in 1784 gives the famous answer to the question, What is enlightenment?: It is the emergence of man from his minority, in which he was trapped through his immature failure to use his own powers of reasoning. The motto of the Enlightenment is *Sapere aude*, "Dare to think."

Kant thinks through to their ultimate consequences the ideas of Lessing concerning the shaping and rebirth of a new man, the expanding of the horizon to include the entire family of mankind, rational religion, and the establishment of a humanly worthy society. We will attempt here only to extract a few kernels from this profound philosophical system as it relates to the image of the future of progress-optimism.

It is a basic postulate of ethical consciousness that man intervenes in the struggle between good and evil in this world and contributes to the victory of the good: the establishment of the Kingdom of God on earth.[7] Even though this may in fact not be altogether so, man must act as if the realization of the Kingdom depended entirely on him. Only if man himself does his utmost may he place faith in an earthly fulfillment with God's help.

---

[6] Lessing's *Erziehung des Menschengeschlechts* (translated as *The Education of the Human Race* [London: Kegan Paul & Co, 1910]) reveals the path towards this new, broad future (1730). See also his famous parable of *Nathan der Weise* (translated as *Nathan the Wise* [London: Cassell's National Library, 1886]), and the publication of the fragments "Eines Ungenannten" *(Reimarus)* (translated as *Fragments from Reimarus* [London: Williams and Norgate, 1879]).

[7] See "Der Sieg des guten Prinzips Über das Böse und die Grundung des Reiches Gottes auf Erden" (1792) in J. Kant's Werke VI, ed. G., Hartenstein (Leipzig: Modes and Baumann, 1838), the related "Ob das menschliche Geschlecht im beständigen Fortschreiten zum Besseren sei" (1792) in J. Kant's Werke I (translated as *The Principles of Progress in Kant's Principles of Politics* [Edinburgh: T and T. Clark, 1891]), and *Das Ende aller Dinge* (1794) in Kant's Werke VI.

Belief that the morally pure man will develop into a world citizen and that the temporal development of history will be towards a future of "perpetual peace" fits naturally into this idea of the progressive betterment of man. A moral community of all men shall comprise the true, invisible church on earth. However scattered and divided this community may be, it will strive for the true Kingdom of God "in everything and everyone"[8] —not, as now, for the kingdom of the priesthood. Kant's *Zum ewigen Frieden* (1795) (translated as *Perpetual Peace* in 1932) was one of his last works, written when he was past seventy. It resurrects not only the older projects for a *paix perpetuelle* of the much-reviled pioneer utopist Abbé Charles de Saint-Pierre,[9] who died half a century before, and similar plans of Leibnitz, but, on a deeper level, the old image of a Thousand Years' Reign.[10] In his philosophical transposition of this idea, Kant no longer makes the Reign of Peace depend on a superhuman power. It is man-guided; not by reason alone, however, but by the will to good. Kant's greatness lies in the fact that he was able to relate the goal of unhindered development of the individual man to the general educational task of the growth of mankind toward self-determination of destiny.

In the split figure of Herder, contemporary and antipode of Kant, we see a tragic turning back to a view of the priority of Germany in this world's spatio-temporal dimensions. Two mutually exclusive concepts concerning the nature of historical development contend throughout his work to the very end. On the one hand, there is the conviction of the progress of mankind towards the divinely ordained

---

[8] These ideas are further developed in the works *Idee zu einer allgemeinen Geschichte in weltburgerlicher Absicht* (1784) in J. Kant's Werke IV, (translated as *The Idea of a Universal History on a Cosmo-Political Plan* [Hanover N.H.: Sociological Press, 1927) and *Mutmasslicher Anfang der Menschengeschichte* (1786), in Werke IV. Here he suggests with Lessing that the internal and necessary goal of historical development in time is the moral perfecting and uniting of man. This is along the lines of his later, more systematically developed *Critique of Practical Reason* (1798) (translated 1909) and *Religion innerhalb der Grenzen der blossen Vernunft* (Konigsberg: Friedrich Nicolovius, 1793) in Werke VI (translated as *Religion within the Limits of Reason Alone* [JII./London: The Open Court, 1934]).

[9] For a discussion of the numerous utopian writings and ideas of this utopist par excellence, who cannot receive special attention here, see Schomann in his *Französische Utopisten*, pp. 94 ff.

[10] No one was more aware than Kant of the half-romantic, half-ridiculous aspect of this idealistic image of the future for human life on earth. He himself draws attention to the Dutch innkeeper who has humorously inscribed *Reign of Peace* on a signboard depicting a graveyard.

"kingdom of humanity" (see *Briefe zur Humanität*). On the other hand, there is the conviction of an organic development within each special folk culture, on the basis of genetic origin, language, *Volksgeist*, and culture. Each of these cultures, says Herder, is the earthly realization of one of God's thoughts. The German people, having had a special call, embody the "best thought."[11] In the course of a century this second, geographically rooted idea gradually gains the victory.

However, it is not Herder, tossed back and forth between humanism and nationalism, but the equally split Fichte who marks the definite turning back of the image of the future from time to place. Another divided man! At first he was a champion of the French Revolution, a supporter of the Jacobites, and an advocate of the most far-reaching views on liberty, equality, and fraternity.[12] He admired both the goddess Reason and the French nation, into whose service he would willingly enter. He was enthusiastic on the subject of the natural rights of man and the doctrine of sovereignty of the people, and held that the state existed only by virtue of a social contract and subject to the will of the people—a basically anarchistic view.[13] His was a vision of the progress-utopia, involving human evolution in time towards a state of freedom and equality.

In 1800, Fichte made a complete about-face and adopted the contrary of the views he had been upholding with such fiery vigor. In this year his *Die Bestimmung des Menschen* (translated as *The Vocation of Man*, 1873) appeared, a plea for law and order to protect man from sin. The seeds of his later "Reden an die deutsche Nation" (1807) are all here.

In this same year, at the midpoint between his revolutionary humanism of 1793 and his conservative nationalism of 1807, he published the utopian image of the future, *Der geschlossene Handelsstaat*,[14] which he himself considered his best work. This utopia is

---

[11] See *Ideen zur Philosophie der Geschichte der Menschheit* (Riga: Hartknoch, 1784—91) (translated as *Outlines of a Philosophy of the History of Man* [London: 1803]); also his highly characteristic *Stimmen der Völker in Liedern.*
[12] See *Beiträge zur Berichtigung der Urteile des Publikums über die Französische Revolution* (Danzig: Troschel, 1793). In this work Fichte gives a parenthetical warning, with true German foresightedness and emphasis, against the ever-increasing and undermining Jewish menace, a menace which announces itself on every hand through the systematic formation of a "state within the state" by the Jews!
[13] See *Grundlage des Naturrechts* (Jena: Cnobloch, 1796) (translated as *The Science of Rights* [Philadelphia: 1869]).
[14] This has not been translated into English.

praised to the skies by the German authors Hans Freyer and Georg Quabbe. It is also discussed, surprisingly enough, by the Dutch theologian Aalders among the five images of the future which are considered representative of five centuries of human thought about the future; it is handled by Aalders with some naïveté. This much-noticed work of Fichte represents a decisive turning back to and fatal version of the spatially limited image of the future.

In his "closed economy" Fichte effects an about-face from the radical individualism of his youth to a radical state socialism which cannot even be labeled enlightened. It can only be compared, and especially with respect to the machinery of coercion, to the later developments of national communism, Lenin-style and Stalin-style, and to the Third Reich of his own country, á la Schacht and Hitler. He indeed deserves full, if dubious, credit for having foreshadowed these developments in his image of the future.

Fichte is not unjustly placed in the category of voluntarism and active influence-optimism. His political "thou shalt" rings out as categorically as the ethical imperative of Kant. His utopia is not fanciful and unrealizable. In the preface to *Der geschlossene Handels-staat* he makes fun, like Marx, of all politically unfeasible and speculative ideal states. As tribunal orator in "Reden an die deutsche Nation-"[15] he makes fun of other utopias as "artifical products of a social machine-art," which are fatal to true philosophy and complete-ly un-German. He calls fiercely on his fellow countrymen to become aware of their vocation not primarily as men, but as Germans—less than half a century after Voltaire, who was blamed for being a man first and a Frenchman second.

The "closed national economy" is not only geographically closed; it also closes off an age. A new spatial image of the future comes into being which is to dominate the next 150 years, and contains enough dynamite ultimately to explode all images of the future oriented toward progress in time.

It was, however, reserved to Macaulay, the clever Englishman, to write the final epitaph for the temporal image of the future in the famous patriotic sneer, "An acre of Middlesex is better than a principality in Utopia."

---

[15] See Hans Freyer, *Die politische Insel* (Leipzig: Bibliogr. Inst., 1936), p. 139.

135

The Utopia as a Powerhouse

The discussion moves closer to our own time. We are now only a century—at the most a century and a half—removed from it. We can therefore experience more immediately the force and impact of these visions of the previous century on our own. In summarizing this stirring period in history which gave rise to so many and such diverse images of the future, we become increasingly aware of the amazing dynamic power of the utopian vision.

The Utopist as Patron Saint and Arbiter of History

It would be interesting to examine and assess the influence exerted personally by the utopian thinkers discussed in this chapter. Sometimes the influence has been immediate; sometimes it has not been felt until long after the utopist has done his work. Just as one can trace the influence of Thomas More on England's domestic and foreign policy, and the influence of Bacon on the development of experimental natural science and technology, so one can trace the alterations in the course of history set in motion by the work of More's and Bacon's successors. Harrington's *Oceana*, for instance, had an immediate impact on France through the work of Abbé Sieyès, who used this utopia as a model for his *Constitution de l'An VIII* (ca. 1789); it was also eagerly absorbed by John Adams and Thomas Jefferson, and emerged in the Declaration of Independence and in various American political institutions. Fénelon's writings were of great importance in the development of enlightened despotism. The oldest type of romantic utopia, the fantasy tales from Vairasse's *Sévérambes*, was read and quoted by thinkers of stature, such as Leibnitz and Montesquieu. The writings of the French utopists, from Rousseau to Morellet and from Fontenelle to Voltaire, are intimately related both to the intellectual revolution in which the Encyclopaedists and the social philosophers participated and to the social and political revolutions that took place concurrently.

Robert Owen, whose thinking had such an impact on the minds of John Stuart Mill, Kingsley, Carlyle, and Ruskin, made his mark both on the cooperative movement and on the snowballing process of industrialization. Saint-Simon left his impress not only on the Industrial Revolution but also on the later "managerial revolution" that came in its train. The development of the successive international projects of Saint-Pierre, Leibnitz, and Kant can be traced in the history of thought about a league of nations, as can the thought of

Fichte's ultranationalistic *Planwirtschaft,* "planned economy," be traced in the nationalistic countermovement. We can see how utopian socialism prepared the way for "scientific" socialism and how "anti-utopian" Marxism prepared the way for modern collectivism, both the nationalist-communist and the middle-class socialist variety. Finally, a rightful place in history should be found for the "madman" Fourier, who, however bizarre and eccentric he appeared to his contemporaries, in some respects was far ahead of his time and has made a contribution of permanent and enduring worth to social thought.

Yesterday's Utopia, Today's Social Philosophy

Much more could be said about the influence of individual utopists as prophets, politicians, and revolutionaries, but that is another story. Attention could also be devoted to the collective influence of the utopists on the growth of social ideas and on the development of socio-political institutions.

One of the most interesting manifestations of the utopian influence has been the persistent attempt to establish utopian communities, both in Europe and in the Americas. These are particularly instructive because they aim to provide a working model of a better social order. Their failures tend to be better known than their not inconsiderable successes, and the political disintegration of these communities, sometimes after a hundred years or more of flourishing communal life, has blinded observers to the influence they exercised on their contemporaries. It is of interest to note, however, that the intentional community movement, as it is now called, is probably growing more vigorously in the United States today than ever before.[16]

We are here concerned not with actual experiments but with the influence of utopian thought as such. Utopian thinking about the future has contributed with equal vigor to the development of social thought and social conscience. Many utopian themes, arising in fantasy, find their way to reality. Scientific management, full em-

---

[16] See Charles Nordhoff, *The Communistic Societies of the United States* (Economists, Zoarites, Shakers etc.) (London: John Murray, 1875); William Alfred Hines, *American Communities* (1878); Ernest S. Wooster, *Communities of Past and Present* (1924); Arthur Eugene Hester, Jr., *Backwoods Utopias* (1950); Hendrik F. Infield, *Utopia and Experiment* (New York: F. A. Preager, 1955).

137

ployment, and social security were all once figments of a utopia-writer's imagination. So were parliamentary democracy, universal suffrage, planning, and the trade union movement. The tremendous concern for child-rearing and universal education, for eugenics, and for garden cities all emanated from the utopia. The utopia stood for the emancipation of women long before the existence of the feminist movement. All the current concepts concerning labor, from the length of the work week to profit-sharing, are found in the utopia. Thanks to the utopists, the twentieth century did not catch man totally unprepared.

The Shift from Superhuman to Human Power

The future no longer lay hidden in the lap of the gods. The recognition of reason as an autonomous governing power in human life had meant the enfranchisement of man. He was now responsible for his own actions. The fact that the evolutionary concept of the struggle for existence at the same time reduced man to the status of animal carried little weight in the face of the liberating power of the machine. Even the exploitation of the uprooted peasants, now huddled together in crowed cities, did not undermine the basic belief that man was born free and could throw off his chains.

The Enlightenment was overflowing with contradictory images of man. He was either beast or angel; he was Homo sapiens, Homo economicus, and Homo universalis; he was *homme d'esprit* and *homme machine*. Made in the image of God, he was also Promethean. The one constant in all these conflicting roles was his new status, his endowment with a new set of rights as human being and citizen.

The Weakening of the Eschatological Image of the Future

The earthward shift from superhuman to human power was not without consequences for the image of the future itself. The conquest of the supernatural strengthened the utopian image of the future and weakened the eschatological one. As man acquired faith in himself, he put this faith to work in improving his earthly existence. The discovery of laws ruling the behavior of natural phenomena led to the search for similar laws ruling social behavior. The world became a mechanism.

Philosophical outlooks revealed the same secularizing tendencies. Kant divorced the establishment of the Kingdom of Heaven from the revealed truth of Christianity, basing it instead on an innate moral

138

sense which calls men to worthy action. The process of liberation was completed by Hegel, portraying the course of history as a dialectic process of growth of the human spirit to a full realization of its own freedom. In Marx the spirit itself, the dawning consciousness of freedom, was replaced by the technology of economic productivity, and the concept of the divine vanished entirely. At the same time the Enlightenment also fathered deism, an important factor in utopism and utopian socialism, with its theme of a natural religion featuring insight and inward piety. These and other anti-Christian and atheistic trends were nourished by a continuing rebellion against the concept of a divinely ordained existing order.

Internal religious quarrels continued right through the French Revolution. Antichurch or antidogma movements toward unity and tolerance were also set in motion (Hugo, Grotius, Castello, Leibnitz, Lessing). In some cases these became a third force between Catholicism and Protestantism; in other cases they allied themselves with various humanistic creeds (Diderot, Herder, Goethe). In addition, there were attacks on traditional Christianity from the outside, stemming either from textual criticism of the Bible (Pierre Bayle, Hermann Reimarus, David Strauss, Giordano Bruno, Bruno Bauer, Ernest Renan) or from the philosophic skeptic's corner. Attacks came also from another philosophical front, not so much from the extremist but innocent French materialistic rationalism (Julien de La Mettrie, Claude Helvetius, Paul von Holbach) as from the fierce German left-wing Hegelianism (Ludwig Feuerbach) and positivistic materialism (Friedrich Büchner).

The social, philosophical, and religious movements all united in one thing only: in undermining the belief in future salvation from earthly misery by divine intervention. The eschatological image of the future was pushed further and further back out of time into eternity. The *eschaton* ceased to exist in time, and became conceivable only as a symbol or a myth.

The Impending Threat to the Utopian Image of the Future

In the end the utopian image of the future did not escape the threat which had already faced the eschatological image, although the causes and the timing were different. In the first place, the feeling that things would somehow work out failed to be confirmed by history. In the second place, the images of the future were themselves at fault, insofar as specific spatial characteristics were mixed into the influence-optimism images. In regard to the first

139

point, the progress-optimism of both liberalism and Marxism was proved wrong by time itself. For the second, images of the future based on influence-optimism suffered from the realities of the Industrial Revolution. As man gradually became aware of the dual character of industrial techniques, technology came to evoke the most pessimisic possible images of the future to contrast with the previously optimistic ones.

Concurrently with this split between positive and negative tendencies, there was an ominous contraction of the social and spiritual consciousness, related to the spatial contraction of the images of the future characterized by influence-optimism. The Industrial Revolution combined with a nationalistically oriented influence-optimism to produce an unprecedented "wealth of nations" and the successive material flowering of England, Germany, and the United States. Particularly in the United States, one special kind of active, expectational optimism—eudaemonism (the ethical doctrine establishing happiness as the highest moral good)—shrank utopia down to eu-topia and enshrined it in the euphoria of the "American Creed" and the "pursuit of happiness." But as a part of the same picture, the ideas of national and imperialistic expansion first promulgated by Herder and Fichte came to dominate the images of the future of all the "young" nations and races of the world. These ideas were rapidly translated into the destruction of the old political equilibria, the formation of new power-blocs, and world wars. While science and technology were busy spanning the earth and welding all men on it into one dehumanized mass-man, the new spatial dimension of the image of the future simultaneously reduced the ideal of a world community in which every man is every man's neighbor, into a series of tight little compartments labeled national self-interest.

This pitiful construition was the sad finale to the Age of Enlightenment, which had begun so promisingly with a tremendous upsurge of new vistas for mankind. The age had outrun itself.

Chapter 13. The Future Becomes Present and Past

The Industrial Revolution sweeps up history and dumps it unceremoniously into the dustbin of modern times. This chapter is a much-compressed history of one small period, reaching to the nineteen-thirties just before the outbreak of World War II. Seen through a diminishing glass, the most interesting part of the period is the turn of the century, which also represents a turning point in the spirit of the times and above all in the thinking about the future.

The trends lightly sketched at the end of the preceding chapter now become sharper. Dialecticism, which thus far had been in Utopia's service, now turns against her. The principle of reversal and revolution, applied *through* the utopia, is now applied *to* it.

Science on the Rebound and the Society of Tomorrow

The essence of the confusion of this age lies in the fact that the same forces are almost simultaneously reaching new highs and unprecedented lows. This juxtaposition of *grandeur* and *misère* is itself worthy of attention as being peculiarly symptomatic for the age. Before indicating how these shifts are reflected in the utopia, some general trends will be discussed.

Science

Spengler and Nietzsche (*ewiger Wiederkehr*, "eternal recurrence") and later Toynbee and Sorokin, in spite of many differences in their views, all unite in describing theories of social dynamics which are in complete opposition to the theory of continuous evolutionary progress. The same thing happens with biological principles. Social Darwinism snatches the theory of evolution away from its biological frame of reference and extends it to the systematic cultivation of a new type of human being through genetics and biochemistry. But is this progress or degeneration?

Technology

The trends in modern technology reveal most clearly the contrasting modes of development in thinking about the future. Technology offers an unprecedented confirmation of the possibilities of the utopia, often far exceeding the utopian fantasies in its concrete achievements. Through technology, Homo sapiens can transform all things; at last man appears to be master of his own fate.

Even as the climax of human autonomy is in sight, however, a road leading back to servitude appears. Some observers see technology as becoming a cancerous growth which destroys the culture it feeds on. Man, in mastering nature, becomes estranged from her and is simultaneously enslaved by a new divinity, the machine. The autonomous has become an automaton.

Politics

In political developments we see the line of thought of Herder, Fichte, and Hegel continued. Evolutionary idealism and influence-optimism are focused on national interest. The old idea of the Chosen People recurs once more, but the goal is not to free the world but to subjugate it. Nationalistic and imperialistic images of the future originally provided a truly spiritual inspiration for the people concerned, especially those minorities held in a state of disfranchisement by ruling powers. In the end, however, they collided head-on with the existing boundaries on the ever-shrinking ball of the earth. The period of tension and conflict has been rung in: first between peoples, then between power-blocs and races, and finally between pan-this and pan-that.

Now all images of the future can be classified according to their spatial position; Eastern and Eastern European are contrasted with Western and Western European. The ascendancy of this new spatial vision of the future in the political heavens sounds the death knell, however, for the vision of the future as such. The genuine vision of the future must contain a critique of the times as well as a model for social reconstruction. But now all critique of the times is silenced as

142

unpatriotic. Even the fictitious romance-utopia is no longer spared by the censor. The creative, free-thinking utopia rapidly degenerates into canned ideology. Even science and art become nationalized.

Philosophy

Here again we find a collision of opposing trends. Bergson opened new vistas with his bold reversal of quantitative time into qualitative time. He distinguishes between *temps-espace*, external time magnitudes in space, and *temps-duré*, internal consciousness of time-duration. This represents a rehabilitation of the temporal as opposed to the spatial image of the future. Influence-optimism is cast in the matrix of the *élan vital*, and essence-optimism is cast in the matrix of the *évolution créatrice*. Bergson's epistemology provides a new substructure for the continuing process of imagining the future.

The pessimism of Schopenhauer, the nihilism of Nietzsche, and aversion to all utopias is only a step away, however. These various streams ultimately find a common outlet in existentialism, which has neither vision nor perspective concerning the future.

Time, wrested from space by Bergson, is now again separated from the future and tied to the present. Once again the Darwinian struggle for existence becomes a central concept. There is fear of life and fear of death; there is a standing on the edge of the abyss of nothingness. All that remains is a tragic-heroic acceptance of one's destiny. One by one all exits to the future are closed off.

Into the Twentieth Century (And Back)

The already-weakened utopia of this period can no longer hold its own. Even while the general trend is still positive and forward, a shifting and wavering can be discerned in the utopia literature.

Full Speed Ahead

Originally the utopia dared only to think as far as the year 2000, sometimes as far as 2500 and 3000. These dates had a definite millennialist connotation. With Ernest Renan, however, begins the era of time-millionaires. Shaw thinks ahead to the year 31,920, Wells to 802.701, and Richard Haldane to 17,864,151 A.D., Stapledon doesn't even bother with counting in one-year units, but deals in roughly calculated eras of tens and thousands of millions of years.

143

This is only possible, of course, if man moves to other worlds in the cosmos with a longer span of existence than is now prophesied for the earth. Once time is detached from earth and coupled with cosmic space, it can be prolonged almost indefinitely.

Without technology, these fantasies of remote space and time would be impossible. Thus technology sometimes seems to steal the leading role from reason in an enlightened utopia.

The genre of time-utopias resulting from this new trend is as extensive as it is diverse. Jules Verne and Walter Rathenau represent the two extremes. Verne, with his fantastic travel-romances through time and space, made available the raw materials to be used by countless later utopists, but he himself was not primarily concerned with utopias, so he will be omitted from the discussion. Rathenau, although no less fantastic in his writings, always kept the utopian theme in the forefront and will be included. In the other selections discussed the utopian theme is given varying importance.

We will begin with Renan's *Dialogues Philosophiques* (Paris: 1876). We are dealing here with a future pushed well along toward eternity, in a setting somewhere in the cosmos. Man has already been perfected into superman through chemico-biological means and is about to merge into God, so that utopism, mysticism, and myth fuse. Renan's position offers a combination of essence-optimism concerning the evolution of man toward perfection and influence-optimism concerning the technological possibilities of achieving this *eschaton.*

Next we shall consider G.B. Shaw's time-utopia, *Back to Methuselah* (Westminster: A. Constable, 1921), written less than half a century after Renan's *Dialogues Philosophiques.* The play opens with Adam and Eve worrying about death versus eternal life. The serpent advises a middle course: accept personal death, but have eternal life through childbearing. The mortal lifespan turns out to be too short, unfortunately, and men die before they achieve full spiritual wisdom. Eventually, a few superior humans do manage, by will power alone, to lengthen their lifespans—at first to a few centuries, finally to thousands of years. In this way a new and higher type of man drives out the older and inferior type. In the fifth and last act, played in the year 31,920, Shaw reaches the limit of his time-horizon. Reproduction takes place oviparously with a two-year incubation period, and the newborn is as mature as a seventeen-year-old of our day. In four years more he has the mature and ripened personality of an old man, without material needs. In this final stage of man the spirit begins to emancipate itself from the body. After the biological conquest of human life comes the metaphysical conquest of human thought.

144

When the final evolutionary goal is reached for man, his spirit will dwell somewhere in the cosmos.

The Last and First Men by Stapledon (1930) belongs to this same cosmic-biological genre,[1] and draws the farthest boundary in time hitherto conceived by man. The eighteenth and last type of man to succeed the primitive Homo sapiens has reached organic perfection by present standards, and is now in a position to improve his species through nonsexual procreation. Here again, human striving is crowned by the achievement of a cosmic eternal life.

One special point of interest in Stapledon's work is his vision of the relationship between time and the future. The last man, who has succeeded in becoming divine, can by means of his own divinity influence his own remote past, the lives of the first and succeeding types of men. The future can liberate and determine the course of history, including the images of the future created in the past. Is this a play with time? Or is it a possibility which may eventually be confirmed by experiments such as the parapsychological time experiments of Dunne?[2] This type of conception has always had a kind of mystical validity within the world of religious experience, best expressed in modern form by the Englishman Charles Williams in his novel *Descent into Hell* (New York: Pellegrini and Cudahy, 1949). The actual possibility of such a relationship does not concern us here, but rather the conception itself, this optimistic view of a time-chain in which the last link determines the nature and quality of the entire chain and redeems the whole in a blending of human and supernatural power.[3]

We turn now to quite another type of utopia, housed in a much cosier time-dimension. Edward Bellamy's *Looking Backward* (1888) represents a continuation of the older utopian socialism. It had a tremendous popularity and led to the founding of an international

---

[1] Although we select only one book by a given writer to illustrate the points under consideration, the same author has frequently written other books on the same theme. Wells in particular has written many books with a similar focus. Shaw wrote many variations on the theme of man, such as *Man and Superman* (Westminster: Archibald Constiable, 1903). Stapledon also has written a number of works in this genre, *Odd John* (London: Methuen, 1935), *Homo Superior, Star Maker* (London: Methuen, 1937), and *Sirius* (London: Martin Secker and Warburg, 1944.), *A Fantasy of Love and Discord* (London: Martin Secker and Warburg, 1944).

[2] See J. W. Dunne, *An Experiment with Time* (London: Faber and Faber, 1927).

[3] For a full discussion of Stapledon's work, see J. O. Bailey's excellent *Pilgrims Through Space and Time* (New York: Argus Books, 1947).

Bellamy Society with national branches and its own periodical, for the purpose of promoting Bellamy's social ideas.[4] The book carries the subtitle *2000—1887* and takes place in the year 2000 in Boston. The main character awakens there after a 113-year hypnotic sleep. He still retains his natural age of thirty and discovers a completely different, socialist society, which he then undertakes to describe. This collectivistic society is a naive and charming mixture of Marxism, pacifism, and Americanism. Society has achieved perfection through technical progress, a notion not to be wondered at in this foremost and best American utopia. What is to be wondered at is that there was room for the utopian conception at all in America. Was it not already itself the new and better world?

This utopia contains a description of the ideal socio-economic system in the best earlier tradition. Technological inventions are perfected to the point where no man needs to carry an individual umbrella when it rains, and sermons can be listened to by telephone. Men and women have economic equality so that all marriages are undertaken out of love.

Bellamy writes at the conclusion of his book, "*Looking Backward* was written in the belief that the Golden Age lies before us and not behind us, and is not far away. Our children will surely see it, and we too, who are already men and women, if we desire it by our faith and by our works." This is certainly influence-optimism!

The utopian writings of Wells are in a class apart. These tales of fantasy and fiction are so diversified that historians come to widely different conclusions about Wellsian utopism, depending on the work under analysis.

Here we will attempt to point up a more general characteristic of utopism, emanating in particular from the divided personality of Wells himself.[5] Like Shaw, he abandoned the Fabian Society of his

---

[4] In America, Bellamy's ideas in his *Looking Backward*, 2000—1887 (Boston: Ticknor, 1888) were chiefly disseminated through the misleadingly labeled Nationalist Movement and through the magazine *The Nationalist*.

[5] Hertzler, Dupont, and Ross all confine their critique to *A Modern Utopia* (London: Chapman and Hall, 1905). Ruyer includes other works but also deals chiefly with *A Modern Utopia*. Quabbe uses *Men Like Gods* (London: Casswell, 1923) and *Open Conspiracy* (London: Gollancz, 1928). Ross does not even mention this last book in his history, but according to Quabbe, the plan for world revolution in this book opens the way to a realization of utopia. Freyer begins his study with a treatment of *Men Like Gods*. He doesn't mention any other work by Wells, and only remarks, lumping Wells and Morris together, *kommt wohl gelegentlich etwas Amusantes heraus.* Doren concludes his work with a note discussing *Men Like Gods*. He doesn't de-emphasize the relationship

youth. Both socialism and Anglo-Saxon liberalism gave way in turn to a kind of enlightened despotism with dictatorial features. He blends scientific positivism with an unbridled play of the imagination. He and Jules Verne together are the creators of modern science fiction.

After twenty-five years of writing about the future, Wells turned to history, reading backwards from the present. Having criticized all the older utopias, he himself in the end wrote the most classical utopia of all, *The Work, Wealth and Happiness of Mankind* (1932). Dispassionate and sobering, shot through with an ironic realism, the work is nevertheless characterized by an indestructible idealism. Although Wells is violently antimilitaristic, he does not shrink from bloody revolutions to bring about utopias, and even foresees techniques of destruction (*The War of the Worlds*, 1898). The divided quality in all his work lays it open widely differing interpretations, depending on whether positive or negative aspects are emphasized.

Wellsian geography is cosmic in its variety. Wellsian images of the future almost always lead away from this world to another, as in *New Worlds for Old* (1908). Considered as only one of many possible worlds, the earth dwindles in size and yet increases in solidarity. The necessity for a world society becomes evident, with an accompanying minimization of the differences between peoples, races, and classes.[6]

At the same time this transition from microspatial to macrospatial magnitudes implies the addition of a new dimension in time. Wells anticipated in his utopian fantasies both the mathematics of Einstein and the philosophy of Bergson. In *The Time Machine* (1895), he has the hero fly through time at will, not only into the future, but also into a past. In *Men Like Gods* (1923), the hero's automobile suddenly drives off the road into another dimension, landing him on an

---

to older apocalyptic-chiliastic ideas. Aalders discusses only *The Shape of Things to Come* (London: Hutchingson, 1933). Mumford includes *The Time Machine* (London: Heineman, 1895) and *The World Set Free* (New York: Macmillan, 1914) (this last is also not included on Ross's list), but confines himself chiefly to *A Modern Utopia*. To understand Wells, it is necessary to rely not on special aspects of individual works but on the sum total of impressions.

[6] Consider, for example, *The Outline of History* (London: Newnes, 1920), which according to Wells himself is replacing narrow nationalist history by a general view of the human record. Shades of Voltaire!

inhabited star hundreds of thousands of years advanced beyond earthly civilization.[7]

A similar motif is found an *A Modern Utopia*, which tells the tale of the earth's cosmic twin-world, much further advanced in time. The hope is held out that the earth will one day achieve this same high level of development. Beginning with an ironic critique of the petty bourgeoisie in his own country, he ends on the brim of eternity. In *The Time Machine*, a Golden Age of the year 802,701 is described. In *The Dream* (1924), an inhabitant of the year 2000 dreams of the past, which is our present. Current events are thus seen through the perspective of the future, and the reader incidentally gets a glimpse of that same future.

In general, Wells establishes the foundation for his pronounced essence-optimism in other worlds and remote periods of time, which offer ample opportunity for the other essential element in Wells's outlook, the purposive influence-optimism. Only insofar as the purposive will is active does man have the possibility of achieving an ideal society. The evolution of man is a conscious and considered process of regeneration (*Mankind in the Making*, 1903). Progress in science and technology is a necessary condition for this evolution. A new mankind will evolve through the perfection of a new biological type.

Wells takes many approaches to the possibility of improving the existing human species. In *The Island of Doctor Moreau* (1896), it is experimental brain surgery; in *The Food of the Gods* (1904), it is a "boomfood," stimulating physical, intellectual and moral growth; in *In the Days of the Comet* (1906), it is a "green vapor wave" transforming human nature from irrationality to rationality; in *The Croquet Player* (1936), he describes the same effect through therapy; in *Star-Begotten* (1937) biological techniques do the trick.

A weaker yet clearly discernible undercurrent in Wells's thinking is the belief in an evolutionary perfectability. Scraps of Darwin, Spencer, Hegel, and Nietzsche all build up a certain image of a Homo superior of great longevity, wisdom, and spiritual superiority. Wells, however, relies not on evolution alone to achieve the desired future, but on utopian activity. Tirelessly he hammers away on the need of

---

[7] Sometimes playfully, sometimes seriously, Wells has through a half-century, concerned himself with the problem of time, from *Tales of Space and Time* (London: Harper and Brothers, 1899), *The Discovery of the Future* (London: Unwin, 1902), and *First and Last Things* (London: A. Constable, 1908), to *The Fate of Homo Sapiens* (London: Secker and Warburg, 1939) and *The Conquest of Time* (London: C. A. Watts, 1942).

techniques for creating men and citizens. In addition to the technologies already mentioned, he suggests methods of child-rearing,
education, and eugenic breeding. Wells, like many of his utopist
predecessors, would establish a controlled system of mating and
childbearing, thus denying equality and individualism as necessary
conditions to the full flowering of the human personality.

Wells rejects socialism and individualism alike, and emphasized the
necessary limitation of individual liberty for the general welfare and
the rule of an élite. He has been reproached with some justice for
preparing the way for fascistic discipline and dictatorship.[8] In *A
Modern Utopia* the Sumarai are given the position of highest leadership and follow a highly ascetic regimen. Progress can come only
through a small, scientifically trained élite which guards and trans-
mits the wisdom of the ages. It is not a hereditary caste but a status
which can be achieved through ability. Twenty years later, in *The
Shape of Things to Come*, little has changed in this picture, although
the élite is now called the "Modern State Fellowship" and the
members appear as technocrats. After constructing a unified world
society according to the principle of "social nucleation," they maintain world-rule in their own hands.

Technology is always of vital importance to Wells, and is used for
the improvement of the socio-economic structure, as in *A Modern
Utopia*. Here is a society in which the working class and the class
struggle disappear in the face of increasing mechanization. Thanks to
technology, everyone has joined the middle class, from which tomorrow's rulers are recruited.

But won't the ruling élite now destroy this vast and inert middle
class, no longer needed as a labor force? This is what happens in the
aristocratic progress-utopias of Renan and Shaw as man evolves
toward the highest level of existence. Wells avoids this turn of events,
which would sweep away the *raison d'être* of all his work, by making
the rulers serve also as high priests of a new cosmic-monotheistic
religion for the middle class.

Walter Rathenau, the German industrialist, politician, and social
philosopher, is a figure one does not meet in the histories of utopias,
and yet he is the uncrowned king of the utopists of the century. He
exceeds all his predecessors in his many-sidedness and in the dividedness of his personality. He is the last great European thinker of this
chaotic time to achieve a constuctive synthesis of the ideas of

---

[8] His autobiographical *The New Machiavelli* (New York: John Lane, 1911)
indeed confirms this tendency.

essence-optimism and of influence-optimism.

How is it that both his name and his work have fallen into obscurity? Is he too much the German or still too near our own time? Whatever the answer, he is certainly a utopist par excellence. Writing in the twentieth century, he weaves together the threads from many older visions of the future to raise utopism to a new height. He follows the classic procedure of More and the utopists of the Enlightenment in first giving a critique of the time (*Zur Kritik der Zeit*, 1912) and then a systematic reconstruction (*Von kommenden Dingen*, 1917).[9]

Rathenau's utopia, stripped to its bare essentials, can be summarized as follows. Our times are filled with distress and misery. This is chiefly due to the unchecked development of capitalism, with its accompanying mechanization of work, man, and culture (*Zur Mechanik des Geistes*, 1913). At this point social philosophy shifts toward utopism; there is a way out through catastrophe, to a new spiritualization of life. The new spirit is already present and spreading. The *Reich der Seele*, "Kingdom of the Soul," is characterized by social consciousness and love.

Rathenau continues the tradition of utopian socialism, especially that of Owen and Saint-Simon, in making a typical utopian reversal in connection with industrialism. Although industrialism has been the source of all evil in the old society, it will also provide the point of departure for the good life of the new society.

In his succeeding works, *Die neue Wirtschaft* (1918), *Die neue Gesellschaft* (1921),[10] and *Der neue Staat* (1919), Rathenau gives form and content to his vision of the new order. He visualizes a new system which, like that of Wells, moves away from both the old individualism and the old socialism towards state capitalism, anticipating modern state planning and labor-management organizations.

Rathenau not only prophesies but rouses man to action. Like Wells, he turns to the intellectual, cultural, and technological-industrial élite on behalf of the general welfare. Rathenau also sets his hopes on a new élite of the younger generation, and addresses his call to the youth of Germany.

German youth, in the process of becoming the national-socialist élite, reacted poetically with "Shoot down Walter Rathenau, the damned Jewish swine." Rathenau was born too soon and in the

---

[9] This has been translated as *In Days to Come* (London: Allen and Unwin, 1921).

[10] Translated as *The New Society* (New York: Williams and Norgate, 1921).

wrong country. Jew and internationalist, creator of one of the last visionary images of the future, he had the misfortune to live on into an age and in a country that returned to a purely spatial Aryan-German vision of a Third Reich.

History now entered a new dialectic phase which harmonized essence-optimism and influence-optimism in a new way. Ironically enough, this new phase was involuntarily inaugurated by Rathenau in the shape of a reaction to his ideas. It nevertheless continued a line of development started before his time and continued in opposition to him, represented by such people as Machiavelli, Fichte, Hegel, Joseph de Gobineau, Nietzsche, Spengler, Ludwig Klages, Albert Sorel, Vilfredo Pareto, and Lenin. The interest no longer focused on human progress, nor on the biological-cosmic evolution of a superior type of man. The interest had narrowed to the selection and promotion of one racial type to a position of world domination.

And yet, are there perhaps two levels of the historical dialectic? Indeed, Rathenau was assassinated, an early sacrifice to the stormy power of the Huns. His ideas were misunderstood and to this day too little known. But although his own life's thread was cut, one cannot so easily cut the thread of history. Many of his ideas about the socio-economic system have become reality in recent years. Rathenau marks not only the high point but the end point in our time of the prophetic-idealistic images of the future.

Hybrid Transitional Forms

The transition we are concerned with relates to the development of skepticism concerning utopian ideas as such. To illustrate this point, three widely differing utopias have been chosen from the writings of Bulwer-Lytton, Anatole France, and Theodor Hertzka. Differing in purpose, spirit, and construction according to the skills and interests of the authors, each one at some point calls us sharply to a halt, either through what they say or through what they do not say.

The Coming Race (1871) by Lord Lytton is the oldest of this genre of twilight utopias. The hero of the tale lives far in the future and deep in the bowels of the earth among an Indo-European race of supermen with a cold sphinxlike beauty and almost divine wisdom. It is Plato's *Politeia* come to life.

The race of supermen naturally possesses a supertechnology, which includes the use of Vril. Vril is both the philosopher's stone and the alchemist's elixir of life, giving both wisdom and power. It is

151

the divine emanation present in every person, and women have more of it than men. Therefore, it is the women (provided with light mustaches) who pay court to the men and are their physical and spiritual superiors. This is a state of affairs which leads to a general harmony. Each person has position and status according to the amount of Vril he was born with. The children, little Vril-monsters who can hardly be told from adults in their precocity and cold sedateness, accomplish all the work of the society as if it were play, with the help of Vril. Since everyone has Vril at his disposal, including its lethal powers, all war and strife is automatically ruled out. Vril is used as a weapon only when it becomes necessary to exterminate inferior peoples.

Within this society there is neither occasion nor opportunity for conflict. Passion has been eliminated and everything is characterized by sweet reasonableness. Erotic desire and love have become so perfectly integrated that literature, stripped of passion and intrigue, has fallen into decay.

Lytton's hero falls in love with two beautiful Vril-maidens and is powerless against their charm and Vril-appeal. Nevertheless, marriage with either is forbidden. Out of mixed compassion and jealousy, one of the maidens transgresses the Vril-laws and helps the barbarian escape to his native country. Home once more and dying of an incurable illness, the hero sets himself to recount the tale of his unbelievable adventures.

While in the happy land of Vril, the hero is at first deeply impressed by this superior society. Gradually, however, he comes to the conclusion that earthly mortals would not be able to enjoy this bliss for any length of time. The author draws this moral from his fable: "If you would take a thousand of the best and most philosophical human beings you would find in London, Paris, Berlin, New York, or even Boston, and place them as citizens in this beatified community, my belief is, that in less than a year they would either die of ennui, or attempt some revolution by which they would militate against the good of the community, and be burnt into cinders . . ."

The difficulty that Wells felt in describing the road to utopia has now shifted to life in utopia. Man may choke on all this goodness.

While Lytton's skepticism is directed against the utopian ideal, Anatole France's skepticism in *Sur La Pierre Blanche (The White Stone)* (1905) is directed against the anticipations contained in the utopian image of the future. The author is directly influenced by Renan. France in the year 2270 is described in the last chapter, at which time a socialistic society has been established, and Paris and the great cities have all dwindled away. The air is more heavily populated than the earth itself, and technology enables every man to live in ease and comfort. There is little that is original in this delineation, but what is of interest in this work is that Anatole France first tears down what he is about to build up. Like Wells, he constructs a utopia and offers a critique of utopias as such.

The scene of the book opens in Rome. It first unrolls backwards toward the stone age and its vision of the future, which we know as antiquity. Then it moves forward to antiquity's vision of the future, all a part of our own past. Finally the scene moves to the present and our own image of the future. Through his historical reconstruction of the future anticipations of past ages, he indicates the relativity of all visions of the future.

To establish this relativity, he uses the ingenious device of having the Romans tell an anecdote concerning the appearance before the tribunal of a certain Jew named Saul or Paul of Tarsus. The story arouses much amusement. Does this man really want to establish a religion for slaves? This is really too funny. But man will surely develop a new and purified religion for an eternal Rome, replacing Jupiter with Hercules.

The author points out that at the time no one could foresee that the little incident involving Paul would influence two thousand years of history. In the course of his argument, Anatole France doles out equal quantities of skepticism about and belief in man's power to predict his own future. The mocking doubt attacks the tenability of the very vision of world peace which his own utopia depicts.

The third and last utopia to be discussed in Theodor Hertzka's *Freiland* (1889).[11] This appeared one year after Bellamy's *Looking Backward*, and the two are often coupled as socialistic utopias. But Hertzka belonged to the ultraliberal Manchester School. Freeland is primarily an economic project, based on the premises of classical economics and the unregulated operations of individual self-interest. This is a new note for the utopia.

Hertzka brings some new materials into his social construction: Owen's and Fourier's voluntary association, Proudhon's credit banks, Henry George's common ownership of land, Cabet's central economic planning, and a generous portion of influence-optimism.

---

[11] Translated as *Freeland* (London: Chatto and Windus, 1894). This really belongs together with an ensuing work entitled *Reise nach Freiland (Freeland Revisited*, 1893).

The influence of his work in Europe was enormous. It was widely translated, and in Austria and Germany a movement sprang up, with almost a thousand affiliated societies, for the purpose of establishing a Hertzka-type colony in Africa. In 1893 an actual effort at colonization was made, but never carried through. Hertzka's influence can be clearly discerned in later Zionist experiments. It is open to question, however, whether one really can say the new state of Israel embodies the ideas of utopism.[12]

Freeland is a kind of handbook for economic development, laissez-faire style. Here one discovers how Africa could become a new America. Hertzka describes an essentially middle-class socialism that never betrays its spiritual father, the essence-optimism of the satisfied bourgeoisie. The inhabitants of Freeland are intensely nationalistic and conscious of their physical and military superiority.

When Negus, military dictator of Abyssinia, has plans for the invasion of prosperous Freeland, a small group of bold and enthusiastic Freelanders anticipate him and succeed in vanquishing the whole of Abyssinia with flying colors. In Freyer's words, they succeed "purely on the grounds of their utopian virtues." Hertzka is certainly prophetic here in anticipating the Italian campaigns against Abyssinia in 1895 and 1935, though these both end, unlike the case of Freeland, in ignominy.

Utopism seems to hit bottom with the introduction of this nationalistic-militaristic spatial orientation. However, Europe, America, and Asia are overwhelmed by the Freelanders' victory and filled with admiration for this tiny African land. After an international conference at Eden, the capital of Freeland, all the countries decide to adopt Freeland's social system *in toto*. Freeland fulfills its world mission by providing the leadership for the establishment of world government and universal peace. With this last contribution Freeland takes its rightful place among the ranks of the utopias.

With all respect for Hertzka's idealism, he leaves us standing with both feet squarely on the ground with his description of the opera-

---

[12] Martin Buber, in his *Paths in Utopia* (London: Routledge and Kegan Paul, 1949), describes this great Jewish undertaking in a paragraph with the modest heading "Noch ein Experiment" as *ein vorbildliches Nichtscheitern* (pp. 222, 231). The work of Hertzka's fellow countryman, Theodor Herzl, is of more importance in this regard. He is the author of *Der Judenstaat* (Wenen: Die Welt, 1896) and the utopian novel *Altneuland* (Leipzig, Berlin: H. Seemann Nf., 1902), and founder and first president of the Zionist world organization. Hertzka's work had the result of shifting the attention of a number of Zionists, such as Israel Zangwill, from Palestine to Africa.

tions of his colony. His view of the future is certainly unreal, but not in a utopian sense, verging rather on the ridiculous. The great utopian vision seems to be petering out in the desert sands of that same continent which spawned Atlantis, ancient source of visions of the future.

The last line of development to be discussed is no longer a transition, but the return trip.

Anticlimax

Four utopian writers who in one way or another point to a road back are Gabriel Tarde, the French sociologist, and three Englishmen: Samuel Butler, the satirist; William Morris, the socialist poet and designer; and W. H. Hudson, the scientist and naturalist. All four were born in the eighteen-thirties and eighteen-forties, and all felt the pull of the turn of the century.

Gabriel Tarde stands in sharpest contrast to Hertzka. In his *Underground man* (English translation in 1905) the transition is complete. Avoiding the spatial dimensions of this world, he leads his readers deep into the bowels of the earth, as Lytton did. His new society is totally noneconomic and purely spiritual. The book not only represents a satire on existing society but also ridicules utopians in general. The choice is now between two evils, and our own world emerges as the lesser of the two.

Toward the end of the twentieth century a great cold front drifts over the world, and entire civilizations are frozen out of existence overnight. A cultural élite of youth retreats to the warmth of the desert and at last goes underground. The only exchange of goods which takes place is a spiritual one. Groups of like-minded people, such as artists or natural scientists, band together in mutual admiration. In this geniocratic republic pure harmony reigns. Family ties have disappeared, thanks to free love. Because of the limited food supply, there is rigid birth control. A woman who gives herself to her lover before he has produced a masterpiece in the judgment of his group is liable to the death penalty.

When men discover how to make bread out of stones, a fatal imbalance in population follows, as a result of the rapid multiplication of births among inferior people. There is also a falling off in the production of masterpieces. The story ends with the ugly suggestion that if the sun ever shines again upon the earth, the most stupid members of this underground world probably will return to the surface, whereas the more sensible people will stay underground.

155

Here is a double moral: there have been troubles on earth and there will always be troubles on earth because of the innate stupidity of men, but things are not better in utopia. Are we returning, after a long utopian detour, to the old doctrine of original sin and man's incapacity to better human society?

The English trend in this direction begins with Butler's famous *Erewhon* (1872) and its sequel, *Erewhon Revisited* (1901). Are these utopias? The formal credentials are certainly in order. They are descriptions of a never-never land, and they are models of axiomatic reversal. In reference to the double function of the classical utopia, there can be no doubt about the existence here of the first, the critique of the times. Butler's pointed critique parallels that of Thomas More, on another level. It is the second function of social reconstruction which is in question.

Butler is a master of the art of inversion of words and of ideas. The setting for this upside-down world is the other hemisphere, where men uphold morals and customs in sharp contrast to our own. The sick are punished as criminals, and criminals are given careful medical attention in public hospitals.

Education is also upside down. Young men learn a hypothetical science and a hypothetical language unusable in daily life in Erewhon. Gambling is taught in the schools, so that children learn from their earliest youth to serve both God and Mammon.

Erewhon's economy is regulated by musical banks which look like cathedrals. They are visited chiefly by women, who make fictitious financial transactions with worthless money, to the accompaniment of sacred music. There is another money for ordinary purposes.

Another interesting inversion is in regard to procreation, which is considered to be a misdeed. The unborn choose willfully to be born and bring great suffering to the couple they choose for parents. The friends of the family gather after a baby's birth, and a notarized statement is set before the baby and read aloud by a "straightener." The statement proclaims that the infant admits the prebirth sin of wanting to be born and asks his parents forgiveness for the trouble he has caused them. After the child has been thoroughly scolded by all the visitors and pinched by the nurse he usually begins to cry, which is taken as an admission of guilt, and the statement is signed in his name.

After this attack on the whole of nineteenth-century English institutional life, what of reconstruction? At first it seems that Butler has been at some pains *not* to offer a system of social reconstruction. The economic structure he points to is one of private capitalistic enterprise. The making of profits is a socially useful activity. Poverty is criminal.

There is nevertheless a kind of reconstruction, although it has the flavor of retreat. The Erewhonians had at one time reached a stage of technological perfection well beyond that of England. Machines replaced the human senses. A learned scholar sounded a warning, however, in "The Book of the Machines," prophesying a kingdom of machines which would enslave men.

In response to this book, a great civil war took place between machinists and antimachinists. The antimachinists won, and all machines invented within the last 271 years (thus, since 1600) were destroyed, except for those preserved in museums. Thus, in two and a half centuries we swing from Bacon's *The New Atlantis*, full of faith in progress, to Butler's *Erewhon*, brimming with disillusionment.

William Morris, author of *News from Nowhere* (1891), represents another kind of search for the road back. With the typical split personality of the utopist, he is at the same time historian, painter, decorator, woodcarver, architect, and spiritual father of industrial design. Socialist to the core, he is influenced by Marx and Ruskin, and is one of the first to take Fourier seriously. Bitterly disillusioned by party strife, he is torn between the desire for a peaceful life of poetry and the necessities of militant urban socialism.

One cannot but respond in kind to this greathearted man, whose work breathes the spirit of goodness. *New from Nowhere* is both charming and artistic, and in fact describes a completely "Morrisized" England. The inhabitants are not only his paper-children, they are replicas of Morris himself.

In this work Morris creates the possibility of escaping despair and an uncongenial environment by entering a world of nature peopled by likeminded beings. He also escapes the new-fashioned world of Bellamy's technological utopia, which he viewed with such indignation. Morris says he would rather lie on his back and tread the air with his legs than face a technological world.

This is a kind of flight, the direction of which is not forward. In the book the hero awakens from a dream to see a completely different world about him. Everything to do with modern civilization has been scrapped. The workers cannot rule this society, for the workers have been abolished too. Where Marx uses the system of production as a means to the establishment of socialism, Morris uses socialism as a means to destroy the system of production.

A carpet of the greenest grass spreads over the ruins of cities,

157

factories, and highways. We are back in the peaceful, unspoiled world of nature with men living in garden villages. All work is done in calmness and joy. All exchange is by barter. There is no central authority, for people rule themselves in small groups. London is leveled to the ground, and the only government buildings left are the Houses of Parliament, which are chiefly used for storage of manure.

How was all this achieved? Here Morris introduces the Marxist model. Revolution and bloody civil war were the necessary triggers. After the revolution, with its accompanying destruction of all dominant powers and institutions, comes utopia—but a most un-Marxian one.

What Morris presents is a combination of Marx before the revolution and Rousseau afterwards, although *le bon sauvage* is a highly cultivated man. He is a blend of artist and artisan, using the group setting of Fourier's voluntary associations, without *phalanstères* or other institutional provisions, with something of Hertzka in them, although without his highly systematized agrarian economy. This is the pure naturalism of the Enlightenment, minus a rationally constructed *code de la nature*.

The ignorance of and indifference to the economic order on the part of the unworldly artist-author devalues the work as a utopia. We have seen that Hertzka allows economic theory to dominate his utopian thinking and therefore make it one-sided. In Morris we see that the complete lack of economic thinking seriously detracts from the value of his utopism. Are there sufficient incentives to productive labor without monetary rewards? Morris answers, "The reward of labor is life." But is it not necessary to give extra rewards for superior work? "The reward for all creative work is the same reward God obtains from His Creation," Morris replies. After all, who would think of presenting a bill for the children he produces? Childbearing is undertaken for pure joy, and so it is now with work. Here, at the very heart of his argument, we see Morris tripped by the little matter of children—because a bill for them is indeed presented. After all, how can a population of approximately forty million souls return to a more primitive state of civilization, which could only support a small part of that number? Did we not just barely escape the Malthusian threat through the great increase in productivity made possible by the Industrial Revolution?

If this were purely a work of poetic fiction, one could simply admire the artist and ignore the glaring defects of his plan. Morris, however, was an outstanding and influential socialist. His utopia is still considered by many to be the purest example of what a modern utopia should be. Regretfully, I must conclude the opposite: Morris's utopia moves a good way along the road to anti-utopism, by retreating into the illusion of a Golden Age of the past, and by failing to take account of modern man's physical and social needs.

The trend towards retreat becomes even clearer in Hudson's *The Crystal Age* (1906). Hudson and Morris hold similar views on nature, but differing views on human nature.

There is a striking similarity of form in the two novels. *The Crystal Age* is a work of art, a fairy tale so sensitively told that the reader is held in suspense right until the final, surprise "unhappy" ending. Like Morris, Hudson the nature-lover manages to depict a world populated by Hudsons. This world is reached by falling with the hero into a deep chasm and returning to consciousness thousands of years later in a beautiful countryside in the Crystal Age. The main ideas are the same as in *News from Nowhere*. There is an idealization of the simple, healthy life in a state of nature.

Certain characteristics of this utopia's social structure are of interest. Hudson is not, like Morris, describing a whole country but a self-sufficient little feudal community centering around a magnificent country house that might have been designed by Morris. The leadership rests with a father, who remains somewhat in the background, and a mother, who takes the active role. The country house is not only very old; it is eternal, like the rock of ages. The inhabitants, at once shadows of the old Anglo-Saxons and men of the future, are strong, handsome, and stately. What is life like here? Through all the color and beauty, there is an overwhelming impression of a static existence. Life is like an eternally frozen lake.

The hero, burning with unrequited love for the maiden Yoletta, finally discovers that these people do not experience sexual feelings. A third solution has been found in this society, midway between that of individual and collective marriage: that of the beehive, with the matriarch as the queen bee. The fiery passion of the people of long ago lives on in her alone, and the burden of an entire generation rests on her beautiful shoulders.

Our romantic knight, no Don Quixote but a genuine Englishman, finally realizes that his desire for Yolette can never be fulfilled. Tortured by the pangs of love, he finally falls ill of his melancholy, but to be ill is a punishable offense. The mother absolves him from punishment, however, and full of motherly concern and wisdom, gives him a cool magic potion. He drinks it, in the belief that it will free him from pain and heal him. Instead, Smith becomes an unwitting Socrates, draining the poison cup because he is a threat to the youth of the community. As the life-currents slowly ebb from his body, the Crystal Age society is secure again from all disturbance and harm.

Not only is the ending unusual, it is unutopian in its conclusion that ordinary mortal man cannot survive in a utopian society. *The Crystal Age*, even more than *News from Nowhere*, sounds the death knell for utopism. It has sunk to its nadir, foreshadowing the mechanical-somatic love relationships of the anti-utopia, such as *Brave New World*. *The Crystal Age* crystallizes the return to a zero point, a negation of all impulse, all emotion. The utopian road is closed off and barricaded.

The Denaturation of the Image of the Future

The term "denaturation" is here used in a double sense. Literally speaking, the utopia is separated from this world, becoming increasingly unearthly and denatured. Figuratively, the utopia is watered down, precisely by making the ties with earth too intimate, through narrow nationalism and false romanticism. Both developments are equally fatal.

The Mythological Utopia

The curious course of development of utopism is all the more striking in that it so closely parallels the previously discussed development of eschatological thinking. First, eschatology assumed utopian characteristics; now utopia is assuming eschatological characteristics. The two lines of thought are converging.

Eschatology was first pushed earthward by the prophecies of the Old Testament. Utopism, on the other hand, becomes increasingly eschatological, as utopists such as Stapledon, Wells, and Hudson describe a kind of evolution of mankind towards spiritual perfection.

If utopia breaks time wide open and strides into infinity, it must in the end come face to face with the *eschaton*, with what Spinoza called substance and Kant called the *noumenon* of the transcendental reality which can be grasped neither by the senses nor by reason.

The Romantic Utopia

As long as romanticism was tied to the rationalism of the Enlightenment it was held in check. Human longings for the future

160

have always had a romantic tinge. Utopism systematized these longings.

Gradually, however, the romantic element became dominant, particularly when irrational factors entered in, such as nationalism. Besides the clearly visible deterioration which nationalism introduced, romanticism has another influence—much less striking, but therefore all the more insidious. In the first place, it tends to seek the future in the past. This withdrawal from the time-stream is to be found in Butler, and most clearly in Morris and Hudson. Nature-worship usually involves a rejection of the existing socio-economic structure, with nothing else put in its place. Add to this images of the future involving nationalistic feelings about a romanticized past, and herein lies utopia's greatest danger.

It is no accident that the Germans, with their romantic historicism, should produce so few genuine utopias. Their greatest utopian writers, Kant and Rathenau, they rejected.

An island like England, on the contrary, is more world-minded, a characteristic of all seafaring folk. Consequently, England has been the most fertile breeding ground, ever since More, for utopia literature.[13] It is therefore all the more to be regretted when the romantic element inserts itself into the English utopia.

Gradually, as the utopia becomes a literary fashion, the novel becomes primary and the utopia secondary. The romantic products of artists in the written word like Morris and Hudson are simply not comparable to the products of social thinkers like Plato and More. The one can be savored; the other must be studied. Perhaps Utopia's greatest misfortune, however, is to receive the attention of writers who are neither serious nor artistic. It then becomes degraded to the level of entertaining adventure stories.

As the spiritualized utopia and the debunked eschatology cross paths, each is moving in a direction which is fatal for the image of the future. A weakened image cannot simply remain a weakened image; it cannot remain without effect on present and future. It is no coincidence that at the end of the period discussed in this chapter, cultural pessimism and fatalism had spread like a cancer through the contemporary society.

It is our intention now to retrace history up to the point of this breach, and in the process to draw conclusions about the nature and working of the images of the future.

---

[13] Se͟ ͟pont, *L'Utopie et le Roman Utopique dans la Litterature Anglaise* (Paris: M. Didier, 1941).

III. Dynamics of the Image of the Future

Chapter 14. The Image of History and the Image of the Future

The question of definitions must now be faced. In general, the confusion of language usage regarding utopia has been deprecatory. In common usage, and even among the majority of the intelligentsia, the utopia is considered imaginary, dangerous, and misleading, in spite of the fact that great geniuses have dedicated their efforts to utopism. Of the many aspects hidden under the one concept of a utopia, one aspect, its imaginary quality, has stamped its mark on the whole and thus distorted it.

The question is not one of name-calling, but of the very nature and meaning of the historical process. The problem is furthermore not only a conceptual one, but concerns the unfolding of the future in its relationship to the present and past. The dispute goes straight to the heart of the problem of the future of Western culture. The disputed concepts need close examination.

Utopism and Eschatology: Untenable Definitions

The best study of thought about the future and of the contrast between utopian and chiliastic thought is still Alfred Doren's *Wünschräume und Wünschzeiten* (1924—25). Doren suggests that the projection of a *Wünschraum* into a somewhere on the boundaries of geographical space, is the most characteristic feature of the utopia, and that the projection of a *Wünschzeit* into a sometime on the boundaries of cosmic time, is the most characteristic feature of eschatology.

Doren mistakes the characteristic utopian device for the basic utopian idea. He further distinguishes between the *Weltnähe* of the

Utopia and the *Weltferne* of eschatology. Both sets of oppositions are inaccurate. Utopias are implicitly set in time, and many explicitly so. Conversely, the *Weltnähe* is frequently very tangible in eschatology. In contrast to Doren's characterization of the utopia as typically spatial we have already emphasized that once utopism takes on a spatial imprint, the beginning of its degeneration has already set in.

W. J. Aalders has built upon Doren's work and in essence taken over his antithesis, with some modifications. Aalders maintains that the utopia is a spatially-oriented wish for the future, and eschatology a temporally-oriented expectation for the future. Aalders differentiates between the wish as an expression of human longing *(Sehnsucht)* and the expectation. This introduces two new elements into the debate.

Psychologically, he vindicates the eschatological projection as the highest, supported by the greatest intensity of belief. On the basis of available historical evidence, the distinction is not tenable. The utopist and his followers may have just as fervent a faith as the eschatologists.

Theological haughtiness emasculates the historical force of the utopia in Aalders's work. Fervent expectation has been diluted to a pious wish, thus also contributing to a decline of the spiritual power of eschatology.

Georg Quabbe goes off the track in another direction. His *Das letzte Reich* (1933) defines utopia as "the picture of a state in which, after the removal of one basic error, human society undergoes a moral ordering which is immediately and eternally effective." He reproaches the utopia for its theoretical error of seeking fulfillment through history when it presupposes the elimination of history itself.

But the real error is Quabbe's. The true utopia is always historically relative. The ideals of utopia are "eternal," but any given utopian pattern has only a relative validity. From Plato to Wells there have been system-builders who have developed several different utopian models even within their own lifetimes.

In Quabbe's definition, the utopia aims at a moral ordering of society. The philosopher-sociologist Hans Freyer considers the utopia to be primarily concerned with a political ordering of society. The title of his utopia is *Die politische Insel*. Freyer makes Quabbe's point about stability with a much more dangerous angle to it. Utopism is not only an attempt to realize a stable order, but a permanent political order. All great utopias refer to a concrete location of a concrete fatherland, and the concern is for the salvation and future of this fatherland. The great utopist, like the responsible statesman, always means his own country. When he speaks of never-never land he means the Greek city-state, or England, or Germany.

Freyer directs the inspired will to a very limited goal, the glorification of his own nation through the realization of the Third Reich. He falls into this trap through failing to distinguish adequately between the two historic functions of the utopia, that of social criticism and that of systematic reconstruction. In the days when only adventurers and explorers overstepped national boundaries, social criticism was naturally directed for the most part to the writer's own country. The utopia's function of social reconstruction, however, in principle operated quite differently. The call for an ideal human society was directed over the heads of the writer's own countrymen to the whole world and to mankind of the future. Specifically, political features are only present in a special kind of utopia.

Only by merging utopism with a purely political nationalism and autarchy *à la* Fichte can it be fixed within the "natural" boundaries of a political entity. In the process, the utopia becomes anti-utopian. After two world wars and a Cold War, fed and led by nationalistic power drives, it is scarcely necessary to point out how this kind of thinking about the future is the deadly enemy of the true utopian idea.

We will turn now to the present day and examine two contemporary writers who have not made specific studies of the utopia as such, yet have in one way or another given a central place to utopism in their work: Arnold Toynbee[1] and Karl Popper.[2]

Toynbee makes a twofold, decisive use of the utopia in his work: first in his discussion of the interrupted growth of the "arrested civilizations," and then again in his discussion of the "disintegration of civilizations" after a period of continued growth, flowering, and breakdown. Each time he introduces the utopia as a disturbing element. He maintains that the arrested civilizations of the Polynesians, Eskimos, Nomads, Ottomans, and Spartans all had one characteristic in common. They all incorporated a "paper model" of a human society on the pattern of the social insects. The ants and the bees achieved their present model society on the basis of a rigid caste-system millions of years before Homo sapiens, and came to a permament standstill.

Here is Toynbee's view of the nature of the utopia: ". . . The action .

---

[1] References are from *A Study of History*, the authorized abridgement of Vol. I—VI by D. C. Somervell (New York: Oxford University Press, 1947).

[2] The discussion of Popper is based on his *The Open Society and its Enemies* (London: Routledge and Kegan Paul, 1952).

which they [the utopias] are intended to evoke is nearly always "pegging," at a certain level, of an actual society which has entered on a decline that must end in a fall unless the downward movement can be artificially arrested. To arrest a downward movement is the utmost to which most Utopias aspire, since Utopias seldom begin to be written in any society until after its members have lost the expectation of further progress. Hence in almost all Utopias . . . an invincibly stable equilibrium is the aim to which all other social ends are subordinated and, if need be, sacrificed."

Because of the overall significance of Toynbee's work, we must go further into a view which the historian of utopism can only label as nonsense. Apparently Toynbee has allowed his entire conception of utopism to be dominated by one special type, the romantic-regressive utopia.

Does Toynbee support his position by producing utopias originating among the Polynesians, Eskimos, Nomads, Ottomans, or Spartans? Far from it. After he has excepted *Utopia* from his argument, with a bow to the genius of More, he goes on to lump together Plato *(Politeia)* Huxley *(Brave New World)*, Wells *(The First Men in the Moon)*, and Butler *(Erewhon)*. He makes a brief (and mistaken) treatment of Plato do for all the others, although neither Huxley's work nor the book of Wells that Toynbee cites is representative of utopism.

Toynbee names four possible ways of thinking and feeling about life and time: archaism, which dreams of the restoration of an earlier Golden Age; futurism, which leaps into the darkness of an unknown future; escapism, which turns away and detaches itself from this world in ways ranging from Buddhism to suicide; and transfiguration, the Christian belief in the rebirth of this world. The first three of these attitudes are all cul-de-sacs. Only the fourth attitude makes room for an "unless"; it is the one possible opportunity for escape from disaster.

Only two of these four attitudes are relevant to the condition of our Western civilization, and these two Toynbee places in sharp contrast to each other. In his antithesis of futurism and transfiguration we recognize our old problem of utopia versus eschatology.

It is clear that Toynbee sees little real difference between archaism and futurism. Both would leap out of the current of the time, and yet both remain in this present reality. They differ only in the direction they take within the time-stream. Futurism is more unnatural than archaism, which at least returns to the once-known, because it turns to an unknown future and thus automatically

165

commands disappointment.[3]

Toynbee makes further distinctions concerning his four attitudes by proposing two pairs of alternative reactions: the antitheses of passive-active and violent-gentle. Archaism is thus passive-violent and futurism active-violent, while escapism is passive-gentle and transfiguration is active-gentle. This completes his definitions but also totally alters the character of his concepts. Archaism and futurism, both characterized as violent, again coincide. The "Saviour with the Time-Machine" reaches as surely for the sword by which he shall perish as does the "Saviour with the Sword" who would establish a world-state.

Suddenly the situation looks very complicated. What we have termed active influence-optimism can also be found in Toynbee's futurism as an active attitude toward life, but in his case it is an activity coupled with violence. More important, in Toynbee this activity is equated with political-imperialistic space-oriented strivings of a military and nationalistic character, features which I have labeled completely anti-utopian.

The fact is that Toynbee is including both archaism and futurism in his definition of utopism. Archaism, "that attempt to peg a broken-down and disintegrating society," and futurism, "one of those attempts at a forcible accomplishment of change which result, as far as they succeed at all, in producing social revolutions that defeat their own purpose by tumbling over into reaction," both end in a pandemonium of violence, unless futurism conquers itself in the Christian faith.

To consider violence the hallmark of utopism does not seem to us to be justified. Because of its revolutionary character, violence may under certain circumstances result from utopism, but it is certainly not its definition. For the great majority of utopias, the central inspiring ideal is that of an enduring peace.

How would Toynbee react to the suggestion that violence is inherent in eschatology? It would be easy to support such a position with the history of the Inquisition, the Crusades, and the extermination of heretic movements. Would he then speak of regrettable but unavoidable secondary effects or by-products? He would probably offer a profounder and certainly more imaginative explanation and apologia; he would indicate how ridiculous and how incorrect it

---

[3] ". . . Futurism as a way of life leads those who seek to follow it into a barren quest of a goal which is intrinsically unattainable . . . Futurism in its primitive nakedness is a counsel of despair which, even as such, is a *pis aller* . . ." (p. 520).

would be to equate Jesus, the Lamb, with the human beings who tear each other apart like wolves.

Gentleness is not a monopoly of Buddhists and Christians, as compared to archaists and futurists. On the other hand, we would not describe all utopists as gentle and softhearted. But they are in almost every case humanitarian idealists. The greatest impact of the utopian idea on the course of history has taken place through its fertilizing effect on social idealism. The revolutionary character of the utopia is directed towards a spiritual (and thus nonviolent) *coup d'etat*, the goal of which is to banish violence once and for all from human society.

Toynbee himself appears as both archaist and futurist in his attitude towards the current process of disintegration of our society: archaist in his rebellion against mechanized industrialization and fundamental democratization, futurist in his plea for spiritualization as a precondition of the beginning of a new order. Toynbee's spiritualization, however, ends in one special form of futurism which transcends itself and becomes eschatology, turning from violence to gentleness while nevertheless retaining its full activism. He maintains that every type of futurism which does not find its ultimate expression in a Christian expectation for the future is doomed to failure.

Toynbee is thus in a very profound sense a greater archaist than any of the archaists on whom he passes judgment. His view is an Anglo-Saxon version of medievalism. Futurism disturbs both his scientific reading of history on the one side and his Christian faith on the other side.

Karl Popper has his own special place among Toynbee's critics. A methodologist who considers the methods of the social sciences regrettably backward, he is roused to undertake his analysis by the problem of the future developments of history, particularly as they concern Western civilization. He fiercely attacks any exercise of philosophy or science which claims to predict long-run future developments as "Historicism," the historical interpretation of events based on so-called natural laws. Hegel, Marx, Spengler, and Toynbee are all guilty of inventing such laws, according to Popper. He also denounces the myth of predestination.

With equal fervor he makes himself the champion of "social engineering." The first line of thought, on the whole, runs parallel to our own basic thinking. Problems arise, however, when Popper begins to spell out these ideas, especially in regard to the utopia. Popper sees Plato, whose "spell" is the subject of the first part of his study, as the source of the cursed historicism. *The Politeia* becomes the

167

focus of Popper's fierce attack on Plato as the enemy of the open society. It also becomes the focus of his attack on utopism, which in the absence of further definition he seems to identify with platonism.[4]

In developing the critique of historicism he also attacks the utopism of Hegel and Marx, which he identifies with "prophetism," attemps to force the predicted future by manipulating present developments. Popper concludes that there is an intrinsic meaninglessness in the concept of "utopian engineering" as opposed to his "social engineering." Apart from the *Politeia* and *Erewhon*, however, there is no sign that he knows the utopia literature, and apparently his chief source of information is Mannheim, whose work is discussed below.

By choosing the term "utopian engineering," Popper jumps from utopism itself to the level of political realization, ignoring the primary function which successive utopias have fulfilled of the gradual maturation of man's mind to the point where it can make a meaningful use of human power in constructing a new social system.

Utopism and Cultural Anthropology

Utopia and Ideology

The task of defining the boundary between utopia and ideology is difficult, and Karl Mannheim has partially confused, partially clarified the issue through his treatment of utopism in *Ideology and Utopia* (London: Kegan Paul, 1936). We will confine ourselves only to those aspects of this profound and erudite work which have reference to the utopia. He himself devotes one chapter to "The Utopian Mentality."

Mannheim sees the utopia as a pioneer in the theory of social organization. According to traditional conceptions, the utopia must remain an unrealized idea in order to deserve its appellation. Mannheim takes the opposite position. He maintains that only those utopias that achieve historical realization can be considered genuine—a judgment which can only be made a posteriori. The basic characteristic of the utopia thus becomes its reality-meaning and the process of revolutionary realization. In opposition to this concretized utopia Mannheim places ideology, transcendent visions which can never be realized.

---

[4] See Popper, *The Open Society,* Vol. I, pp. 157 ff.

This mode of defining the utopia has certain advantages in that it throws light on several traits of the utopia which had been previously misunderstood. To that extent Mannheim's thinking parallels our own. In his survey of utopias of the past which fulfilled his definition and achieved historical reality, he demonstrates forcefully the intimate connection between image of the future and the future.

Building on these insights, Mannheim asserts, countering Toynbee, that the great transformations in the historical process have been pre-eminently the result of the effectively "acting" utopia moving outward from the intellectual élite to the social consciousness of the masses. The social consciousness of the masses receives its primary nourishment, then, from this utopian substratum. The most significant historical structural shifts in society are correlated with shifts in utopian awareness and utopian world image. There are, however, utopias which have never become a reality, and there are images of the future which have been realized but which cannot be considered utopias. The utopia is a thing *sui generis*, with its own existence apart from its operation.

This is not an academic question of definition, but rather a question of the conceptualization of the future itself. Reviewing Mannheim's theory, he recognizes four types, or constellations, of utopian awareness in Western history: Baptist chiliasm, liberalism, conservatism, and socialistic communism. It is immediately evident that he pushes the utopia toward the socio-political sphere, making it the foundation of a science of politics. He who wins has the utopia on his side; he who loses, has ideology.

This degrades the utopia to a matter of practical politics and interest groups, and the trend is accented by Mannheim's identification of the utopia with the suppressed, upward-striving classes and ideology with the ruling, conservative classes. To the extent that this succeeds, we no longer have the Marxian class-ideology, but the Mannheimian class-utopia.

Now from a socio-psychological point of view it cannot, of course, be denied that the ruling classes are always inclined to label any attempt at changing the existing order as utopian—impossible of realization—and that the rising classes consider the arguments for the maintenance of the existing order "ideological." But this brings us back to the problem of terminology. In fact, the majority of utopias, including the socialistic utopias, have originated among the élite.

Ultimately Mannheim weakens utopism not by undervaluing it, but by overvaluing it. He does not give sufficient consideration to the image of the future, and makes it carry the entire burden of the actual future. The result of Mannheim's conceptualization of his subject matter is to bring ideology and utopia together over the same common denominator: the social myth. Ideology is the social myth of the dominant class, which wishes to maintain the existing order. The utopia is the social myth of the upward-striving class, which wishes to establish a new order. This intellectual reduction places us once more before the problem of an earlier time concerning the relationship between utopia and myth.

Utopia and Myth

There is increasing divergence of opinion concerning the definition of the concepts "myth" and "mythology." Professor Gerardus van der Leeuw has undertaken studies of this in connection with primitive thought and religious phenomenology.[5] Ernst Cassirer has traced the development of these concepts in philosophical thought from Plato to Friedrich von Schelling, and published a number of works on the subject.[6] Georges Sorel has introduced the concept, "social myth,"[7] and this has been pursued further by Rosenberg.[8] Two opposing lines of development have focused more and more interest on the idea of the myth: on the one hand the spreading myths of national socialism, fascism, and Soviet communism;[9] on the other hand, the renewed attempt at demythologizing the New Testament.[10] The movement "away from the myth" has moreover evoked a countermovement "back to the myth," as witness Berdiaiev and others. Modern existentialist philosophy reflects the precipitation of this turmoil and tries to incorporate these opposing myth-trends in its own way.[11]

---

[5] Gerardus van der Leeuw, *De Primitieve Mens en de Religie* (Groningen: J. B. Wolters, 1952); *Phänomenologie der Religion* (Tübingen: Mohr, 1933).
[6] Ernst Cassirer, *Das mythische Denken* (Berlin: Bruno Cassirer, 1925), translated as *The Myth of the State* (New York: Anchor Books, Doubleday, 1955).
[7] Georges Sorel, *Réflexions sur la Violence* (Paris: M. Rivière 1912), and in Willem Banning, *Moderne Maatschappij Problemen* (Arnhem, 1950), Chap. 8, "Sociale mythen en hun betekenis."
[8] Alfred Rosenberg, *Der Mythus des zwanzigsten Jahrhunderts* (München: Hoheneichen, 1936).
[9] Theophil Spoerri, *Die Götter des Abendlandes* (Berlin: Furche, 1932).
[10] See Gerrit Jan Heering, *"De Verwachting van het Koninkrijk Gods* (Arnhem: Van Loghum Slatarus, 1952), pp. 110 ff; also Rudolf Bultmann and others in the collection *Kerygma und Mythos* (London: 1953), and T. Dokter, *Het Mythologische, het Theoretische en het Bijbelse Wereldbeeld* (Den Haag: Boekencentrum, 1951).

Under these circumstances it goes without saying that the myth would need new and extensive study. This lies outside our realm of competence, because a much-disputed concept of metaphysical and religious structure lies at the heart of the problem. But since the utopia is so often (and wrongly) labeled myth today, a closer consideration of the problem is inevitable. Without going too deeply into the analysis of the myth itself, we shall try to illuminate the essential features of the mythical consciousness of man as contrasted with the utopian consciousness.

The myth explains the unknown and the feared, and establishes contact between man and the supernatural, forming the bridge between the here and the beyond. It is therefore sacred. Mythical "explanations" are not rational. Other categories than those of logic are used, and other conceptions of space and time. The form is poetic and aesthetic.

Two factors are striking in the development of the myth: first, a shift from the beginning of time to the end of time; second, a refinement of the conception of the influence of superhuman power on human life. In explaining that everything happens as it must happen, it produces a theodicy out of a theogony.

Myth and the utopia both create images of the future, but the differences are great. The utopia may in fact be considered one of the oldest and purest examples of demythologizing. The development of a utopian consciousness implies and presupposes a shrinking of the mythological consciousness. The appearance of the utopia on the scene of history represents the Copernican revolution in the image of the future, shrouded in mythological origins. The essential difference between the two lies in the world-view and philosophy of life which each reflects in its assessment of the relationship between human and superhuman power. The myth is absolutistic and sacred; the utopia open, indeterminate, and relativistic.

The confusion between myth and utopia could never have developed if certain ideological concepts had not taken on the character of social myths. At that moment the myth and the utopia appear to have acquired a common goal at the social level. However, the *auctor intellectualis* of the social myth was very much aware of the difference between the two.

According to Sorel, the social utopias *cherchent à établir un*

---

[11] See Albert Camus, *Le Mythe de Sisyphe, Essai sur l'Absurde* (Paris: Gallimard, 1949).

171

modèle auquel on puisse comparer les sociétés existantes pour mesurer le bien et le mal qu'elles renferment, while the social myth is an expression *de la volonté d'un groupe qui se prépare au combat pour détruire ce qui existe.* The social myth is thus an expression of a mentality which infuses force into its wishes through the formula of Sorel's well known "direct action." Sorel is thus the creator of the suggestive "propulsive idea," the refined propaganda, coupled with drastic over action. He maintains that only those ideas are true which are fruitful and that the social myth contains truth insofar as it can inspire and mobilize the masses to action.

We have already encountered this argument of the anarchist Sorel in the later work of the democrat Mannheim, except that what Sorel correctly labels social myth, Mannheim incorrectly labels utopia. If we take the trouble to analyze the main elements of the social myth, we can see that they are basically those of the original myth; we can see also that they are practically identical with what Popper also attacks so fiercely under the misnomer of utopia.

Utopia and Politics

The relationship between utopia and politics has already been discussed in connection with Freyer, Popper, and Mannheim. The intimate relationship which they would establish between the two belongs to politics and the social myth rather than to politics and the utopia. They have been led astray by the *Politeia,* by the fact that professional statesmen were also designers of utopias, like More and Bacon, and also possibly by those revolutionary chiliastic movements which leapt into power politics. In spite of the special genre of "mirrors for monarchs," the utopia is really on the side of Don Quixote and not Don Carlos.

Remarkably enough, there is, to my knowledge, only one writer on utopism—Quabbe—who has perceived that utopism and politics are mutually exclusive. *Der Gegenpol der Utopie heisst Realpolitik* runs the first—and perhaps the best—sentence of his book. The advantage which politics has over the utopia, he goes on to say, is that the former really exists. But then this is its only advantage. The utopias, on the other hand, have for thousands of years suffered from the disadvantage that they have never really come to life. But then this is their only disadvantage. Therefore, he concludes, *ist der utopistische Gedanke von der sogenannte Realpolitik so unendlich weit enfernt, wie Vernunft und Sittlichkeit von der heutigen* [1933] *Politik Europas.*[12]

Utopia and Art

There is an artistic element inherent in the utopia. But in giving full recognition to this fact, it would nevertheless be incorrect to shift the utopia into the realm of art: aesthetics is not the primary motivating power of the utopia, but rather the medium of expression. Not only are the inward necessities and compulsions that move utopist and artist different, but the outward forms of expression are also different and often of a contrasting nature. The light which falls on the phosphorescent semidarkness of the twilight town of Amaurote in More's *Utopia* is not the same as the "metaphysics of light" in Rembrandt, the gradation of color as opposed to dark shadow in his "Nightwatch." The rational construction of a utopia requires specialized economic and sociological knowledge as well as a feeling for organizational detail and subtle structural relationships such as is seldom found among artists. It also requires the patience to study and make use of enormous amounts of social data which the artist would not feel aesthetically justified in incorporating into a work of art. This is not to say that profound sociological insights have not been embodied in literary works of the highest artistic merit and that such insights have not influenced social thought. The relationship between the science of society and the art of the novel is a complex and important one, and aesthetic intuition plays its role in both. But the work of systematizing and ordering concepts so that they can become useful tools in working with and reconstructing the social order does indeed lie at the opposite end of the creative continuum from the intuitive insight. When the utopist, in his work of fiction, neglects his systematic task and allows himself to be carried away by intuitive insight, aesthetic style, or both, the utopia as such goes downhill.

Utopia and Ethics

We come to the conclusion, then, that the utopian consciousness is motivated by ethical, and primarily social-ethical, impulses, rather than by aesthetic ones. Does the utopia then becomes ethics, or a special category of ethics?

[12] *Das Letzte Reich, Wandel und Wesen der Utopie* (Leipzig: Meiner, 1933), p.1.

In our opinion the entire discussion of inward drives and motivations, on whatever level, explains the origin and to an extent the dynamic working of the utopia, but not its essence. There is certainly a point of contact between utopism and ethics, because ethics too concerns itself intensively with the image of man, his values, and the dreamed-of fulfillment of humanity. The utopia, however, has a unique synthetic aspect which combines the civic, the political, the socio-economic, the humanitarian, the cultural, and the religious. It offers a total plan for human regeneration.

Utopia and Science

Insofar as science is directed to the discovery of laws which will enable man to predict future developments, it can be said that it also strives to form an image of the future. The social sciences, then, are working towards a social image of the future. This was first true of economics. Later sociology, psychology, and education followed suit, as well as demography, the science of history, and cultural anthropology. The replacement of causality by statistical probability does not in principle alter this trend. The modern theoretical world-image built up from Newton to Einstein is also reflected in the development of the social sciences and their successive images of the future, which are products of the imaginative mind in a quite literal sense.

The problem of demarcating and differentiating between the social science images of the future and the social-utopian images of the future here presents itself. This is all the more important because a scientific element is included as an essential part in some definitions of the utopia.

Ruyer's highly original definition of the utopia as an *exercice mental sur les possibles latéraux*[13] brings it immediately into the realm of theoretical thought. Ruyer's analysis puts the utopists in company with the scientific makers of the modern world-image. The utopia, which questions and thus liberates itself from the given reality, is the beginning of science. Thus both Newton and Einstein were led to the threshold of their new ideas through utopian representations of an other world. Ruyer particularly sees a parallel between the geometric work of Nikolai Lobachevski and Riemann, and the intellectual play of constructing a systematic utopia. Even if the non-Euclidian thought-experiments had not led to highly signifi-

---

[13] *L'Utopie et les Utopies* (Paris: Presses Universitaires, 1950), p. 9.

174

cant results, they would still in themselves have been just as amusing and critical a satire as any utopia.[14]

Ruyer's concept makes the utopia a product of a specific type of theoretical science. While this is undeniably true, and certainly very flattering to the utopia, this reasoning results in some distortion of the utopian concept.

For the utopia is not only an intellectual and creative play with new hypotheses. Ruyer neglects the ethical-idealistic motivation of the utopist, and his special mental orientation. The utopist is not only concerned with *that which can be*, in theory (although this is a necessary precondition for the realization of a utopia), but with a voluntaristic *that which must be* (*Seinwollen* and *Seinsollen*). He is not creating a mere counterimage, a sample social order, for society's amusement, but a serious ideal image, and example, to be considered and followed.

For those who take the traditional view that science is concerned with explaining that which is, and that the realm of the ought belongs to religion, ethics, metaphysics, and the philosophy of value, the utopia is immediately eliminated from the field of science by this extension of its scope. In our opinion, however, this does not follow.[15] Whenever social scientists introduce concepts of mechanistic functioning with respect to the social order, they are incorporating mythological values into their thinking. Whenever they insert a justification for a *Seinsollen*, for a course of development which man himself could influence into their axiomatics or interpretations, they are incorporating values of a utopian character. Once the sharp distinction between scientific knowledge and value has been challenged, it becomes much less simple to draw the boundary between scientific and utopian thinking.

[14] The Riemannian thought-world has been translated for the layman by other mathematicians in utopian fashion, represented as a two-dimensional world populated by beings without height. There have been similar attempts at describing other planet worlds, inhabited by beings without weight, or by beings who have no notion of the heavens or other heavenly bodies because their sky is constantly overcast. Two books by the outstanding physicist George Gamov, *Mr. Tompkins in Wonderland* (Cambridge: Cambridge University Press, 1950) and *Mr. Tompkins Explores the Atom* (Cambridge: Cambridge University Press, 1961) give a humorous utopian introduction to the new world-image of space and time and to modern atomic physics.

[15] See our *Kennen en Keuren in de Sociale Wetenschappen (Knowledge and Valuation in the Social Sciences)* [Leiden: H. E. Stenfert Kroese, 1948].

Chapter 15. The Unchanging Historical Task of the Changing Utopia

We have seen in the preceding chapter that while eschatology and utopia both belong to the genre of positive images of the future, there are important differences between these two types of thinking. Utopism differs from eschatology in respect to each of the three major components of the positive image of the future. It differs in respect to its view of the future as an expression of the human spirit, in respect to expectations concerning the course of events as they move toward the future, and in respect to the manner in which these various conceptions and expectations are woven together into a specific image. We will now explore these differences further, and then briefly review the basic characteristics of the utopia and its changing historical forms.

Essential Characteristics

Dualism is an omnipresent but insufficient condition of the utopia. A similar dualism exists in almost all expressions of human culture. But the utopia, in addition to being dualistic, is also demiurgic: it creates the Other world.

The utopia has a revolutionary character, although this is not to be equated with violence, in spite of the role utopism played in the French Revolution. The revolutionary potency of the utopia lies primarily in the spiritual power of a new idea. It encompasses social policy, but is more radical in intention and design than any plan of practical policy, within whatever political framework.

176

The dualistic thinking in counterimages concerning the Other is by nature dialectical. The utopian dialectic is often incorrectly thought to be limited to the Hegelian or Marxist variety, a threefold movement ending in an enduring synthesis, and the utopia is therefore criticized for its static character. This view rests on a doubtful interpretation of Plato's *Politeia.*

The utopia is always historically relative. It carries within itself the seeds of its own elimination through progress in time. The vision which it holds up of the best conceivable future at any given time, is by definition a vision subject to change, and utopias do change both in form and content with the course of history.

The typically dualistic mental structure of both the utopist and his utopia finds its best expression in a mapping of two roads of essence-pessimism and influence-optimism. The utopia demonstrates to man how he is continually demolishing his world and how he can reconstruct it. The function of essence-pessimism is primarily negative. It springs out of rebellion against the existing order and gives expression to "divine discontent."

It is utopia's function of influence-optimism which ensures its place among positive images of the future. In stating the possibility of a better order than the existing one, it replaces determinism with an open future. It does not leave man helplessly standing at a door opening on a vista of many possibilities, however. Utopia's influence-optimism assigns to the human conscience the task of choosing among various possibilities for society, and choosing that possibility which will most closely approximate the ideal as any given group of men sees it. The utopia aims at the development of human dignity, requiring that man make his own history and order his own society according to rational and moral principles.

The final and not least important aspect of the utopia as a positive image of the future is the image itself, stemming from a free search of the intellect. The intellectual requirement of axiomatic reconstruction must be applied to imaginary material. More than in the traditional practice of science, then, a continuous blending of intellect with other faculties rooted in the emotions is required.

The Lesson of Three Thousand Years

In describing Utopia as an ideal-type, we have been attempting to give a picture of the unchanging essence which lies at the core of changing external manifestations, the *ruhender Pol in der Erschei-nungen Flucht.*[1]

The first task of the utopia consists in holding up two mirrors: one to reflect the contemporary generation, and one to reflect a counter-image of a possible future. As an eternal questioner, the utopist is also the prototype of the revolutionary and radical spirit. His thorny questions penetrate the crust of bourgeois self-satisfaction, giving all vested interests the uneasy feeling that their ramparts are being breached.

The utopia is a milestone in the history of the liberation of man through the self-liberation of the mind. It opposes predestination with the conviction of human freedom in shaping the course of history. Several times the utopia helped to bring about a major turning point in history, through a change in the image of the world and the image of man. If offers a firm foothold for historical idealism and poses questions to Homo sapiens in order to activate Homo faber.

Utopism is the forerunner of all modern conceptions concerning social policy, social organization, and social peace. All the art of social engineering could not place one stone upon another in the social edifice if the broad outlines of the system as an idea had not been projected long before, and if the seeds of the motivating ideals had not early been sowed in the hearts of men.

Both before and after Comte it was the utopia which took unto itself the task of *prevoir pour pouvoir* (foreknowledge is power), a task from which the practitioners of the social sciences shrank back. Not social science but the utopia is the spiritual father of modern planning in all its variations. Its axiomatic exercise and thought-experiments must enable it to construct logical and structurally complete social mutations.

This aspect of the utopia's function becomes increasingly important with the passage of time. History reveals again and again how

---

[1] See Schomann, *op. cit.*, for a discussion of French utopias. For a comprehensive overview of Anglo-Saxon literature, see Dupont, *op. cit.*, who includes 75 utopias, with Wells's works counted as one, as opposed to only 21 English utopias mentioned by Schomann. Ross, *Utopias Old and New* (London: Nicholson and Watson, 1938), mentions 285 utopias, counting Wells's works separately. He also includes some general philosophical, economic, and political systems that are embodied in published works, such as the Communist Manifesto, writings by Mikhail Bakunin and Petr Kropotkin, and by Mussolini and Hitler. If we subtract the 35 such works included in his enumeration, 250 remain, and the list is still not complete.

long new ideas must gestate before they become the common property of a people. The now generally accepted concepts of social security and full employment first took shape centuries ago in utopian images of the future.

There are three possible roles in which the utopia influences the course of history: as buffer for the future, as a driving force toward the future, and as a trigger of social progress.

Like speculation in futures on the exchange markets, the utopia forms a buffer between the colliding powers of past and future. It is a cheerful shock-absorber in the social market of ideas. Its active influence-optimism, its eternal questing, gives an impulse to dynamic social-humanitarian action. The imagined tomorrow is today's idea.

In its unremitting attack on signs of social decay and in its constructive planning, the utopia has been a powerful lever of progress through time. Practically everything which twentieth-century man thinks of as different and better in the realm of social action has originally been a part of or the fruit of utopian thought-experience.

The utopia itself, it is true, shows traces of decline, nor is eschatology the force it was in the Middle Ages. There where images of the future formerly carried on their work, a vacuum now threatens—but it cannot long remain a vacuum. That space will be filled again with social myths, ideologies, and pseudoeschatology, all inducing man once more to submit to supernatural powers.

The decline in the utopian images of the future reflects a lost faith in human self-determination in our own time. The utopia joins its attackers and becomes anti-utopia; its previews become post-mortems.

But the present decline of the utopia is not relevant to an assessment of the role of the utopia in its prime. On the contrary, we may well ask ourselves if the decline in utopian thinking is not also a decline in social progress itself.

Part Two
Iconoclasm of the Image of the Future

IV. Devastation of the Image of the Future

Today all images of the future, utopian and eschatological alike, have been driven into a corner and out of time. They appear to be the victims of a common conspiracy, and yet they themselves set in motion the processes of their own dissolution. The denaturing process first began within each of these movements. Why this strikingly parallel development in both eschatology and utopia? Is there a hidden factor at work which drives both images to self-destruction?

The most remarkable aspect of this entire development is the blindness of our generation in regard to it. How is it possible that this abrupt breach in our times, occurring midway through the century and already challenging the future historian to find a new label for this period, goes unnoticed? We could easily find indications of the shape of coming events from the course which the dominating images of the future of the last thirty centuries have taken in this era. We have failed to see these indications because part of the disintegrating process lies precisely in this, that we can no longer interpret the messages which our own images of the future give us. We thus find ourselves caught in a vicious circle. We do not understand and respond to the degeneration of our images of the future because we do not understand their function; our lack of understanding and response hastens the silent death of our visions. We might say that the future speaks a foreign language to us today.

The rejection and destruction of old images of the future is not the basic phenomenon with which we are concerned. This is a historical process which has always gone on. The unique aspect of our present situation is the existence of a vacuum where the images had once been. There is a literal aversion to images of the future as such, whether of a natural or supernatural order.

183

The contemporary fashion of imageless existentialist philosophy, analyzed from the point of view of religion and even theology, is but the reverse side of the splintered coin of the image of the future. This philosophy effectively removes both God and the power of humanistic ideals from any influence on the course of human events.

But let us not blame everything on existential philosophy. Theology, ideology, art, science, social movements, and socialism—in short, the entire style and structure of our society—breathe the spirit of this new time, this radical change in attitude toward the future. Many speak of the decline of our culture, but to our knowledge, no one has laid his finger on the gaping wound from which the lifeblood of the culture is draining away, where the pulsing and impassioned images of the future that have always moved man and society now lie torn and still.

Chapter 16. De-utopianizing

We are taking up the phenomenon of de-utopianizing before that of de-eschatologizing because the de-utopianizing process is more overt. De-eschatologizing is a subtle process, remarked only by a small circle of scholars. But while the novelist and the theologian may seem worlds apart, they have both participated, each in their own way, in the same process. They have sat at the deathbed of the image of the future.

The Historical Development of the Anti-utopian Utopia

In one sense the anti-utopian utopia is as old as the genuine utopia. Its intellectual origin lies in the split nature of utopian thinking, which turns in upon itself and sees its own thinking about the future in the critic's mirror. Its spatio-temporal origin lies in Greek antiquity, right in Plato himself, spiritual father of utopism.

Plato's *Politeia* is not really a utopia according to our own definition of the term.[1] One important element is lacking: Plato does not give a fictional portrayal of his scheme as already in operation somewhere in the past, present, or future. His book is rather a program for legislation and the establishment of a certain social structure, based on reason and justice. Nevertheless, countless utopian writers since Plato's time have made use of the -many fertile ideas in the *Politeia*, so that it is in effect part and parcel of the utopian

---

[1] Doren "Wunschräume und Wunschzeiten," in *Vorträge der Bibliothek Warburg 1924—1925* (Leipzig: B. G. Teabner, 1927), and Ruyer in his *L'Utopie* also take this view.

literature. Plato himself made explicit use of his own ideas, thus becoming his own first disciple, in *Timaeus* and *Critias*. Both these writings achieve three things: they present the future in fictional utopian form, they give a contrasting picture of the future which divides it sharply from the present, and they depict an anti-utopia at the same time that they depict the utopia.

Plato deliberately relates *Timaeus* to the *Politeia* by having Socrates mention one of the outstanding features of the latter at the very beginning of the new work.[2] Then two contrasting kingdoms are described. One is the *Politeia* come to life, as something which according to this tale already existed a thousand years ago in Attica as an ideal arch-Athenian city-state with a population of virtuous citizens. The other is the kingdom of Atlantis, a mighty world power overflowing with luxury, a land where all self-discipline is lacking. It is strongly reminiscent of the old legends about the land of the lotus-eaters. Atlantis's thirst for power brings the two kingdoms into conflict, and Athens is victorious. However, both conquerors and conquered are destroyed by Zeus, who causes Atlantis to be swallowed up in the sea.

In *Critias* Plato works out the lightly sketched utopia and counterutopia with a more detailed description of Atlantis, a once noble kingdom which gradually degenerated.[3] Plato uses the device of counterutopia to explode the myths of the Isles of the Blessed and as a foil for the true utopia, which describes an ideal society of sober and just people.

Theopompus imitates this procedure in a fragment of his *Philippica*, one of the oldest Greek fictional utopias. The peaceful and flourishing city-state of Eusebes is inhabited by wise and perfect men possessing no material technology. Opposed to it stands the rich, warlike, power-mad city-state of Machimos, striving for world domination.

With the Renaissance the utopia comes to life again with a genre of travel-romances and its complement of counterutopias. One of the oldest of these is Bishop Joseph Hall's *Mundus alter et idem* (1605).[4] The description of a land called Crapulia becomes the occasion for

---

[2] He says, in effect: In the *Politeia* we have seen how ideal beings look in a state of inaction; now we will see them in action, and see of what they are physically capable.

[3] See Dudok, for a topographical comparison with More's island of Utopia, pp. 33 ff. and pp. 95 ff.

[4] This was published in 1643 in Utrecht, together with Bacon's *Nova Atlantis* and Campanella's *Civitas Solis*, Ultraiecti (Utrecht: Joannem à Waesberge, 1643).

penetrating social satire. As Ross[5] summarizes it, "Government is democracy gone mad, democracy by all the people, with no one obeying, government only when drunk, government whose chief virtue is anarchy. He who eats and drinks most is regarded as the most noble and at his death his corpse is donated as a great delicacy for his servants to eat at a service to his memory. To be sober, to be moderate, to be reasonable, is a crime; man is subject to woman, fatness is the only criterion of fitness for high office and the public schools are in reality public houses."

According to Ruyer,[6] Swift's *Gulliver's Travels* is *la première utopie anti-utopiste*. He is thinking primarily of the description of the island Laputa with its great academy of Lagado. This work unquestionably contains anti-utopian elements,[7] even as do the earlier works of Rabelais and the later works of Lytton, Butler, Hudson, or Tarde. But these men have not intended to create counterutopias, although they have furnished the materials for the genuine anti-utopia from the earliest times.

A work that is plainly intended to be a counterutopia is the English physician-skeptic Bernard Mandeville's *The Grumbling Hive or Knaves Turned Honest*, which first appeared in 1705 and became better known in later years as *The Fable of the Bees, or Private Vices Publick Benefits*. His main point in *The Fable of the Bees* is that only man as he is, with all his fearful shortcomings, can build up a great civilization; if man should succeed in going against his own nature and becoming more virtuous, which God forbid, he would be quickly and irrevocably doomed to destruction. By giving a central place to human egoism as a prerequisite for the general welfare ("private vices publick benefits") he becomes, via Adam Smith, the founder of the "dismal science," classical economics, which in turn becomes the great enemy of the social utopia.

The Fable of the Bees was translated into many languages; one could buy an abridged edition for half a penny on almost any street in Europe. Mandeville followed this book up with *The Moral*, in which he further emphasized the utility of the human qualities of greed, dishonesty, and idleness.

---

[5] Harry Ross, *Utopias Old and New* (London: Nicholson and Watson, 1938),
[6] *L'Utopie et les Utopies* p. 193.
[7] This element becomes even more pronounced in the writings of Swift's earliest imitators; for example, *A Voyage to Cacklogallinia* (London: J. Watson, 1727) by Samuel Brunt, and *A Trip to the Moon* (Dublin: 1728) by McDermott. See Dupont, *L'Utopie*, pp. 271 ff.

Montesquieu makes use of this same anti-utopian conclusion in his allegorical tale of the troglodytes, in the *Lettres Persanes* of 1721: a certain minimum amount of virtue is necessary, but a well-conducted monarchy frees itself from the bonds of a too-stern virtue, thereby making possible a wealthier and more refined civilization.

Another work which can be reckoned among the older counter-utopias is Samuel Johnson's *Rasselas* (1759). A withering critic of his times, he was an even more withering critic of utopian optimism: "Ye who listen with credulity to the whispers of fancy, and pursue with eagerness the phantoms of hope; who expect that age will perform the promises of youth, and that the deficiencies of the present day will be supplied by the morrow, attend to the history of Rasselas, Prince of Abyssinia."[8] Rasselas becomes restless in the Happy Valley where he dwells, and sets off on a trip around the world. This gives Johnson the opportunity to pass all manner of ways of living before the reviewing stand, and to discredit all utopian striving. In the last chapter, "The Conclusion, in which Nothing is Concluded," an unhappy and disillusioned prince finally returns home to his own valley.

A whole century elapses before any more counterutopias appear. A renewed spurt in the nineteenth century produced *Two Thousand Years Hence* (1868) by Henry O'Neil and *Across the Zodiac, the Story of a Wrecked Record* (1880) by Percy Greg. William Mallock's *New Republic* (1877) may be included with a few reservations. It was challenged as an anti-utopia by no less than G.B. Shaw, who in his younger years published *Socialism and Superior Brains: A Reply to Mr. Mallock*.

The nineteenth century was rounded off by the publication of two books by Wells, with anti-utopian features which cannot be ignored: *When the Sleeper Wakes* (1899) and *The First Men in the Moon*, (1901). Both these works describe a terrible exploitation based on a highly developed technology.

In the second quarter of the twentieth century a perfect flood of anti-utopian novels appear, inspired successively by World War I and the Russian experiment; World War II; the dictatorships of Mussolini, Hitler, and Stalin; the atomic bomb; and the Cold War. Outstanding in terms of contents and pioneering impact is Aldous Huxley's *Brave New World* (1932), with its frightening vistas of the future.

Among the most original of the writers to follow Wells and produce a catastrophic flowering of this particular genre, are George

---

[8] Cited in Ross, *Utopias Old and New*, p. 13.

Orwell, with *Animal Farm* (1946) and *Nineteen Eighty-Four* (1949); Arthur Koestler, with *Darkness at Noon* (1940) and *The Age of Longing* (1951); John Palmer, *The Hesperides* (1936); Virgil Gheorghiu, *The Twenty-Fifth Hour* (1949); Walter Jens, *Nein, Die Welt der Angeklagten* (1950); Curzio Malaparte, *La Peau* (1950); Evelyn Waugh, *Love Among the Ruins* (1953); and, once again, Aldous Huxley, *Ape and Essence* (1949).

The swelling ranks of anti-utopian novelists form a solid front against the two remaining "formal" utopists of this century, Wells and Stapledon. As far as we know, there have been no genuine utopias written since World War II. Already back in 1871 George Meredith, the benevolent agnostic, had advised Chapman and Hall against publishing the manuscript of *Erewhon*.[9] Published in spite of this advice (by another publisher!), it survived many reprintings. But it is extremely doubtful that any true utopia (which *Erewhon*, after all, was not) could find either publishers or readers today. The fact that any counterutopia, of whatever quality, is eagerly received, is symptomatic of the changing spirit of the times.

When it became evident that the pseudo-utopian pretentions of liberalism and marxism could not be maintained, man did not turn back to the true utopia, but to a third type of pseudo-utopia, that of fascism, national socialism, and communism. These promised an ideal kingdom in the tradition of Mandeville, Machiavelli, Fichte, and Hegel, in terms of national and imperial greatness, power, and wealth.

Counterutopism in Different Keys

In order to understand the particular turn that historic counterutopism has taken in our own time, it is necessary to trace its previous journey.

In antiquity, the question was basically one of a choice between good and bad utopias. The individual was himself responsible for an intelligent choice between the two.

Gradually we see the counterutopia develop as an instrument to be used as a warning against *all* utopian possibilities.

Disutopia

Already, in Mandeville, we have seen the black-and-white alterna-

---

[9] Mentioned by Ross, *Utopias Old and New*, p. 16.

tives of the utopia being reversed. Using utopian techniques, he turns the platonic argument upside down. Hedonism is the only truth, and the wrong choice is precisely the *summum bonum*.

In our terminology, it can be said that Mandeville strikes at utopia by replacing essence-pessimism plus direct influence-optimism with the essence-optimism of the theological doctrine of justification of the ways of God to man. The result is a cynical apology for the existing order.

Pseudo-Utopia

Mandeville's book became a scandal and was forbidden by the authorities, but the ideas became incorporated in the new economic thought of the times. Both liberalism and Marxism opposed the utopia, and functioned themselves as pseudo-utopias. Both maintained that utopian goals can best be realized through the laws of nature already operating in society.

Semi-utopia

The counterutopias have left their mark on the genuine utopia. They have compelled the application to utopism of newer technologies, and they have also aroused a rebellion against the unspiritual negative utopia. As a result, the utopia is in danger of losing its specific character. Between the influences of science and spiritualism, it becomes an unrecognizable object.

The scientist's ideal of a differentiation between what is and what ought to be, condemns the social utopia to a nonscientific status as a useless pastime when it is judged by the standards of empirical science. Insofar as utopism aspires to scientific standing, it assumes the character of an extrapolation of existing trends. It then differs very little from social planning. Social planning, with its emphasis on reform, works with the existing order and moves only one step at a time.

The utopia betrays itself in quite another direction when it fails to stay within its own province of human society on earth. Recent utopias have moved right back to metaphysics and myth, reaching to the farthest limits of eschatology. Thus they overshoot the age-old goal of the utopia. Where Mandeville does not even recognize the possibility of divine intervention and the elevation of natural man, Wells and Stapledon go on a search for the divine into the farthest reaches of space. To them man is only a mite in the myriad spiral nebulae of the starry infinite, for which time-space distances are reckoned in trillions of years.

With the genuine utopia in its death throes, the semi -utopia gave birth to a new genre, science fiction,[10] which has had its greatest impetus from America. It has spread all over Europe, along with Hollywood films, jazz, and bebop, as a part of "the American way of life." Science fiction is a hybrid product, usually neither science nor fiction, and first cousin to detective stories and the comics. It had in part crowded these out, and in part swallowed them up. Its career has been a stormy rise from newspaper serials to magazine fiction, then to books and at last to anthologies. On the whole, science fiction is a highly commercialized product. In pocket-book form it has reached printings in the millions and has grown into one of the largest pulp industries. Film, radio, and television have further widened its range of communication. This front of "coca-coloniza-tion" has even penetrated to France, which is already familiar with *fantascience* and has its Parisian Club des Savanturiers.

What is this new comet in the American skies? In design and feeling science fiction continues to remain uniquely American. It is American in its pioneer-type philosophy that nothing is impossible. It is also American in its mirroring of a new tone which has crept into this pioneer philosophy: it represent a retreat from unbridled optimism about the future into a rapidly engulfing pessimism about tomorrow—a real future-neurosis. On the one hand science fiction is a continuation of the swashbuckling, romantic frontier adventures of the westerns. The frontier is now in space, and the new worlds to conquer are literally other worlds. The escapism is into the future, rather than into the past; there is no idealization of what has been, but an emphasis on what is to be. There is also a shift from a major to a minor key, with an accompanying kind of space phobia, a hysterical attitude towards all that is far away and "foreign," which conceals an even more acute time-neurosis: a fear of the onrushing stream of time with the ever more drastic changes it brings, a fear that the unknown may be undesirable.

All this is suggestive and interesting, but relates chiefly to the special developments in the American image of the future. Within the

---

[10] For an excellent treatment of this subject see O. Shaftel, "The Social Content of Science Fiction," *Science and Society* (Essex: Chelmsford, Spring 1953). Compare this with S. Spriel, "Sur la 'Science-Fiction'" *Esprit* (Paris: 1953). See also Basil Davenport, *Inquiry Into Science Fiction* (London: Longmans, Green and Co., 1955).

frame of reference of this work we must confine ourselves to those aspects of this development which also apply to the course of Western European thinking about the future.

The forms which science fiction takes are so numerous and diverse that it is not easy to reduce the shifting patterns to one basic figure. For example, it has in part penetrated straight into the inner sanctum of science itself, as reputable scientists and writers with scientific training make use of this medium to try out their ideas. Perhaps its significance can best be explained by reasoning back from the tremendous attraction which this genre has for the masses. What is the nature of the attraction? For one thing, science fiction offers an exciting set of new sensations to prick the jaded appetites of today's bored public. It succeeds, in a time when the astonishing fails to astound, in eliciting the breathless reaction "How can such things be!" The common ingredients are the shocker-thriller à la detective, technocracy, pornography, sadism, and escapism in space and time, with a breath of Freud-Kierkegaard-Nietzsche-Spengler-Sartre and a sauce of Prometheus-Icarus-Columbus-Jules Verne-Wells. There is also a generous admixture of melodrama (in American terminology, space opera), technology, monsters and subhumans, rockets and robots, planeteers and pin-ups, noble aspirations and tingling sex appeal.

What are the main themes of science fiction at the present time? In spite of the vast army of writers at work producing these books and the tremendous possibilities for imagining new and ingenious devices or recombining old ones, the number of themes is definitely limited; the stories tend to be somewhat monotonous, the flights of imagination disappointing and the human element unvarying. No matter how far they fly into space, the planeteers are disconcertingly down-to-earth. A few of the main variations will be suggested.

An important theme is war, both international and intergalactic, with fantastic weapons and radioactive materials that cause gene mutations and an accompanying degeneration of the human body. Another theme is psychic control over the individual and the masses by soul-engineers, with a similar degeneration of the human spirit. Then there are interplanetary adventures, with invasion of the earth by beings from other planets, often with an accompanying subjection and exploitation of man. Or the enslavement of man by tyrannical robots (the Frankenstein motif), or the supremacy of mechanical supermen, as in the Cartesian formula, "I think, therefore I am," is applied to thinking machines.[11] Or the Malthusian motif of increasing overpopulation of the earth and the ultimate extinction of man through starvation is employed. There are also other themes, all in a minor key, all centering around the doom of man and civilization as a result of improbable technological achievements and a complete failure in the realm of moral, social, cultural, and political achievements. Science fiction projects the existentialist categories of fear, suffering, and death into the future, making it look so alarming that man can be glad to live in the relative security of the gray and comfortless present. It is not, after all, as bad as one had thought.

Another paradoxical outcome of the semi-utopia is that science fiction ends as antiscientism. It also comes to include in its utopias just those elements which eschatology is throwing out of its scheme of things, especially mythology. It makes so crystal clear what the fatal consequences of the continued development of science and technology might be that it revives the old idea of a moratorium on further scientific research.

Most of all, science fiction mirrors the uncertainty of the times about the future. There are still traces of the old progress-optimism and enlightened nationalism concerning the possibilities of improving the world through science, lingering on in figures like Einstein. There are traces of the old influence-optimism, active and direct. Something of Promethean man lives on in literary superman. Thus, science fiction leaves its readers helpless between hope and despair.

Let us draw up the balance sheet for science fiction. On the positive side goes all that the semi-utopia has preserved of the vitality of the genuine utopia, including the critique of the times. Sometimes this is cast in the classical form of the encounter between superior beings of another planet and earthlings, despised by the superior beings for the feverish preoccupation with trivial affairs. This humbling lesson strengthens a feeling of historical relativity and guards the road, however narrow, to the open future.

Science fiction also carries on the tradition of the systematic construction of another world, and thus prepares for the onrushing postindustrial revolution.

On the negative side stands the antiscientific and anticultural focus of the genre as a whole. Its culture-pessimism points away from progress, and its development is on the whole antihumanistic.

---

[11] See Isaac Asimov, *I, Robot* (New York: Gnome Press, 1951). This describes a new type of robot with built-in controls according to the newly-discovered "laws of robotics."

The negative utopia combines all the aspects of the previously mentioned anti-utopias, to an extreme degree. It is the very oldest platonic anti-utopia in modern dress, but it has no positive counterpart. It is the disutopia of Mandeville with cynicism carried to a *reductio ad absurdum*. It is the pseudo-utopia both in its liberal and Marxian Social Darwinism, and in its treatment of dictatorship (for example, Virgil Gheorghiu). It is the semi-utopia, with its technology, its quasi religion, its deification of the leader (Ford as Lord in *Brave New World*), and its substitution of fairy tales for religion in the spiritual diet of the masses.

Borrowing from the genuine utopia the satiric technique of axiomatic reversal, it outdoes Cyrano, Holberg, Rabelais, and all the portrayers of the world upside down to Lytton and Butler. However, the negative utopia turns upside down not this world but the world of the utopia itself. The negative utopia is a caricature of utopia.

In a tremendous increase in essence-pessimism, the general feeling is that all Faustian human power, whether of good or evil intent, inevitably produces something far worse than the original *status quo*. Utopian striving is not only meaningless but disastrous.

It is not so much that utopia is impossible, in this view, as that man is impotent. The negative utopia makes a direct attack on the Achilles heel of all utopism. In the moment that man makes use of his own power, which is the essence of all utopian striving, his lack of power becomes painfully evident. In this sense every utopia as it unfolds into the future operates as an anti-utopia. Thus it is that the "brave new world" is neither brave nor new. nor even a world, but an embryo factory.

Iconoclasm of the Images of the Future

We have just seen in what ways the de-utopianizing of the utopia has taken place. What had once been the essence of utopism, the satirical critique of the times and the systematic reconstruction, have now become weapons to be used against the utopia itself. The positive has been negated, the future defuturized, and the image demolished.

Negation

The contrast device, a utopian technique from the earliest days, comes gradually to be used with a different emphasis. Now it is the existing order which receives the positive accent and the utopia the negative accent.

It is clear that the utopia has contained a double charge, first exploding the Middle Ages to burst into modern times and then exploding modern times into smithereens (and itself along with it). Every utopia is historically relative and carries within itself the seeds of its own decay. The power of the utopian idea, however, has until now seemed constant. Now we are for the first time faced with the problem of whether the utopia as such is at an end.

Defuturizing

We mean by the term "defuturizing" a retreat from constructive thinking about the future in order to dig oneself into the trenches of the present. It is a ruthless elimination of future-centered idealism by today-centered realism. We have lost the ability to see any further than the end of our collective nose.

The horizon is perhaps a bit narrower for the practical politician, a bit wider for the socialist: narrower for those who are concerned with immediate policy decisions, whether in government or business, wider for those concerned with overall planning. But everyone takes the existing situation as the basic point of departure. The daily paper summarizes not only the day but our times. We are no longer willing or able to peer around the corner of the century, or even to peer into the next decade, except when it is a question of dealing with millions of years and vast distances in space. The very size of such time dimensions renders them harmless and nonthreatening to the present.

Deimaging

The process of destroying the image of the future reaches a climax in the negative utopia, which is a caricature of the future and at last delivers us into the realm of comic books. It is not true that modern man no longer thinks in images, but those images now have quite a different referent. Insofar as they still refer to the future, their content is nihilistic and full of despair. It is only a step from the caricature of these chimaerical images of the future to the rejection of all images of the future.

There remain, then, only those images which depict the world as it is or those which are based on the world as it is. There are four ways of depicting the existing world. Three are realistic: the scientific, the

195

technological, and the political. The fourth is an escapist technique, involving the use of the mass media. All of these are intimately related to our own time. Anyway, is there really a future? If there is, why waste time in fruitless speculation about something which is subject to so many unforeseeable variables that we cannot possibly make any predictions about it? If there is not, as we are being told more and more of late, so much the worse for us. Negative images of the future have made us spiritually ripe for a visionless existence bounded by today.

Having described this threefold process of negation, defuturizing, and deimaging, we find ourselves still on the surface of the phenomenon of the iconoclasm. We have not penetrated into the heart of the de-utopianizing process. In the last analysis we must be concerned with the changing relationship between man and time, which is expressed in a new image of man and a new spirit of the times.

When modern man limits his time-consciousness to the present, we may term this a weakening of utopian awareness, the source of all thinking about the future. This utopian awareness, as has been repeatedly said, operates on the basis of two inward drives: the split nature and polar tension of the spiritual life, and the urge towards self-determination of our own destiny. The changes in the spirit of the times and in the attitudes of mind of modern man strike at the heart of these two drives. These changes could be labeled dedualizing and dehumanizing.

Dedualizing

Dedualizing is a phenomenon that is especially characteristic of the natural sciences. The habits of thought of the natural scientist tend toward monism. He considers only one aspect of a complex phenomenon, and chooses to treat that aspect as if it contained the significance of the whole. He seeks the object without its subject, the fact without its value judgment, the quantity without its quality. As it happens, this type of natural-science approach has been elevated to the position of ultimate standard for all scientific work, with an accompanying tendency to regard the nonscientific as of no significance.

This positivism has been greatly accentuated by technological developments. Everything that can be measured, registered, and controlled is valued. This has led to the specifically modern habit of matter-of-factness which Albert North Whitehead has termed "the fallacy of misplaced concreteness." There are not "more things in heaven and earth ... than are dreamt of in your philosophy." The modern Horatio, in fact, only does his dreaming on the psychoanalyst's couch or at the movies.

Spiritual existence is more and more forced back into the one dimension of the present, of that which envelops us (Jaspers's *das Umgreifende*), and of the concrete situation which is always for every individual "that which is mine" (Heidegger's *Jemeinigkeit*). Life is flattened out; it lies inert, without depth, meaning, color, or value. It amounts to nothing more than an insect society equipped with airplanes—highly mobile, but stagnant in time.

Life's basic challenge, the breach between the is and the ought, has received the most ignominious treatment of all: it has been annulled.

Dehumanizing

The destruction of dualism leads to the destruction of humanity. Not only does monism exclude the possibility of the *Umwertung aller Werte*, but the confinement of the spirit to the tangible fact leads to the devaluing of all values. Let us not make the mistake of romanticizing the past. There was never a time when man en masse was overflowing with altruism and spirituality. The utopian critique of every age reveals quite the contrary. Otherwise, Rousseau would have felt no need to present us with the image of the "noble savage," or Swift the image of wise and noble horses. Or, to go back considerably further, we should never have needed the symbolic figure of "old Adam" (and his Eve!) . Does nihilism, then, new in name only, represent a phenomenon as old as sinful man? Does the imbecile in Bernanos perhaps belong to all time, and also Camus's *peste* and Sartre's dirty hands? What is there to indicate that the great mass of humanity is any more stupid, wicked, or doomed today than it ever was?

Indeed, there are no objective criteria for the measurement of the progress of human insight in various ages. Empirical science, with all its techniques, has not yet brought us so far. It may well be, however, that there are indicators in each age which point to trends. Nihilism is not an isolated system of ideas but part of an organic whole which we label the spirit of the times or the style of a culture. In our opinion it is neither mass-mindedness nor materialism which gives such a menacing character to the times, but their intimate relationship with technology. The mechanization of life, not only in working hours but in our leisure time, extending beyond our manual to our mental activities, extends the influence of technology far beyond its original scope and threatens to enslave mankind.

When the course of events failed to confirm the optimism concerning technological power, bitter disillusionment set in. This disillusionment fell into a spiritual vacuum, for complete reliance on this same technology had already undermined the spiritual resources with which man had previously met his disappointments. The will to recover was gone.

The dehumanizing of man is basically the loss of belief and confidence in man's own worth. As a result of the Industrial Revolution, man is incapable of conceiving that anything can move except through the pushing of buttons. Now he is faced with a machine too vast for him to comprehend, with buttons he has no strength to push. Once again, we have the philosophy *il monde va da se*, only with a complete change of emphasis: the world no longer runs for man's benefit, but against it.

What can man in all his smallness, small in spite of his mass-identity, do in the face of the powers which he has helped unleash in the world? He stands as *l'Être et le Néant*. Everything goes from nothingness to nothingness. Nietzsche and Kierkegaard, Heidegger and Sartre, each interprets in his own way this same basic modern spirit, which in its Western nihilism paired with inaction comes very close to the Eastern Nirvana, with its rejection of the world and the flesh.

When man's utopian aspirations to develop his own humanity die out, then man himself dies.

Chapter 17. De-eschatologizing

Pontius Pilate did not succeed in putting the true Jesus to death, but in the ensuing two thousand years Christian theologians have been slowly but surely achieving just this in their efforts each to save his own version of Jesus. The general outlines of the de-eschatologizing process parallels the de-utopianizing process.

Historical Development of Anti-eschatological Eschatology

The teachings of Jesus have already been discussed in Chapter 7 as a proclamation of an imminent Kingdom of God. Problems of historic authenticity aside, it is clear that the image of the future evoked by Jesus, as revealed in the records of the first three Gospels, on the one hand is closely connected with the image of the future taught by the Jewish prophets who preceded Him, and on the other hand makes a historic breach in the existing situation of His day. This second aspect was the heart of the Glad Tidings. Jesus did not teach His disciples to pray, "Thy Kingdom come," in reference to a far-off ultimate event. It had the implications of a total reversal soon to be revealed. This element of revolutionary realization of an Other and better world here on earth "as it is in heaven" also entered into our definition of pure eschatology.

Such a definition is not acceptable to the great majority of Christian theologians today, however. A long drawn-out regressive movement in theology has resulted in the building up of an eschatology without an *eschaton*, and, as in the fairy tale about the emperor's new clothes, no one dares to admit not seeing what isn't there. This undermining of eschatology is not the product of any competition

199

either to adorn or to distort Christian thought. Rather it stems from a profound human need for rationalization after the fact.

Two factors have set this eroding rationalization into motion. The first is the disappointment of the expectations concerning the speedy return of Christ. Could Jesus have been mistaken concerning the time of His Coming? Here exegesis must take over, and it began already in the time of the Apostles.

The second is a gradual impairment of the capacity to believe. Modern man after some two thousand years represents the culmination of a new point of view concerning God, human life, and the world which makes it impossible for him, even in his role as a good Christian, to believe in a re-creation of an earthly Kingdom.[1]

We have said that these two factors forced theology into a rationalization after the fact, in order to save what could be saved of the Glad Tidings. This is true, but it is not the whole story. Of equal and possibly greater importance is what cultural sociology might label an attempt at rationalization before the fact by theology. It is not true that the theologian is perpetually being pulled along by the modern believer in a vain race with time. He sometimes takes the lead. Again and again a theology of crisis develops which is not only an answer to the times, but itself a challenge. It is a challenge in two ways corresponding to the above-mentioned negative factors. It dehistoricizes, and it descandalizes the religious records. The dehistoricizing aims at purifying the sayings of Jesus and the Revelation of John of any elements of precise time-computations, and at making the evangelical "soon" relative and reassigning to it the meaning "someday"; its goal is to force the biblical prophecy of fulfillment out of the concrete time-flow into an abstract eternity. This process is coupled with an attempt at dematerializing with respect to earthly prospects and focusing attention on the beyond rather than the here through a general spiritualizing process. Time and space undergo a similar negation, as the Kingdom of God is moved out of historical time and spatial events.

This dehistoricizing was, at least in the beginning, mainly a process of transposition. The descandalizing, however, was almost from the very start directed at elimination of the incriminating subject matter, for the latter undermined precisely that which Paul singled out as

---

[1] The strongest evidence for this is perhaps to be found in England and America, particularly the latter. The theme of "Christian Hope" in the Assembly of the World Council of Churches in Evanston, Illinois, in 1955 reflects this development.

unique in the new Christian teaching, that which was therefore a stumbling block to the Jews and a foolishness to the Greeks. Here we come face to face with a fourfold paradox, perhaps the most enormous and least understood paradox in the history of Christian culture. This is what it implies:

1. There has been a continuous attempt to replace the divine wisdom taught by Jesus in his language and for his time with the human (and particularly theological) wisdom of this century, in order to purge the teachings of Jesus of what have now become stumbling blocks and foolishness even for Christians.

2. This attempt has been characterized by a thoroughgoing exegesis which has had the ironical effect of negating the Jewishness and Greekness of the gospels.

3. Christianity's first theologian, the Apostle Paul, himself began this process (in spite of the wisdom expressed in 1: Cor. 2:6-16) and opened the way for a later negating of his own doctrines and the development of a long chain of eschatological interpretations which in the end resulted in a progressive de-eschatologizing.

4. This development, which continued on from primitive Christianity through the Roman Catholic Church, has been supported both by Reformation and Counter Reformation. Today it seems to have gone farthest in Protestantism, in which the extremes of ecclesiastical orthodoxy and a liberalism which borders on humanism appear to meet. In fact, however, the Catholic Church has also been inwardly affected by these spiritual currents.

Paul himself laid the foundations for a Christology in which the man Jesus made way for Christ, the Lord, and in which the teachings concerning the Kingdom made way for teachings concerning salvation. Next, Paul was himself interpreted according to the Fourth Gospel of John, whose Christ-mysticism assisted in the Hellenization of the Jewish-apocalyptic strain of the teachings of Jesus by covering them over with Greek *logos*-metaphysics. The death, resurrection, and exaltation of Jesus as the Christ came to assume a central place in the sin-grace-salvation schema, while the life and heroic-ethical mission of Jesus, the prophet, and the good news concerning earthly renewal proclaimed by Him, receded into the background. The Kingdom of Grace came to dominate over the Kingdom of Glory.

At the same time there was a shift from belief in a cosmic re-creation to belief in individual salvation. Individual redemption came to be valued more highly than the collective salvation of society. This shift also encompassed a shift of orientation from future to past and to present: toward the past, in a preoccupation with the sacrificial death on the cross of Jesus, and in a preoccupation with the renewal which in that moment took place; toward the present, by virtue of the factual presence of Christ for those who through the renewal of conversion and faith lived with Him daily. This was a presence both in the spirit, through the Holy Ghost, and in the body, through Holy Communion. The bodily presence extended further to the presence of the Church as the Corpus Christi. These are further shifts drawing emphasis away from the flesh and toward the spiritual body, signs of a progressive spiritualization through transubstantiation of the Christian doctrine.

The Roman Catholic sacraments are visible signs of this same process. The Eucharist, which brings about communion between the resurrected Saviour and man, is the most significant sign. The priestly attendant is the mediating instrument of Jesus, lending Him tongue and hands that Jesus may continue to bestow grace upon man. The believers come into fellowship with Christ through these sacraments, and He affects their day-to-day lives by virtue of His past being present always and everywhere. It is mainly through the Church that this sacramental present receives more and more stress whereas the eschatological future evaporates. In the sacrament the *parousia* is as if it were already realized; in the Holy Mass the death on the cross is actualized over and over again, and the *donec veniat* (1 Cor. 11:26), literally meaning "till He comes," is more and more neglected in comparison to the present-perfect "I am come."

The *regnum Christi*, incorporated in the Church, has already begun, and expands with the growth of the Church through Roman Catholicism, through evangelization, through missionary work among the heathen, through the Crusades, and through the Inquisition against unbelievers, nonconformists, and heretics. The extension of the temporal power of the Church is an extension of the Kingdom of Christ. The Kingdom of God, the *basileia tou theou*, is in the meantime, as we have said, slowly fading into the background. Man need no longer wait for a future announcement of election to the community of believers in the new order of the Kingdom of God; he can receive his salvation now through the visible Church.

Even before the Reformation broke loose against the Roman Catholic Church, cosmic eschatology had largely been reworked into individual and ecclesiastical eschatology. The Christian Church was increasingly proclaiming itself as the accomplished eschatological fact of salvation.

The reformers Luther, Melanchthon, Zwingli, and Calvin were not protesting this point of view. Whatever differences they had with Roman Catholicism and among themselves concerning Protestant versus reform orientations, and however much the Bible was re-examined as a literal proclamation of the Word become flesh, no questions were raised concerning the teaching of Jesus about the coming Kingdom, nor concerning the Revelation of John. On the contrary, while they vied with each other in proclaiming God's mercy in Christ, and although they bitterly and fanatically fought each other in religious wars, they united in a merciless battle to put to the fire and the sword the heretics who held fast to Jesus's promise of the near establishment of the Kingdom.

Neither the Reformation nor the Counter Reformation destroyed the fundamental position that Christ, the only-begotten Son of God, has already come, and that the Holy Ghost has been present among man ever since. The idea of the predicted Second Coming was blurred and finally blotted out.

The theology of the last five centuries exhibits all the characteristics we note in the general development of science. It took several centuries to wipe out the models of thought of the Middle Ages, and then the dominating conceptions of the eighteenth and nineteenth centuries had to be successively erased. Now in the twentieth century we are preoccupied with rubbing out the last Judaic and Hellenic traces in theology, thus killing eschatology off as an idea.

Jacob Taubes concluded his interesting study on *Abendländische Eschatologie* (1947) with a discussion of Hegel, Kierkegaard, and Marx; this, in his opinion, seems to close the subject entirely.[2] Shortly before World War I, Troltsch had already issued his famous statement, "The eschatological bureau is closed these days." This was not entirely true, however. There remained a spiritualized belief in the coming of the Kingdom of God. This was introduced by philosophical eschatology as the expected end-result of a gradual evolution toward ideals of brotherhood and justice through the growth of an internal kingdom of the human spirit. And in 1906 Schweitzer's monumental *The Quest of the Historical Jesus* was published, representing the rediscovery of the eschatology of primitive Christianity in the person of the historical evangelical Jesus.

Theology attempts to remove the stumbling block, the scandal. It is not difficult to begin the destruction of the scandal, but it is very difficult to end it. In its beginning the process appears both innocent and reasonable. It is a question of separating out the precious and

---

[2] *Abendländische Eschatologie*, p. 191.

203

imperishable contents from the rough and perishable wrappings. The historical Jesus, it is explained, used an image-rich language which was easily comprehensible to His own contemporaries. His words need to be translated and His time-bound images reinterpreted so that modern man can derive meanings from them which will be equivalent to their original meanings. The first step in this process is to purify this language and eliminate the Jewish dogmatism and prophetic apocalyptics which were current at that time, as well as the messianic symbolism and Eastern gnostic mythology. Then the later graftings of Greek metaphysics and Johannine *logos* -mysticism must be carefully removed in order to make the teaching of Jesus understandable and acceptable to the modern mind.

This secularizing process has progressed from an attack on the outer trappings of Christian teaching to a subversive penetration of its inmost core, in the attempt to make it conform to modern ideas. But what is this inmost core? For the orthodox fundamentalist it is all core, down to the last "a," "and," and "the" of the Bible. From the religious point of view, this position is perhaps both the simplest and the strongest. At the same time, if even one word is seriously questioned it turns out to be the weakest, for then the whole structure collapses. There has in fact been a gradual retreat on all fronts. The Catholic Church has been the one to hold on the longest to miracles, to the Immaculate Conception, and in general to a *credo quia absurdum.* But how long will it be possible to cling to a belief which is absurd in the face of modern thought?

The iconoclasm ends with the destruction of the *eschaton* proclaimed by Jesus. First it destroys Jesus, the historical man, then it destroys God Himself. Here again the attack was originally directed at the biblical use of images. It concentrated itself against the image of the intervening God of Abraham, Isaac, and Jacob.

A gradual process of elimination is involved: God is ejected from His heavenly place (divine housing shortage!), ejected from the course of history, and removed to an existence to spatially distant that it permits of no personal communication of son to Father in prayer. He has evaporated into the Spinozan primeval source of all being, into the platonic idea and philosophic faith (Jaspers), into the inconceivable Holy Name which expresses the inexpressable.

The theologians are seeking diligently but vainly to square the circle. They try to retain the Bible as divine revelation while throwing out the ballast of the biblical image of the future; to retain the Christian faith minus stumbling blocks, keeping the mystical Christ and the ethical Jesus, but throwing out the Prophet; to retain God as the primal source of all things, while abandoning the final goal; to make Him first, but absent.

Countereschatology in Disguise

The striking parallels between counterutopism and countereschatology will be pursued in this section. The emphasis will be on comparison, rather than on a complete analysis of countereschatology, and we have chosen certain characteristic categories of this phenomenon as the framework for our discussion.

Thoroughgoing Eschatology

Schweitzer, one of the most profoundly influential figures of this century, drew certain conclusions from his study of Jesus which are of greater importance for us than his actual view of Jesus. He maintains that the New Testament, and especially the Synoptic Gospels, must be read in the way of "consistent eschatology": we must think ourselves back into Jesus's own thoughts and emotions through a process of mystical communion and historical resonance. Once we have identified ourselves with the speaking and acting Jesus, we realize that He was completely filled with one idea, that of a speedy coming of an earthly messianic reign. Jesus did not think that He was to bring about this reign immediately, but He expected and proclaimed it.

Jesus's dominating motive was not the redemption of individual man, but the salvation of mankind. Presently, says Schweitzer, Jesus was doomed to the bitter discovery that He had been mistaken and misled by His dreams: the prophesied *parousia* failed to come about. The natural course of events disavowed His metahistoric idea. Jesus then attempted to compel God to make this dogma triumph over history by taking the role of the suffering servant and provoking His own suffering and death. The death of the Messiah was to ensure the coming of the Messiah. The sacrifice on the cross was a deliberate messianic act, inspired by and in fulfillment of the Old Testament prophecy. Only if we read the gospel as the story of a thoroughgoing eschatology can we understand and experience it.

The goal so far in Schweitzer's writings has been to experience Jesus and the gospel anew, in our time. But just at this point comes the great and unexpected countereschatological turning point, inaugurated by Schweitzer himself. Having demonstrated at some length the extent to which Jesus was transported by this *idée fixe* of an imminent coming of the Kingdom, and having made the point that we can really only understand and unite with Jesus if we enter into His own thinking about this, then he goes on to say that it is impossible for modern man to go back to the image of the future which Jesus had. This image of the future is the product of a "naïve" train of thought embodied in a cultural mode and in primitive materials of presentation which are time-bound and inextricably linked to the eschatological story of salvation. This imagery is secondary, and the essential eternal message, equally valid for our own time, must be separated from it.

Schweitzer feels that the primary thing in the teachings of Jesus is the expectation of a coming Kingdom of redemption from evil. Should Jesus return in our own time, He would preach exactly the same expectation of the Kingdom of God and an essentially similar way of life for man. But He would do it in a modern way, leaving out ancient Jewish supernatural imagery and dogmatics.

It is up to us, Schweitzer concludes, to translate the naïvely imaginative depictions of Jesus into modern thought, taking a free approach to history and a liberal approach to an ossified theology.

Why is this ethical-eschatological revision of the gospel basically countereschatological? The point of departure seems little changed in this translation, and the recommended course of action for man is a familiar one. But the ultimate goal has fallen away. Schweitzer no longer speaks of a coming Kingdom, and in fact can no longer do so. The reason it that the Kingdom will not come by an act of divine intervention in history, but through the moral striving of man. God Himself is changed. Like Hegel's rational world-spirit, Schweitzer's God is a moral world-will. This moral world-will resides in man. The Kingdom is not transcendent, but immanent.

In our terminology, Schweitzer continues the development from religious to philosophic chiliasm in the tradition of Reimarus, Lessing, Kant, and Friedrich Schleiermacher, with a shifting of the theological accent from apostolic and dogmatic Christianity to a philosophical system of ethics. But he also eliminates the *eschaton* of the Last Things and replaces it by humanistic goals of self-fulfillment for man, a philosophical act with far-reaching consequences. The goal is set by man himself, under the inspiration of Jesus.

The ultimate goal postulated by Schweitzer continues to bear the same name bestowed by Jesus on His vision: the Kingdom of God. But it is in fact little different from and scarcely more than an ethically secularized residue, *à la* Kant. Schweitzer's gospel contains no single messianic idea which could give the slightest pause to modern rationalistic thought. His ethical voluntarism can easily be translated into the direct influence-optimism of utopian thinking about the future.

For this very reason, this de-eschatologizing takes on a tragic-heroic character. The transition from eschatology to utopia, as a necessary adaptation to modern thought, takes place just at the beginning of a period in which this same modern thought is directed toward de-utopianizing. This reduction, then, must inevitably have negative consequences. Schweitzer himself is in part aware of this. He points out that modern man lacks the capacity for resonance with the eschatological (read utopian) *Weltanschauung* of Jesus. The nature and will of Jesus must remain alien to us, because our intellectual and emotional life contains no equivalent to His moral conviction concerning the general fulfillment of mankind. A living communion with the true Jesus is no longer possible, not because of the Jewish accoutrements of His faith, but because of His basic human convictions concerning an Other world.

Beside Schweitzer another figure emerges, this time from the house of reformed orthodoxy: Karl Barth, whose equally consistent eschatology has placed its mark on the theological thought of our century. One would perhaps not expect a man who has returned to the work of Luther and Calvin, and thus to the Holy Writ itself, to play a role in the de-eschatologizing process. It is not so surprising, however, when one considers that the great reformers were already retreating from eschatology in their fight against the chiliasts, and that Barth is primarily a disciple of Kierkegaard.

Barth reestablished the Kingdom of God as God's Kingdom, as the final outcome of God's will and the outpouring of divine mercy on sinful man. Not only must man live in faith and hope of this ending, but, while accepting God's judgment concerning his human unworthiness, he must let this expectation rule his life continuously. Barth's thoroughgoing eschatology maintains that man is permanently caught in the polar tensions between this sinful world and the Other holy one. "Permanently" means that he feels this intensely from minute to minute unceasingly during his entire earthly existence. This unremitting tension places man every moment before the ultimate choice.

This tensed expectation concerning the Coming of the Kingdom, which gives direction to human life, is independent of the historical stream of events. The Coming is entirely independent of the future. The Coming is not measurable by any human time-categories of soon or late, will not be fulfilled in historical time, and is not involved in the passing of centuries. For Barth the Kingdom of God is here since God's eternity stands over time as the horizon stands over the revolving earth. Therefore, the *parousia* is also here-and-now, since Christ is always present, always with us unto all eternity.

All talk of the perpetually postponed *parousia* is therefore meaningless. That which can never come in time, can even less stay away in time. The biblical expression "The Kingdom of Heaven is at hand" means nothing more or less than that the eternal Kingdom of God stands before us, within our reach, deciding our life and commanding our decision.

Does the banner of thoroughgoing eschatology camouflage a contraband cargo? He who does not shrink from a sharp answer could say that this eschatology is consistent because it completely eliminates the old eschatology, preserving only the empty hull.

The two kinds of thoroughgoing eschatology described here, that of Schweitzer and that of Barth, different as they are, became the prototypes of further countereschatological developments. Almost all later ramifications and patterns are implied in these prototypes.

Endless Eschatology

Modern theology had already tried in the nineteenth century to separate the historical Jesus and His time-bound proclamation from the spiritual Christ beyond time, and from the eternally valid idea of which He was the incarnation: the ideal of human existence on earth. The sensational work of D. F. Strauss published in 1835, the *Leben Jesu,* made a sharp demarcation between idea and reality. Its thesis that the historical figure of Jesus was to a great extent a product of imagination and fiction gave a tremendous impetus to the destruction of the Jewishness and the historicity of the image of Jesus. It pushed aside the temporal and accidental, the human coincidence, for the sake of the divine and eternal. This is a Hellenistic metaphysical trend which fits in well with the *logos*-Christology of Paul and John.

Althaus continues to work along these lines in his *Die letzten Dinge*, which reveals the influence of both Schweitzer and Barth.[3] The two dominating motifs are a critique of the expectation of the Kingdom of God as the end of history, and an axiological-metaphysical eschatology.

[3] Paul Althaus, *Die letzten Dinge* (Gütersloh: Bertelsman, 1922).

In his axiological eschatology he contrasts the realm of ideas and highest values with the empirical and historical world. This realm of values he identifies with the Kingdom of God. History is placed in opposition to eternally valid values which may guide man from moment to moment in history. The nearness of the Kingdom of God consists in the continuousness of the presence of these values.

Formless Eschatology

Rudolf Bultmann[4] gives a further impetus to the countereschatological movement. He is influenced by Schweitzer's method of historical biblical criticism, Barth's Pauline dialectical theology, and Heidegger's existential philosophy. These three approaches have one thing in common: dehistoricizing. Bultmann develops this into a system of his own, which is best known under the label of demythologizing.

The New Testament is primarily mythical in its mode of presentation, says Bultmann. The myths which adorn the contents of the gospel message come in part from the Old Testament, which in its turn borrowed from other heathen myths, and in part from other Eastern sources. The contents of the gospels are not acceptable or believable for modern man in this antiquated form. That form comes in direct conflict with his scientific knowledge (his new image of the world), with his historical experience (the perpetually postponed *parousia*), and with his self-awareness as man. He no longer believes himself to be the prey of supernatural powers which have chosen the world as their workshop and playground, but rather grasps after these powers for his own use, on the basis of that scientific knowledge in which alone he now places his faith.

How should we understand "mythical" in this connection? Bultmann considers all those ideas mythical which present the non-worldly as visually and tangibly experienceable in this world—for example, the Son of God, the virgin birth, the expiatory sacrifice on the cross, the bodily resurrection, and the ascension of Jesus. Salvation itself is not tangible, nor is the content of the Christian message empirically "demonstrable." All "demonstrable" facts of salvation are mythical and thus a stumbling block or a scandal to modern, nonmythical thought. In order to retain the core of the gospel, the *kerygma*, "message of salvation," a radical demythologizing must take place.

---

[4] Rudolf Bultmann, *Neues Testament und Mythologie* (Hamburg: Reich und Heidrig, 1948).

This radical demythologizing, directed against the imagery of the Bible, affects the image of Jesus, the image of man, and the image of God. All these must be purified. Bultmann considers the cult of the historical and synoptic Jesus an illusion. In reality we know nothing of Jesus except that He came. This is sufficient. The human person of Jesus, His teachings, His life and sufferings, His words and His deeds, are from the Christocentric point of view irrelevant. No communion is possible with the Jesus who was indeed once a living man but who has long since been dead. Communion is only possible with the spirit of Christ. In this dehistorizing, dematerializing, and depersonalizing of Jesus, the only remaining concern is with the eternal ideas and the spiritual truth which He represents. The crucified Christ of the past lives in the present, and only in the present. There is no other Christ to return in the future.

Bultmann would retain the Acting God as an admitted "mythological residue," but this God does not promise any other future. He is only present through the spirit of Christ, a silent witness to the struggles of man—man who may or may not surrender. Thus all images are actualized, spiritualized, and transposed in the metaphysical language of existentialism. The New Testament is modernized by presenting its present-perfect and future tenses as one single and simple present.

In modern eschatology all that remains, according to Bultmann, is the conception of the cross and the resurrection. The total of this eschatology is comprised in the preaching of these events, in the Church itself, and in man in the act of existential surrender. But this mythological purification is plainly a subjective one, for Pauline *kerygma* and Christology, as interpreted by Bultmann, also contain materials from Hellenic and gnostic myths concerning resurrection and salvation. A residue of Jewish mythology also lives on in the concept of the acting God. Bultmann's method of demythologizing, which cuts the beating heart out of the message of salvation—ostensibly in order to save this message—has cut loose from the moorings of the Christian religion and opened the way for all other interpretations, including non-Christian ones. He has therefore opened the way for a more systematic dumping of those mythological conceptions, which he himself wants to retain in an implicit sense. It is not to be wondered at that Bultmann's disciples felt that his demythologizing had not been radical enough, and went on to exceed his efforts, with the inevitable result that the *kerygma* he wished to save was not spared.

The countereschatological effect of the work of Bultmann and his followers was the indirect result of their demythologizing mission. This mission was aimed at the form of the biblical message. A second movement soon followed, aiming directly at the de-eschatologizing of the contents of the message. The so-called Berne School was a part of this movement, including such writers as Martin Werner, Fritz Buri, and Ulrich Neuenschwender. These three men all build on Schweitzer's work, and all take as their point of departure the "perpetually postponed *parousia.*" Each of them surpasses his teacher in the logical applications of his technique, and yet each is determined to retain the term "eschatology."

The conclusions of Schweitzer's consistent eschatology of primitive Christianity form the basis of Werner's *Die Entstehung des christlichen Dogmas* (Bern, 1941). He demonstrates systematically the de-eschatologizing process as it has continued uninterruptedly since St. Paul and particularly St. John. He shows how Christology and ecclesiology have progressively distorted, spiritualized, and destroyed the eschatological message of Jesus and robbed it of its prophetic, heroic, and cosmic proportions. He describes the bourgeoisification of Christianity as the doctrine is whittled down to a concern with individual rebirth and a sacramental *logos*-doctrine.

Werner takes the same, somewhat unexpected turning which Schweitzer took before him, but it is even more sharply delineated. We can never return, he says, to the primitive Christian eschatology. But neither can we accept the deviation of the Church in this respect. The position into which even primitive Christianity was coerced as a result of the unrealized return of Christ, has become increasingly uncomfortable. It has crumbled, rather than been strengthened, under the impact of an altered *Weltanschauung* brought about by the course of time and scientific developments. Werner argues that therefore we must now move forward along this same road of de-eschatologizing—we must systematically clear away all remaining fragments of eschatological metaphysics. The implication is that a new Protestant dogmatics must be developed which completely abandons the time-bound eschatology of Jesus. The work must be done, unafraid, in the spirit of Jesus Himself.

Buri, one of Werner's disciples, has developed this "consistent countereschatological" point of view in more detail. He states that the de-eschatologizing of Werner must go on to the demythologizing of Bultmann. We must dare, says he, the leap from the beyond to the here-and-now, from transcendence to immanence. Only by making the above combination can Bultmann's mythological-eschatological residue be logically and radically eliminated. Then even the *kerygma*, inconsistently retained by Bultmann, can be courageously removed.

But Buri too retains an eschatological residue. Reality as given is ethically indifferent, encompassing both sense and nonsense. The Christian eschatological element which Buri retains is the will to fulfillment of life, which gives meaning to man's meaningless existence in his *Daseinsnot*. In his choice between two possible worlds, one meaningless and the other meaningful, man must choose the latter. In other words, Buri travels the road from theocentric to anthropocentric determination of destiny, and thus from indirect to direct influence-optimism. Having demonstrated that the eschatological consciousness is waning, he issues a call to the utopian consciousness, unaware that this too has been equally undermined. Existential eschatology contains, by its very nature, an insoluble antinomy. As an expectation of future fulfillment, it can never be more than a negative eschatology, a caricature of itself, since the *eschaton* has first been carefully removed.

Meaningless Eschatology

Buri's existential eschatology is separated by the thinnest threads from a meaningless eschatology. Buri himself described biblical eschatology as *eine positiv zu bewertende Illusion*. It is to be valued positively because of its inspiring ethos which Buri, with Schweitzer, would like to retain as the will toward a meaningful fulfillment of life. But is not such an eschatology-without-*eschaton* equally an illusion, particularly for the believer?

This impression is strengthened by Walter Nigg's aforementioned *Das ewige Reich, Die Geschichte einer Sehnsucht und einer Enttäuschung*, a work written under the influence of the Berne School. He points out that the chiliastic struggles for the realization of the *Reichsmythes* on earth were always condemned to failure. The disappointment over the unrealized *parousia* was continually and inevitably followed by new disappointments. But the *Sehnsucht* remains, and although the myth may alter, Nigg hopes that the pathos can nevertheless be retained and find new modes of eschatological expression and fulfillment. If it is retained, however, it must be with the knowledge that the goal itself has vanished.

212

The last major trend to be discussed reverts to the other extreme. It is based on an interpretation of Augustine's *The City of God* and strongly resembles the Roman Catholic conception of the Church as the body of Christ. The partial fulfillment of the Kingdom with the First Coming of Jesus is gradually extended to the view that this was the total fulfillment. The Kingdom has come once and for all time. Any expectations for the future are illusory, not because they can never be realized, but because they already have been realized.

This last position is found predominantly in English theology, and especially in the work of the Cambridge New Testament scholar, C. H. Dodd.[5] His concept of a realized eschatology has been developed in a number of works. With the Swiss School at Berne, he maintains that eschatology is central to the gospels, as a proclamation of the Kingdom of God. But while Schweitzer and others hold that this expectation has not been fulfilled and is, in principle, nonfulfillable, Dodd says that the expectation has been fulfilled and that the Kingdom of God has come.

Dodd bases his position on Paul and the Gospel of John, thus on the "purified" gospel, rejecting the "futuristic eschatology" of the Synoptic Gospels and Revelation. In the Fourth Gospel the Kingdom of God is correctly represented in mystical fashion as the eternal order in which we participate by living in Christ.

The realized eschatology is a pure negation of eschatology as an image of the future. It is sheer caricature to speak of realized salvation in this age. The Berne School is empty and the Cambridge School blind when it comes to the future. The one is disillusioned over what has not happened in history, the other immobilized by what has supposedly already happened, and mankind is left dangling in a vacuum.

Iconoclasm of Images of the Future

This overview of theological developments equips us to perceive

---

[5] *New Testament Studies* (New York: Charles Scribners Sons, 1954); *The Gospel Parables* (Manchester: Manchester University Press, 1932); *The Apostolic Preaching and its Developments* (London: Hodder and Stoughton, 1936), Appendix about eschatology; *The Gospels as History* (Manchester: Manchester University Press, 1938); *According to the Scriptures* (London: 1952) (Stone Lectures, Princeton Theological Seminary).

the remarkable parallel developments of de-utopianizing and de-eschatologizing, which have so far escaped the notice both of theologians and sociologists.

We analyzed the iconoclasm of utopian images of the future under the headings of negation, defuturizing, and deimaging. These same elements leap to the eye in an analysis of the attack on the eschatological image of the future.

Two further factors which we identified as crucial in contributing to the decay of the utopian images, dedualizing and dehumanizing, are found to be crucial here also, as dedualizing and dedeifying.

Negation

The clock of our theological time is continually striking the note "de." The modern view of life requires a de-antiquating in general, and a descandalizing of the Bible in particular. This "de" process, however, is not intended to be negative. On the contrary, the intention is to save the positive values of the past from the relentless tooth of time. But subjecting these values to the trimming shears of modern civilization is like peeling a potato: it becomes more palatable, but some of the essential vitamins are destroyed.

In the end it makes little difference whether one takes the *parousia* which has not come as the point of departure, concluding that it will never take place, or whether one begins with the appearance of Christ almost two thousand years ago and comes to the opposite conclusion that the *parousia* has already taken place. The image of the future is smashed between the hammer and anvil of "never" and "already." The desks in the Eschatological Bureau are piled to the ceiling with eschatological studies, but the office remains closed.

While the untenability of fundamentalism has been demonstrated, the tenability of any form of modernism has not been established, for theology itself has sawed off the only limb of the tree of knowledge on which modernism could find a secure foothold: the limb of the image of the future.

Let us examine the progressive negation of eschatology at the point of defuturizing.

Defuturizing

The history of Christianity is the history of man's struggle to free himself from the fundamental message of Jesus: "The Kingdom of God is nigh." Its failure to come posed man with a time-problem

214

which has not diminished with the centuries. Jesus placed a heavy burden on the shoulders of the future. How can a good Christian free himself of this burden? Here begins a never-ending exegesis. There are three protagonists in the ensuing struggle against the future—the Church, theology, and time itself—and three foci of attack—man, Jesus, and God.

The Church, as we have already seen, would solve the time-problem by expanding, first as the Kingdom of Christ, and finally as the Kingdom of God itself.

Theology has always supported this development by softening Jesus's revolutionary message concerning the Coming of the Kingdom as much as possible and concealing it under a haze of mysticism. It remained for Kant to arouse theology and provide it with a philosophical content for the message.

There are three connected time-elements in the gospel message concerning the Coming of the Kingdom, all of which can be ascribed to Jewish futurism. The first is the prophecy concerning that which is to come; the second is a time-computation associated with this prophecy; and the third is a philosophy of history inherent in this prophecy.

All three elements are defuturized. The first attack is on prophecy as such, a Jewish tradition from which Christianity must be freed. The gospel is acceptable as *Wahrsagung*, "truth," but not as *Weissagung*, "prediction."

The attack on the apocalyptic elements of Christianity is less far-reaching than the attack on the prophecies. The proclamation of the Coming of the Kingdom of God must be retained, since it is an irrevocable promise made by God. Only the computations concerning its imminence are at fault.

The most far-reaching defuturizing takes place, not in the attack on the forms of prophecy and apocalypse, but in the attack on the content of the message, on the idea of the Coming of the Kingdom of God. This idea, it is maintained, comes from late Jewish dogmatics. The whole complex of concepts concerning the end of time are Jewish in origin and in tradition. This Jewish cosmology rests on a theodicy concerning the ultimately beneficent workings of God in history. The Jewish conception of salvation in history is unacceptable in the modern *Weltanschauung*. Christian theology must liberate itself from this Jewish theology.

De-Judification then combines with dehistorification: true religion exists apart from time. Therefore we must free ourselves from the historical Jesus, not only because He thought in Jewish terms, but more generally because His message was time-bound. We must reconstruct the eternal Jesus, apart from His relationship to His own time.

The defuturizing is complete if one accepts the view that the God who revealed Himself in Jesus Christ is eternity itself, incommensurable with time and history. The Realm of the future then becomes an eternal category.

De-imaging

Paul condemned two attitudes in respect to faith: "The Jews seek signs, and the Greeks seek wisdom." He himself began the process of casting off Judaism, but adopted Greek modes of thought. Modern man does not bring the *sacrificium intellectus* to faith; rather he sacrifices signs on behalf of reason. Any sign which actualizes the Other-worldly in this world is objectionable. Demythologizing is basically de-imaging.

All visible signs of the invisible are rejected, including the signs wrought by Jesus. The resurrected Jesus appeared in the midst of His disciples and said to them, "See my hands and my feet, that it is I myself; handle me, and see; for a spirit has not flesh and bones as you see I have." De-imaging dismisses both the negative (the empty grave) and the positive image (appearance and recognition of the resurrected Jesus). The great questions are: where do the boundaries of the image lie, and once the de-imaging process has begun, can it be halted at any point?

It is not surprising that the oldest of the Christian Churches, the Roman Catholic, still clings to all the biblical miracles, the image-worship, and the rich imagery of cathedral architecture, religious art, and liturgy, nor that it kept to the Ptolemaic image of the world as long as possible, as being most consonant with the biblical image. Even today the Roman Catholic Church has retained concrete images of choirs of heavenly angels. Mary, Mother of God, Immaculate Virgin, receives an increasingly exalted place in Church doctrine. The Catholic Church has evidently felt, and been confirmed in its feeling, that once the iconoclastic process has begun, there is no stopping place short of a second final crucifixion of Christ Himself. Nevertheless, the Church had to accept Copernicus. Will it be able in the long run to resist the creeping secularization of the modern image of the world?

The more rapid progress of iconoclasm in modern Protestantism is not to be interpreted as intentional sacrilege. Descandalizing always seeks to find a compromise between old and new. It is not the

216

intention simply to scrap the image-rich language of the New Testament, but to translate it into an appropriate form for modern man.

Images can be preserved by giving them symbolic meaning. Why should we not consider the cross and the resurrection as symbols of reconciliation and redemption, and Christ as the symbol of the God-concept? According to Jung, such symbols are the archetypes which live in mankind's unconscious. But de-imaging, combined with a technique for the exposition of symbols, in the end deprives the biblical book of images of its unique and specific character, whatever the intentions of the expounders.

Symbolic interpretation greatly intensifies the shift from Jesus toward Christology and Christ-mysticism, and from the Old to the New Testament, begun already by Paul and John. The iconoclastic spiritualization leads to a progressive depersonalization of the image of Jesus. Remarkably enough, this de-Judification of the images of the Bible might seem to lead straight back to the purely Jewish "hearing" of the Word, and to the imageless God of the Jews, who is but a holy name for the Jewish "ear of the world." There is, however, a heaven's breadth of difference: this modern way of rewording the gospel message divests it of imagination, including imagining the future.

The image of the future is not only the matrix of faith, but also its alma mater. Faith without an image of the future lacks the dynamic power of the believing imagination. Losing itself in this world, it ends by losing the original image of God. These two processes, closely related to defuturizing and de-imaging, can be described as dedualizing and dedeifying.

Dedualizing

The reader who has had the patience to follow the preceding analysis of the undermining of biblical imagery will now be rewarded by perceiving the key to the drama of de-eschatologizing and the related collapse from within of the Christian faith. It is clear now that this process of self-destruction cannot be explained entirely by the delayed *parousia*, nor by the modern scientific *Weltanschauung*, although we suggested these two current conceptions as possible hypotheses. For nineteen successive centuries the delay of the Lord's return did not have the deeply troubling effects which we now observe in this twentieth century. Also, the scientific image of the world has been developing and changing ever since the sixteenth century, but—until the beginning of our century—without affecting

217

the core of eschatological expectations. Moreover, the latest developments in physical science do not exclude the possibility of "wonders," such as a cosmic transformation.

The eschatological consciousness has withered on the vine because the religious consciousness has sustained serious injury. Two foundation stones of religion in general and eschatology in particular have crumbled: the dualistic view of two opposing forces in the real world, and the optimistic view of such dialectical movement leading to the final high goal.

The dualistic attitude of mind lies at the very core of religious thinking. It divides all existence into two orders. They can be labeled the here and the beyond, and a distance which is something more than purely spatial is involved in that distinction. The dualistic-optimistic *Weltanschauung* adds that in this struggle, good will ultimately win over evil.

From the very beginning, the theology and theodicy of the budding Christian religion struggled with this dualistic *Weltanschauung* which could never be made entirely consistent with monotheism and its associated concept of omnipotence. If an almighty God rules this world, how is it that this same world does not yet belong to His Kingdom? Augustine's answer was to formulate a systematic monism by the introduction of *The City of God* into the existing order through its earthly representative, the Church.

This was the first great breach in the *Weltanschauung* of antiquity. But the old dualistic views of the future lived on for centuries in the religion of the people, periodically exploding in chiliastic movements. Optimism, the other great foundation-stone, remained; its ties with dualism were not so stringent. Therefore, the image of an Other and better world could live on. It was even strengthened by the later development of evolutionary optimism and related ideas concerning natural progress.

But inevitably the second foundation-stone also had to give way, and this heralded the second breach and made a general reversal inescapable. As long as optimism dominated, whether it was pure essence-optimism or indirect or direct influence-optimism, a positive image of the future was still tenable. But as soon as essence-pessimism gained the upper hand, strengthened by influence-pessimism, and allied itself with a monistic *Weltanschauung*, the eschatological image of the future collapsed.

Modernistic theology (at least the Protestant) has taken over not only this monistic-pessimistic terminology, but also the underlying principles. This means that the *parousia* is rejected not simply be-

218

cause it has been so long delayed, but because the modern Christian can no longer believe in it at all. Monism compels theology back to the idea that Christ is already come, and away from the idea of a return as a specific future event.

Dedeifying

The countereschatology of modern theology results in dedeifying. In his excellent study of modern eschatology, Heering tentatively raises the question of whether the arguments of his colleagues, such as Schweitzer, can be supported by a genuine religious faith and are consistent with it. What Heering raises as a point of doubt, we offer as an inevitable conclusion.

Heering cites—hardly noticing the implications—a meaty saying of Karl Heim: *Gottesglauben und Endglauben sind unzertrennlich.*[6] In our opinion this remark is strikingly to the point. God's omnipotence is meaningless, at least for human thought, if it is not directed toward the goal of some kind of fulfillment at the end of time.

This states the positive view. We are now already in the negative stage, however. We must dare to think the reverse. The iconoclasm of the image of the future has crushed the belief in the end. But this also means the beginning of the end of the belief in the God who reveals Himself in time and history. The many images of the divine encounter which form the core of the Christian faith in God then become meaningless. A shift from a theocentric to an anthropocentric world-view has taken place.

De-Judification aimed at, and achieved, the somewhat hasty exit of the God of the Old Testament. When he disappeared, the God of the Covenant disappeared from the world stage.

The progressive elimination of wonders draws ever closer to the negation of the last and greatest wonder, that of divine mercy and salvation. Defuturizing is nothing less than the recognition that the bonds between the temporal events of this world and God must be cut, since God will never establish a Kingdom here.

With the death of the eschatological consciousness, there is indeed a sense in which we can say "God is dead"—to man.

---

[6] *De Verwachting van het Koninkrijk Gods* (Arnhem: Van Loghum, 1952), pp. 205—206. Cited from Karl Heim, *Jesus der Weltvollender* (Berlin: Furche, 1939), p. 172.

V. The Breach in our Time

Ce n'est que faute de
savoir bien connaître
et étudier le présent
qu'on fait l'entendu
pour étudier l'avenir.

Blaise Pascal[1]

Our preliminary study of images of the future is concluded. This historical narrative of the *grandeur et décadence* of images of the future was meant to give us a better insight into the present, that we might also possibly have a more trustworthy foresight into the future. Now we will have an opportunity to test these insights.

The prevailing situation in the mid-twentieth century may be characterized by the following paradox. The images of the future, particularly those of eschatology and utopia, each gave expression in its own way to the idea of a coming turning point in time. The de-utopianizing and de-eschatologizing of these historical images of the future have indeed brought about a turning point, but in reverse of that which had been historically envisaged. The change is not the upward flight of an arrow released from the hunter's taut bow, but the headlong fall to earth of a bird with clipped wings.

And yet contemporary man is scarcely aware of this pitiful collapse. He believes himself to be still standing with both feet firmly planted in the present. He does not know that he is standing on an earth fault which is ready to shift and split wide open at any moment. But the historian of the future, looking back, will see our age as a transition to a fourth period to be added to the sequence antiquity-Middle Ages-modern times.

---

[1] Lettre VIII, décembre 1656, à Mlle de Roannez, from *Pensées et Opuscules* (Paris: Hachette, 1897), ed. Léon Brunschvicg, p. 223.

Chapter 18. Timeless Time

Once time was divided into past, present, and future. The past was mirrored in the reconstructed images of history. Foreshadowings of the future were seen in constructive images of the future. But our time knows only a continuous present. Between the present and cosmological time lies nothing; a vacuum. Qualitatively speaking, time is not the same as formerly. The age-old interplay between images of the future and the course of time has been abruptly broken off.

Fulfillment and Self-Defeat of the Images of the Future

It is scarcely possible to overestimate the extent of the tremendous spiritual reversal which has so silently taken place in our day. We must fully appreciate the fact that never before in the history of human civilization, as far as we know, has there been a period without any kind of positive images of the future. This in itself is already the breach in our times.

Thus far we have been able to identify the life-style and behavior patterns of each period from its images of the future. But our period is chiefly recognizable by its lusty attack on all images of the future. There are other characteristic phenomena of this age, but none of such far-reaching significance as the iconoclasm of the images of the future.

The invalidation of images of the future not only affects our own time, but also stamps the future in its own peculiar fashion. The decades around the middle of this century may be commemorated by future generations as the definitive turning point from its flowering to its decline. Our study of time and the future will find its completion by elaborating the relationship between the historical dynamics of culture and the flowering and decline of images of the future.

In this and the following chapter we will examine the following four propositions:

1. The fact that the processes of de-utopianizing and de-eschatologizing are strikingly similar, not only in broad outlines but in details, points to one structurally related underlying process.

2. These deeper-lying forces are upsetting a long-standing historical equilibrium with a resulting obliteration of all thinking about the future.

3. The breakdown in our time *is* a radical breakdown, not simply a temporary wavering of the historical process, for reasons unique to this age.

4. In the absence of a diligent application of counterforces, the defunct condition of current images predisposes Western culture to breakdown.

The Expiring Realm of the Future

Image-negation has affected the utopian and eschatological image in strikingly parallel fashion, but only these two image-generating areas of Western culture are so affected. In other words, the defuturizing and de-imaging are not total but specific. Other types of thinking about the future are left undisturbed.

There is no general tendency toward iconoclasm. On the contrary, eidetic representation by means of images has never been as popular as it is today. Via the mass media, visual imagery plays a more important role than ever before. The novel of the future is among the best-sellers of our time as a caricature of utopia, as semi-utopia, and as science fiction. There is furthermore so much interest in planned developments of every kind that ours has been termed the age of planning. Finally, the secularized eschatology of Marxism and liberalism has given rise to other political forms of pseudo-eschatology and social myths which have attraction for large parts of the world's population in our time, particularly when coupled with nationalistic and imperialistic representations of the future.

There is no doubt that de-imaging and defuturizing are focused on utopian and eschatological images of the future. These two modes of viewing have always been seen to exist on different levels, apparently

223

mutually exclusive. It was not conceived that the two might complete each other and coexist peacefully. It now appears that if they cannot live together, they will probably have to die together.

To what genre of images of the future do utopia and eschatology belong, and what are their basic points of correspondence? We have earlier referred to the genre in question as that of positive images of the future; that which they have in common is the optimistic and concrete representation of the totally Other and better society to come in the course of time. The basic difference between utopia and eschatology concerns whether this Other is to be brought about by God or man.

The dualistic conception of the world has suffered very seriously, and it is surely this conception which is the most essential prerequisite for a split between the present and that future in which the great transformation must take place. But our age has substituted an actualistic monism for this futuristic dualism.

This essence-pessimistic, monistic view of the world as a given and unchangeable reality eats into the other elements of the culture like a corrosive acid. It labels every idealistic attempt at radical improvement of the world as irrational and impossible. In other words, every faith in the future, whether utopian or eschatological,. is intellectually and philosophically untenable, because any belief in goals, and particularly belief in an ultimate goal, is untenable.

Labeling this world meaningless can be considered just as arbitrary as labeling it meaningful. That the validity of meaninglessness is nevertheless so generally accepted by the modern mind is due to the fact that a simultaneous attack on meaning has been launched from an entirely different quarter. Human striving is thought to be an illusion and divine intervention a myth. An innate *hubris* in man leads to a perpetual cycle first of overestimation of human power with all its disastrous consequences, and then of abject conviction of the complete impotence of human power.

The destruction of the positive image of the future finally represents the reverse side of another image of the world. Nihilism forms the counterimage of the dehumanizing and dedeifying discussed in the previous chapters on de-utopianizing and de-eschatologizing. These processes are intimately related in their common denial of any power, human or superhuman, which can create anything new under the sun.

The new scientific view of creation has the consequence of embalming this world as it is and atrophying that fruit of the centuries, the vital split-awareness of the future, whether seen through utopian

224

or eschatological lenses. If we can find a satisfactory answer to the problem of why the currents of thought about the future developed over a period of three thousand years of human history, have so abruptly reversed themselves, then we will have a clue to the underlying nature of the crisis of Western culture.

Untenable Explanations of the Breach in Time

Why has the age-old dialectic of optimistic and pessimistic images of the future apparently come to a stop? The solution lies in going straight to the core and working outward from the images of the future and their development.

A paradox is thus revealed: historical images of the future have contained an autodestructive force which was a part of the very nature of the historical images; this effect can therefore not fully be explained by the fact that the historical images of the future have not worked (the "disillusionment theory") inasmuch as their ultimate decay was implied in their fulfillment. There is then, after all, a dialectical process but a dialectic of drastic self-liquidation, a dialectic of thesis and antithesis without synthesis.

The historical images of the future contain a double charge: they propel the present into the future—which is their obvious function— and they provide the successors which they themselves have reared with a built-in time-bomb. Not only have they eliminated themselves for the sake of later redemption through newer images of the future, but they have already in their own operations and partial realization worked against their successors, setting in motion a process which ends in the exclusion of *all* images of the future. This puts an end to all renewal in time of current images of the future.

As time moved forward, the images of the future also leapt ahead, in consonance with their historically relative character. This was particularly true of the utopian images, but even eschatology was subject to continued revision and reorientation, in spite of its shell of absolutistic dogma.

Let us consider these somewhat cryptic remarks more closely.

Father Chronos Devours His Children Anew

Effective new images of the future, which in their turn redeem the pledges of the older images they supersede, carry out one essential task: they propel time forward.

Whenever a new image of the future itself grows old and hardens into infallible orthodoxy, the danger of hypostasy sets in, and a ball and chain is fastened to the fleeing foot of time. The Christian Church of the Middle Ages threatened to dig itself into the existing order. Talmudism repeated itself in scholasticism, Phariseeism in Christian hypocrisy. The image of the future which does not move forward with its own time loses its vital force and must seek underground methods of self-realization. But its procreative power is not thereby destroyed. Again and again, it arouses for its own self-preservation those counterforces and movements which are in rebellion against a standstill of time.

Just as Jesus revived the fading Jewish image of the future, so did sectarian chiliasm attempt to revive the weakened Christian image of the future by counteraction directed against the Church. The rebellion which developed during the Middle Ages and found expression in the Reformation was much more a reformation of the Church than a reformation of the image of the future, even though it represented a movement back to primitive Christianity. The Middle Ages themselves were burst asunder by the regenerating images of the future of *rinascimento* and *risorgimento*, and these images laid special emphasis on rebirth and resurrection.

After this there followed a rapid succession of renewed, renewing, and sometimes contradictory images of the future, influenced by and influencing new currents of thought: rationalism and romanticism, revolution and evolution, individualism and collectivism, Christian restoration and humanistic secularism. These new images inaugurated new periods or introduced new currents into existing periods. The unbroken continuation and bringing up to date of images of a possible and desirable Other world increasingly made another world of this world, as profound structural changes took place in response to one set of images after another.

The double charge which the images of the future carry, first for self-multiplication and then for self-destruction, released itself via these fundamental structural changes, of which the images are both producer and product, cause and effect. The changes—economic, social, and cultural in nature—need not be analyzed here. They can be summarized in the concept of a fundamental change in *Weltanschauung*. After each encounter of image with reality, man, the world, and God are changed, because time itself has changed. The key to our crisis lies in these sudden mutations of time.

The images of the future influence these changes in the image of the times in a threefold manner: through a tremendous acceleration of tempo, through an unparalleled increase in the intensity of the "charge" in even the smallest segment of time, and through the releasing of that charge in a kind of cultural nuclear fission.

The first point, concerning increase in tempo, has already received a great deal of attention. One symbol of the general acceleration of tempo as compared with the Middle Ages is the fact that clocks and chronometers must now be able to measure fractions of seconds with great accuracy, at the same time that astrophysics and archaeology are working with millions and trillions of years. Today, centuries count almost as days. Instruments for the measurement of time dominate our whole lives. In the Middle Ages man had time. Now, time has man.

Our second point is that every moment is charged with the highest voltage and reaches the most acute intensity. We have said that the centuries are as but days. But there is also a sense in which each day is as a century, coupled with the tension of every moment in an almost unbearable insecurity. Every man stands at every moment before the *kairos*. Man's mind is ready for sudden and drastic changes, coming at ever-shorter intervals. Vistas and horizons have been radically shortened. Although the lifespan is lengthened, a lifetime is shorter than ever before. Who can complete a life's work in the one-day lifetime of our butterfly-existence? The boisterous clock which noisily ticks away the seconds of our life, has replaced the silent hourglass and the reverberations of eternity sounded by church bells. The smallest segment of time has come to dominate time as a whole, just as the weakest link in a chain defines the strength of the whole. And it is the present moment which is the weakest link in the entire chain of historical time.

Our third point is that the time-chain is already broken. Time is unchained. Those forces whose energy has been conserved through the centuries, sealed up in time itself, have now been set free. All brakes have been removed, all restraining ropes untied. This liberation of time is mainly the work of the emancipating images of the future. But whereas the older ones still kept time in check, the new ones successively loosened earlier bonds.

In our earlier historical review of images of the future we have observed the progressive freeing *of* time, *in* time—a process which has accompanied the coming of age of human thought. We have also observed that this development has never received attention as a logical, step-by-step evolution leading to certain inevitable consequences. Gradually the wrappings in which time was swaddled have been loosened by images of the future until finally they were

227

discarded altogether, first by the utopia and then also by eschatology.

Older and mainly eschatological images of the future would have kept the wrappings tight and held a firm grip on the future by making it subject to a predestined course of events. The utopia also bound itself by divine or natural laws. But now all historical lines of development converge on a time from which yoke and reins have been removed, a completely free time. Free from what, and for what?

Free, first of all, from guidance, whether for good or ill, by a supernatural power. Now the way is apparently clear for man's self-determination of his own destiny, for the exercise of human freedom and responsibility. We have repeatedly indicated a shift from indirect to direct influence-optimism, from pure eschatology to a manifold utopism with an active, purposeful social-ethical approach to the problem of achieving a humanly worthy society. It was always the intention to make time free for man, to put it at his service, that he might direct future developments toward desirable ends.

Now all obstacles to progress have been removed. Man's power over hostile nature is almost unlimited. His skill in social and economic planning has enormously increased. And yet, at the very zenith of his outward power, his awareness of inward impotence has reached a dramatic low point. Just as the way seems entirely open, man suddenly finds no way out to the future.

Obviously something unforeseen has happened; some other counteracting force must have come between man and his future. We see now the fatal miscalculations of man. In his successive images of the future he has gradually liberated time from all its bonds, both present and future. Dialectics and determinism have been swept away. But at the very moment when man stands ready to redirect the redeemed time-potential according to his own wishes, time refuses to be ruled and turns against its old ally and liberator.

The double explosive of human images of the future has been completely discharged. After successfully bursting asunder the rigid restrictions of the existing order with the first rounds, the concealed second charge has gone sadly amiss. At first it left a queer vacuum. There was no longer any superhuman power present, as far as man could see, to guide the course of events, and human power was not quick enough or able enough to guide events in the right direction. The swirling waters of undammed time now filled up the vacuum in their own fashion, with malicious caprice.

Man is out of it altogether. All that remains to him is withdrawal

228

from the all-pervading present through various forms of escapism. Man has not lost his split mentality nor laid aside the old Adam, but only subjected them to the requirements of the times. The split no longer runs between present and future, but straight through the present itself. The man of today is a moment-ridden man. The mass media grant temporal passes that permit man to spend short "leaves" in electronic limbo, removed from the ever-present urgency of the world's woe. But even then there is no escape from the increased tempo of living and the high tension of each moment of time to which man has become addicted.

Whether in kindliness or in scorn, time does indeed permit man to squander his free hours in all sorts of worthless ways. Free time now plays the role of the devil creating mischief for idle hands. Ever more free time is bestowed on greedy man, and for lack of time he can scarcely fulfill his task in time. For modern man's "free time" is indeed an optical illusion; this time is chained, chained fast to the present.

An increasingly irritated reader may now ask with some sharpness what he is supposed to do with an explanation like this. What is the meaning of this personification of our time, of the "powers" of this time? Have we not, after all, set a trap and only caught ourselves? Have we not replaced one riddle with a greater one? In short, is this figure of speech which refers to the present time as an autonomous and personified category, anything more than that? The reader cannot be put off with the famous philosophical answer which Augustine gave to the problem he himself propounded, "What is the time?" He answered, "When no one asks me, I know, but when I must explain it to someone who asks, I do not know." After which apology, Augustine proceeded to give his nevertheless famous explanation.

Metaphysical explanations aside we mean here no more and no less than that the very essence of time, for the most part under the influence of preceding images of the future, has undergone a radical conceptual change. Previously, present-day time had no independent significance or existence of its own. The present owed its existence solely to the dimensions of past and future. But now, on the contrary, the present sucks all existence in time up into itself. Between the microscopic reduction of the moment-bound now and the macroscopic dilation of an endless universe, lies a void. This vacuum marks the spot where the present swallowed past and future. Our time has brought a new type of moment-ridden man into being and drilled him into perfect obedience. This modern incarnation of

Paul Revere does not ride time, but is ridden by it. Our problem is whether he chooses, or still can choose, the dignity of a human existence powered by the human will, or whether he prefers to submit to the effortless laissez-faire of an ethically indifferent course of time.

It is man himself who is responsible for this double charge concentrated in his positive images of the future. Its autodestructive activity, although certainly not intended, has nevertheless come about through man's cooperation, even though this consisted chiefly in what he refrained from doing. Man stands guilt-laden before the breach in time which he himself has made through his voluntary enslavement to the present. Again and again when we speak of the present time, today's moment-ridden man looms in the background. It is this development of modern man we must explain, or more modestly describe, according to the course of development of man's images of the future. These images themselves can be explained (or described) only in terms of an interaction of endogenous and exogenous factors in the course of history as it moves toward a new human conception of time.

VI. The Broken Future of Western Culture

In the previous chapter we attempted to suggest a satisfactory explanation for the great change in our own time, unique in the history of Western civilization for the absence of persuasive positive images of the future. We have tried to show how this radical breach took place as the logical consequence of a movement in time which revolutionized time itself, as images of the future from the past worked themselves out.

Now we are looking ahead in an attempt to foresee the consequences which this breach may imply for the future.

Chapter 19. The Future of the Christian Belief-System

It would be a highly important undertaking to write a history of the future of religion in general, as a world problem. There is no doubt that the great religions of the East—Buddhism, Hinduism, Confucianism, Judaism—have been reached by the challenge of new futures and a changing present. These changes are also of crucial importance for the West in the coming encounter between the Christian and non-Christian religions.

Since our study concentrates on the future of Western culture, we will confine ourselves to the future of Western religion, defined as the prevailing Christian belief-system, which includes a belief in God.

We will consider this Christian religion as much as possible as a whole, without distinguishing between Roman Catholicism and Protestantism, and focus on a general trend which is the sum of the various forces and counterforces at work in the field.

The sociology of religion has made little progress as a science since the time of Max Weber. In particular, there have been, so far as we know, hardly any major examinations of the subject which also deal with future developments. This lack of systematic thought on the future of the Western Christian belief-system is not so strange after all. For Christians there can be no discussion of a future in which there might be no Christianity. Christianity, resting on the belief in the authority of God's word, is enduring by definition. It is possible for a Christian to recognize that the outer forms of worship and ritual and even some of the dogma might conceivably change, but never the essence of Christian faith, which has eternal validity.

For non-Christians, on the other hand, Christianity is often either something already outgrown or something to be outgrown. In either case, there seems to have been hardly any stimulus for discussing the

232

future of the Christian belief-system, though in our opinion this subject is crucial to the future of Western culture as a whole.

What follows is an attempt to demonstrate how in our time the split mind, which sought integration in and through images of the future, tends to cut its bonds with an Other reality and withdraw completely into the one world of the present—how dualism is changing into monism.

The Death of God

The future of the Christian belief-system is a question of the development of faith and worship in historical time. A grasp of this development can only be achieved, in our opinion, through an understanding of the almost complete reversal brought about in the relationship between the entities God and time.

When Nietzsche wrote his famous words "God is dead," he said at once too much and too little: too much, in that even now this God lives for countless people, albeit as a blurred and faded image; too little, in that God has since then died many deaths as the manifold functions related to the image of a personal god living and acting in time were cut off one by one.

At first with diffidence, finally irresistibly, the conviction has grown that the Christian God owes many of His traits, if not His existence, to older religious-mythical ideas from ancient Eastern sources. These images gradually and increasingly came to be perceived as incompatible with modern Western ideas. A purification of the image of God was undertaken, with demythologizing as the goal. Various points of view contributed to this process, and for the most part they carried German labels, such as demagicking, de-Judification, demetaphysicizing, or de-apocalypticizing. The intention was to revive God for modern thought, to make Him live again.

Gradually modern man uncovered one biblical image after another as mythical in nature—the resurrection, heaven, hell, the hereafter—precisely all those respects in which God was thought to be active for the future salvation of man. But in the modern view the human reality is given by nature. The transformation into the Other is a myth. To that extent the Son of God is a myth, and also God the Father, the Creator and Fulfiller.

The encroachment upon the old image of God is spatio-temporally extended to the universe. God is deprived of the heavenly sphere as His personal place of habitation, and His new domicile is left in the air. This is but a symptom of a more profound spiritual and intellectual revolution which overthrows God as First Architect, Builder, and Mover of the Universe. This revolution not only affects His creative function, but most especially His task in and power over time from alpha to omega.

The old images of chaos and cosmos, the immeasurably distant poles which God was thought gradually to be spanning through the work of His creation, are now outmoded. The universe develops on the basis of immanent, demonstrable, and definable powers, not through the inscrutable operations of transcendent powers.

In the older view of a God who revealed Himself in history, the stream of events in time mirrored God's disposition towards man. The course of history was permeated with divine meaning, and the pattern fixed. Now the evolution of human thought regarding the future has liberated historical time from an intervening superhuman power and leaves it to its own destiny. Time is autonomous, and the future is no longer determined and directed by a higher hand.

God's removal from history is intimately related to His removal from this world. God has died not only a social death, but also an axiological, ethical, and cultural death.

At the same time that Pascal went over from the God of the philosophers and scholars to the God of Abraham, Isaac, and Jacob, Spinoza was exchanging the Jewish-Christian God for a metaphysical God as the really existing and eternal but impersonal God to whom man is in fact bound by the *amor Dei*. Then, closing off a long period of philosophical demonstrations of God, Kant, a century later, removed Him from philosophy on the grounds that this was a science of "pure reason," rationalizing only that which could be empirically known, and that God overstepped these bounds. He placed Him instead, as a postulate of "practical reason," in the separate field of religion. Modern philosophy has in general continued this trend of not-knowing, emancipating itself from biblical revelation and Christology. Here agnosticism predominates, but with a few exceptions, such as the phenomenology of Max Scheler and Catholic existentialism, even the retention of a philosophical or metaphysical faith goes hand in hand with a rejection of the Christian belief in a personal God. The theological point of view has in general made way for the anthropological point of view: God has made way for man.

In the work of Karl Jaspers, a theologian who was continually concerned intensively with Christianity, nothing remains of the Christian image of God but the mystical "ground of all being," a "shapeless all-shape," a "silently speaking" or a "nonrevealing" transcendence; in short, a completely imageless idea.

And how does this hidden deity work for the future of mankind? Is He merely the ground of all existent being, or is He also the lodestar and goal of the not yet existent? No, indeed, however much man may try, this God will not permit Himself to be seized or bound, precisely because He is God. He and the future remain for man a closed book.

In our age every man is a Sisyphus, rolling his stone in vain. He cannot rise above himself, above his temporality and his essential existence-to-the-death. To philosophize is to learn to die, and the only meaning to be found in life is a resigned *amor fati*.

In response to this mood, modern theology has moved from rationalization after the fact to rationalization in advance, approaching the farthest extreme of a science of godhood without God. This iconoclasm takes place in the mistaken belief that God, through being made imageless, can be better served or even saved. The destruction of the divine image of the future has extended to the destruction of the image of God as image.

According to our theoretical position on the role of images of the future in the creation of the future, the *eschaton*-less Christian faith of the present has no future. This prediction will only hold insofar as no counterforces are brought into play which can bring new life to the religious image of the future. It is true that earnest attempts are being made from every side to modernize the old conceptions, to translate them into our own language and modes of thought, to adapt and clothe them in a manner appropriate to our time. But this is mainly true of the images of religious behavior. The images of the future have not been treated in this manner. These have been hollowed out and mechanized to the point where they are nothing but a contentless and meaningless ritual.

Is it still possible that religious images of the future might be revived? There is no reason why this possibility should be excluded in advance, but the chances of such reversal in trend seem fairly limited. Apart from an improbable actual Second Coming (which would meet the fate predicted), there remains the possibility of the future appearance of a new prophetic figure through whom God would speak and give man a new religious image of the future. The more Christianity is mechanized and the God-consciousness of men minimized in accordance with the spirit of the times, the less chance there is of successfully giving a new content and form to eternal truth as an adequate and timely answer to the challenge of the future. A new prophet would not be crucified; he would simply be

235

ignored or laughed at. *C'est le ridicule qui tue.*

What of the ecumenical movement and its leaders? This movement has faith in the future of its ideal of unity. But although this ideal is of course associated with religious motives, it is not as such a Christian image of the future. In this respect it is more a means than a goal in itself. Assuming that at some time the ideal of unity will be realized, which Christian faith will this unity then serve? As long as the road to unity is still being traveled, this question is not as disturbing as it will be when the goal is once reached. What image of the future will then be offered? International unity is a necessary precondition, but a precondition of what? Where does it lead? What does it want to achieve? Unity considered in this light certainly contains a remedy against external crumbling, but in no way prevents internal disintegration resulting from a threadbare image of the future.

The same applies, *mutatis mutandis,* for the many other counter-forces which are at the moment working in and for the renovation of Christianity. Whatever hopes one may cherish for these movements, they are unfortunately negligible in respect to the Christian image of the future as an overwhelming conviction which might once again dominate Western Christianity, whether Protestant or Catholic. That another religion on the same level and of the same type as Christianity will emerge, as some thinkers suggest, is a possibility we would rule out, at least within a foreseeable time.

What kind of equivalent faith might step in to take the place of this waning one? Neo-Buddhism, evolutionary vitalism (Alexander, Julian Huxley, Haldane), philosophical faith (Jaspers), humanism or even superhumanism (Nietzsche's Übermensch), Camus's *pensée de midi,* or a religious syncretism? We do not know. But one thing must not be forgotten: if the present trends of thought prove capable of destroying Christianity, not only as a social institution but also spiritually in and through its own adherents, then there will remain little hope for substitute currents of a religious or cultural nature. All the structurally related and associated expressions of Western culture are equally threatened; the total pattern of culture is at stake.

Chapter 20. Other Cultural Components and their Future

Progress is the realization of Utopias
Oscar Wilde

A very brief examination of key areas of Western culture is undertaken here in order to bring out clearly the structural unity of the diverse elements of culture as they are touched by the wand of time. Philosophy, the queen mother of the sciences, gives the clearest indication of the reversals that have taken place in our images of the future. The philosophies of science, logic, and mathematics rank first, and thereafter the philosophies of religion, law, art, and history; the philosophy of man himself comes last of all.

Philosophy

Philosophy had a future so long as it created an image of the future which could endure in time. It matters little, in principle, how the Other is labeled or defined. There is more meaning, however, hidden in the world-shaking struggle in medieval scholasticism between conceptual realism and conceptual nominalism than modern man has been willing to admit, for nominalism was the great attack on the actual existence of this Other reality, an attempt to characterize it as simply a "name." Two great figures, whose influence and significance were only perceived after their time, led the way towards this futureless future: Schopenhauer and Nietzsche.

For Schopenhauer the ground of the world's being—*das Ding an sich*—lies in the intrinsically groundless will to live. The world is our will, and our image of the world is conceived by this will. It is the

237

worst of all possible worlds, but man can neither leave nor redeem it; he can annul the world by destroying its creator, the will.

Nietzsche does not go this far, and yet goes further. While he would not destroy man, he would destroy God instead *(Thus Spoke Zarathustra).* His *Beyond Good and Evil* has the subtitle *Prelude to a Philosophy of the Future,* but by denying the transcendent and articulating the idea of eternal recurrence, he in effect undermines the basis of all future philosophy.

The influence of Schopenhauer and Nietzsche in reshaping later conceptions of reality can scarcely be overestimated. It is felt in Comte's positivism. It has affected the blending of Hume's empiricism, Marxian historical materialism, and behaviorism. It has further affected Wilhelm Dilthey's vitalism and is to be found in the pragmatism of Dewey and James.

These developments find outlets today in two distinct currents. The first makes short work of traditional philosophy and includes the Vienna Circle of Moritz Schlick, Rudolph Carnap, and Otto Neurath. These men assign parts of the matter of philosophy to the various branches of science, reject a part as not amenable to scientific treatment, and retain philosophy per se only as the analytic instrument for the unity of science. This serves to reduce philosophy to a formal combination of linguistics and logistics.

The second current, modern existentialism, also contributes to the liquidation of philosophy. We will discuss Heidegger, Sartre, and Jaspers as representatives of this movement.

Heidegger's goal is still to develop a metaphysics of true being. The essence of man is his *Dasein,* "existence," but the meaning of man's existence is determined by its temporality. Thus the only possible anticipation of the future consists in living with one's face set towards death.

Sartre proclaims his atheism more boldly. Since God gives no sign of life, there is in effect for us no God. Man is alone with himself, and the world stands opposed to him, indifferent and unconcerned.

Jaspers takes an intermediate position. With Heidegger, he gives the existential existence of man a central place. Man's existence, however, becomes truly existential only to the extent that man rises above himself. At the same time, transcendence itself can never be achieved by man, and all his striving is illusion. The meaning of life consists in the acceptance of the perpetual failure of every attempt to transcend the here-and-now. In attempting to understand modern existentialism, we find the oft-made comparison between existentialism and gnosis significant. There is indeed a striking coincidence

238

of terminology and symbolism in the two philosophies. The main difference, in our opinion, lies in the fact that gnosis, with all its worldly pessimism, had an image of the future, and existentialism has none.

The contrast between the Gnosticism of antiquity and modern existentialism will be examined further for the insight it gives into the flowering and decline both of philosophy and of Western culture in mutual interaction.

Gnosticism

Dualism here achieves its most extreme expression. This world cannot be the work of God, and is not to be justified by any theodicy. But God's existence, however passive, and that Other reality, however invisible, are basically positive. It is true that man has been thrown into a demon-possessed world, but there is also a Thrower.

The dialectic of this line of thought is nihilistic in regard to this world, but in the synthesis the Other reality plays a positive role. Gnosticism combines an essence-pessimism for this world with an influence-optimism for the Other world. This philosophical doctrine of salvation was finally condemned by the Christian Church as a heresy.

Existentialism

Here man is thrown into a world which is not hostile but indifferent. Man is free to determine his own destiny, but his choices are meaningless, for they all lead to . . . nothing. Man is not only thrown into the world, but abandoned there—thrown but without a Thrower.

Existentialism keeps pace with Gnosticism in fundamental pessimism regarding earthly existence, but their ways soon part, for there are no polar tensions in existentialism to provide dynamism and movement. But even if we accept the conclusion that existentialism has eliminated its own future, we need not conclude that philosophy as such has reached a terminal point in the development of Western culture. Countermovements are always possible. In fact, such countermovements already exist, even in existentialism itself, as in Jaspers, and Christian existentialism. Where have these brought us?

Edmund Husserl's phenomenology was an attempt to develop a

strictly scientific philosophy which is nevertheless metaphysics in the Kantian tradition. Husserl believes it is possible to perceive the essential nature of things intuitively. This means a *zurück zu den Sachen*, "back to things," which, however, requires a preliminary *Einklämmerung*, "setting in brackets," of observed reality. Thus we would appear to arrive at a sort of intermediate entity or sphere between this and an Other reality. It would then become possible to demonstrate the essential laws of this purified reality. We must confess that this method of examining reality *(Wesensschau)* has remained somewhat of a mystery to us, but many thinkers today claim to make use of it. Phenomenology is hardly in itself a sufficient justification for the claim to objectivity and adequacy.

At the beginning of this century, expectations of a spread of Bergson's dualistic philosophy might still have been cherished. Since then, however, the optimistic image of the future contained in "creative evolution" and the *élan vital* that also penetrated into the cosmic –religious area *(Les Deux Sources de la Morale et de la Réligion)* has gone the way of all positive images of the future.

Christian existentialism is a counterstream which offers more hope, since it runs with other main currents of the age. The one characteristic common to all is the leap from purely subjective existentialism into the transcendental and thus to a form of absolute truth. Now the great question remains as to whether this development stems from the obvious attempt to infuse new life into existentialism, or from the attempt to synthesize with Christianity. The answer will depend on whether, after further consideration, these entities appear to be compatible, or whether existentialism ultimately does not negate all transcendence. We gladly note that Gabriel Marcel entitles his existential system a metaphysics of hope, but pure existentialism leaves no room for hope. The earlier Christian hope is also seriously weakened. Could the combination of existentialism and Christianity under these circumstances possibly be stronger than the separate parts? Nevertheless, this attempt deserves our sympathic attention, and it is certainly true that it contains more potential force for the future than other movements, because of its attempt at synchronization.

Catholic thinkers are the main contributors to Christian existentialism. A noticeable revival of the Catholic doctrine of Thomism has taken place in the last half-century, under the influence of Étienne Gilson, Jacques Maritain, and Antonin Sertillanges. Apart from the great following which Maritain has, as "humanist," however, this somewhat isolated philosophical phenomenon can scarcely be considered part of the general developmental trends in Western philosophy.

There remains the ethical voluntarism, based on reverence for life, formulated by Albert Schweitzer. Unfortunately, while his person is respected as almost none other in our age, his teachings, uniting *humanitas* and *caritas*, remain a philosophy completely outside time.

This is the age of skepticism and pessimism, and at the moment no single philosophical countermovement has a serious chance. But what of the future? Will the cyclical movements of history bring us to an upturning of mood again? This is the critical question.

Human consciousness is not an accordion, to be squeezed and then stretched out again at pleasure. One cannot push the metaphysical consciousness back into a purely physical consciousness without suffering the consequences; it will not simply spring out again of its own accord in time. If anything at all has emerged from our previous discussion, it is that there is an intimate relationship between the religious—particularly the eschatological—consciousness and the metaphysical consciousness. The relationship is not a purely intellectual one; it is also emotional, the fruit of the creative imagination. It developed through the religious consciousness of the last centuries in a direct line from Pascal, Rousseau, Kant, and Chateaubriand right up to and certainly including Nietzsche. The gradual growth of a religious and antireligious attitudes kept pace with the growth of the ametaphysical and antimetaphysical consciousness. Existentialism is not just one more philosophy which chanced to develop in this time, but the exit line to a cultural tragedy.

Science

At first glance the development of science appears to be in the opposite direction from that of religion and metaphysics. What has been taken away from the latter seems to have been added to the former. Does this mean that there is a limit to man's intellectual capacity, so that development in one area must inevitably take place at the expense of another, with the result that a decline of religious and metaphysical thought is the price that must be paid for the flowering of scientific thought? The answer lies in a consideration of images of the future.

Science has flourished in the course of the last five centuries as a result of a powerfully generating image of the future, itself both fruit and seed of a basically changing image of the world. This develop-

241

ment in Western science is coupled with the general development of Western culture as a whole. One of the greatest obstacles to a better understanding of this relationship between science and culture lies in the fact that there is no general agreement on the precise meaning and content of these two entities.

Development of the Sciences According to Their Images of the Future

Scientific thought was part of a cultural whole until far along in the Middle Ages, and sharp differentiations between different areas of thought were not made.

The earliest and most decisive breakaway from the former encyclopaedic whole of religion, morality, philosophy, and science was undertaken by the natural sciences, especially from the sixteenth century on. By means of an extraordinarily fruitful combination of empiricism and theory construction, the natural scientists took their future into their own hands. Bacon was an amazing forecaster of this development.

This image of the future has not weakened or faded in the course of the centuries, but has grown stronger. Applied science and technology have bestowed a halo on the basic sciences and have transformed the idea of unlimited possibilities into concrete reality. The revolutionary turn of affairs that set in with this independent development of the physical sciences has been felt far beyond the realm of science itself. The pressure of the physical-science thought-model on all thought, including social-science thought, has steadily increased. Whose name should we lend to the hopeful image of the future of these new sciences? Where Bacon gave the natural sciences the motto "Knowledge is power," Comte provided the social sciences with the slogan *Prévoir pour pouvoir* (Foreknowledge is power). With Comte, who declared sociology the queen of the sciences, the star of the image of the future rises again, and furthermore a balance between the physical and the social sciences is ensured.

However, by the time of Comte, the balance of power had in fact already been destroyed by the impact of the Industrial Revolution. Later writers maintained that sociology must contribute to the restoration of this equilibrium. It was a crisis-science. Nevertheless, both Comte and Marx, and all their followers, were themselves dominated by physical science thought-models.

Comte introduced positivism, Marx social determinism, and Spencer Darwinistic evolution, into the thinking of the social

242

sciences. But this physicalism and naturalism, both in the extreme forms of Marxism and liberalism and also in the more neutral intermediate positions, created obstacles to the full development of these sciences, since their methods were not adequate to the complex subject-matter.

The overwhelming success of the physical sciences forced scientific and philosophic thought towards a new all-embracing monism. The movement towards the "unity of science" has a great appeal for modern thought.

In economics, econometrics; in sociology, sociometrics; in philosophy, probability theory—all contribute to the neopositivist trend toward general systems theory.

This monism calls forth its own antithesis, and the social sciences rebel against the limitations of physical-science techniques. The prophetic warning of Goethe still sounds: *Wer will was lebendiges erkennen und beschreiben sucht erst den Geist herauszutreiben.* It is a fact that culture itself as an object of study has been gradually removed from the cultural sciences. Cultural sociology is a dying species of sociology, in spite of the culture-crisis. An independent science of culture has never emerged. On the other hand, empirical sociology has flourished, but it has little status from the science-of-culture viewpoint.

The gulf between those social sciences which are still resisting, and the physical sciences themselves, is steadily widening, partly through increasing specialization. Man's uniquely human qualities are destroyed by the chill hand of mathematics, which reduces a living reality to a series of functional relationships. Placing a social reaction in a test tube produces only inaction, for social chemistry cannot survive in the vacuum required in the laboratory experiment. A fatal split thus develops between the warring camps of science. The earlier integration has vanished. Only by placing the development in context with the relation to the image of the future of science itself, however, can any clarification of the crisis be arrived at.

From Utopism to Counterutopism

Scientific images of the future are the intellectual fruit of the general thinking about the future of a given time and are rooted in it. We have already discussed the manner in which utopian thought prepared the way for a renovation of a cramped scientific tradition, by providing a model for critique and reversal of fundamentals.

Initially, the intellectual climate which utopism helped create

243

strengthened utopism itself as well as science. Ensuing scientific developments also shed their aura on the social sciences, from which equally exciting things were expected. Ironically, the dialectics of history, which do not spare science, caused the influence of the physical sciences to operate on the social sciences in a wholly contrary and unexpected direction, going from utopism toward anti-utopism.

Imitation of the classical models of physical-science thought led the cultural sciences to an extreme use of quantification, resulting in a capitulation to positivism and the ideal of value-free judgments. This not only involved a preference for the observation and measurement of easily quantifiable phenomena, and for extrapolation of current trends; it also involved the reduction of scientific research to an evaluation of alternative means to given goals.

If this doctrine of scientific objectivity had been equally feasible for the social sciences, no harm would have been done. But what happened was that the social scientist set himself up as an impartial observer even while he was unconsciously cementing all the officially banished values into the very foundations of his work—camouflaged. The result was a supposedly neutral, but basically bourgeois and conservative, social science which used the values of the established order as its point of departure.

In the physical sciences valuation was indeed irrelevant for practical purposes: earthquakes, eclipses, and volcanic eruptions took place without regard to human judgment. But in the social sciences hidden value-judgments on the part of researchers gave scientific sanction to certain types of events. Marx quite correctly unmasked much of this kind of science as class-science, but then he used for his own antibourgeois valuation exactly the same untenable procedure of incorporating his value premises into a system of his own. By this apparently legitimate scientific reconstruction, he strengthened the trend in social science toward anti-utopism and counteridealism. Liberalism and Marxism, however opposed in other respects, were united in that they assumed that society was regulated by discoverable scientific laws.

The consequences were fatal. On the one hand, the practitioner of the social sciences had to refrain from pronouncements concerning goals on pain of banishment from his professional brotherhood. On the other hand, science itself was drawn into the struggle between the Marxist and liberal schools of thought, the image of science itself was obscured by political considerations, and scientific research was sucked up into various ideological currents. The situation was never

244

made explicit because of the taboo on values and ideals. Progressive thinkers could only be classified as nonbourgeois, and therefore Marxist, thinkers. The time-honored utopian method of axiomatic critique was narrowed down to a forced choice between the extremes of ultraliberalism and ultra-Marxism in science.

A rebellion against this rigid attitude was inevitable. Revolutionary minds have risen to the challenge: "scientific humanism" represents a modern version of that evolutionary optimism of the previous century which the forces of disillusionment had displaced. Scientific humanism forms part of a different stream of thought emanating chiefly from Great Britain (with Bernal, Huxley, Hogben, Mannheim, Haldane, Russell, and others). It can be recognized from the bold new look of a systematic planning for the future.

The fact that the representatives of this school have ties with either Marxist communism, atheistic humanism, or both, presents an obstacle to unbiased analysis of their ideas. Established religious and political forces in Western society have tended to regard these modern utopian ideas as unfair competition and have reacted with an upsurge of counterutopism and antifuturism. Not infrequently, progressive thinkers are also personally attacked as disloyal and dangerous to the welfare of the country. In this respect these thinkers must pay the price their utopian forerunners paid. But if the result is that regenerating images of the future from progressive minds can no longer come up for honest analysis, then this means the systematic cutting off of these vital sources of social nourishment.

The Age of Science, or Science of This Age?

One important link is still lacking for a considered judgment concerning the future of science: the link between the situation in science and the prevailing culture-crisis. Since science and culture interact, the relationship between the ups and downs of Western science and Western culture is complex.

Science and Society

If we look back several hundred years and compare the situation then with that of our own time, the most striking change that has

245

taken place is the gigantic growth of the influence of science on society.[1]

This influence operates on society as a whole as well as on the individual, affecting social structures and culture patterns as well as minute events of daily life. This is, after all, the age of science. Now the crucial question for the future is, where is the direction and leadership for continued progress coming from, the age or the science? If we anticipate ourselves and simply answer that the *primaire agence* is the age—that is, our own time—then we have touched the core of the inconspicuous and yet revolutionary development of the last centuries.

Our earlier explanation concerning the double charge in the image of the future—the first carrying the image to new heights, and the second exploding the heart out of it—applies especially in the field of science. The scientific images of the future were among the first to liberate themselves from the past and to free their own age. But this free age now holds captive that very science which worked so hard to free it. This is the core of the reversal. Time—our time—has hired science.

This modern phenomenon of a spiritually enslaved science has implications for science itself, for society as a whole, and for the university in particular. The scientist has always been the child of his own time, and science has often served kings, nations, or special interest groups—becoming, in Marxian terminology, class-science. But in our time the highest bidder can purchase scientific power for any enterprise. He who pays the piper calls the tune. Science is the modern Babylon, the biblical "mother of whores."

Science has proved itself to be useful, modest, and ingenious. It supplies logical reasons for our behavior, individual and collective. Psychoanalysis has descended to the deepest subcellar of man's soul and lovingly nurtures all the excrescences that grow there. Man's work and his chances for promotion are both under scientific supervision. His recreation and education are in the hands of mass-media technicians; specialist staffs supply the weapons for economic conflict of interest. A suitable scientific theory stands ready for every political action, whether in economics or biogenetics, whether in central planning or geophysics. Warfare too finds not only its scientific techniques but also its ideological justification clothed in scientific garb.

---

[1] See Bertrand Russell, *The Impact of Science on Society* (London: Allen & Unwin, 1952).

Even culture has found a scientific-philosophic basis which lends itself to the transformation of the abnormal into the normal (existentialism), or to the anaesthetizing of the current crisis by labeling it a transition stage from a lower to a higher level of social existence (Sorokin). Whatever our generation does, or fails to do, is done in the best scientific manner. The indulgences of faith are now replaced by the general passport of science.

On the other hand, the modern scientist has, generally speaking, a diminished prestige and authority. The work of a science become subservient to society is carried out by an equally subservient intelligentsia. In fact, the entire concept of the intelligentsia has become devalued as its members take on employee status in business and government. Frequently the scientist-servant is forbidden to publish his work independently or to express himself freely. *Il y a des accommodements même avec la science.*

Science still has its independent advance outposts of unimpeachable integrity. Their relative influence however, is declining. Unorganized in a highly organized society, scientists now face being pushed even further down the ladder. In times of depression, the unemployed brainworker is the most drastically disinherited. It was in the thirties that the term "intellectual proletariat" became common in Europe. In times of prosperity the economic value placed upon the intelligentsia lags increasingly behind the rising standard of living, so that the brain-worker is frequently worse off than the skilled laborer. Is this simply a question of demand and supply?

In our opinion the decline in the social value placed on the scientist weighs more heavily here than the purely economic explanation. The loss in status is the crucial element in the situation. For the public, the authority of the scientist, working in the seclusion of his study or university, has been transformed into the sinister menace of the man in the white jacket, a demonic blend of Svengali, Fu Manchu, Caligari, Frankenstein, and Dr. Knock. From the economic point of view it is at the same time indispensable and without value, since it is as available as the air we unthinkingly breathe.

Differences in status or standing, although still in evidence within the world of scientists and university graduates, are more and more leveled off in public life. There, little distinction is made between the university-trained individual working in industry, business, or government, and the scientist who makes a profession of scholarship and research. Gradations and nuances disappear under the common stamp of subservience.

How does the intelligentsia react? The term "unattached intelligentsia" in part describes the situation. It forms a group apart, half withdrawn into voluntary isolation, half forcibly banished by society. Politically shelterless, socially adrift, they are spiritually "displaced persons." Outside the narrow borders of their own specialties, treading the terra incognita of human relationships in society, the scientists fall prey to the general crisis of science.

This unattached intelligentsia consists largely of frustrated intellectuals. In the course of their professional activities they have been led into conflicts of conscience and tensions which have exploded in rebellion against the existing order and into the extremisms of the ultrarevolutionary or the ultrareactionary. In Europe particularly, fascism and national socialism has attracted a number of these unattached intellectuals. It is then not to be wondered at that many of the most intelligent and sensitive intellectuals have later succumbed to the fascinations of Eastern European ideology.

What is it that drives this unattached intelligentsia toward totalitarianism but a deeply felt, passionate sense of social and cultural responsibility? Its protest against our bourgeois, complacent science grows out of an attitude of self-criticism which should in itself be acknowledged with respect. The tragedy is that it knows that the present political communism for which it is working may leave it only the choice between submission and death. Moved by a fatalistic self-contempt, it is apparently ready for both. It has lost faith in itself and in the future of the intelligentsia as a source of social progress. Its image of the future is negated. This intelligentsia is the greatest enemy of the intellectual, undermining the very basis of his existence. In deep horror of American influences in Europe, which it considers anticultural and hypermechanistic, it does an about-face and gives its allegiance to another, equally anticultural, mechanistic extreme.

The drifting intelligentsia do not sufficiently discern the general relationship between the specific crisis in science and the overall crisis in culture. The neglected science of culture thus has its revenge in our scientistic age, in which critical philosophy with its accompanying synthesizing conceptions has been destroyed.

Unfortunately our movement is circular. We call for reconstruction and reform, but reform always matures far in advance, in the ideas of a small number of creative intellectuals. Now, however, the idea of an intellectual élite is rejected. Intellectuals no longer constitute an élite and do not want to be a minority; on the contrary, they too become swallowed up by the masses. The trend is rather for scientists and scholars to move away from an involvement with future reforms. The training of the intelligentsia at present strengthens the cheap optimism of the *vis medicatrix naturae*. Young budding intellects are herded like so much livestock into an enclosure fenced with barbed wire. The sign on the gate reads *Caveat intelligentsiam*. Such stock-farms are feeder stations for annual fairs called universities, which can be recognized by the pedigrees they issue in forms of diplomas, handed out by the miserable collection of types known as a faculty.

Science and the University

If we add the university to science and society in our analytical scheme for determining the changes which have already entered into our culture, we find that the contradictions within modern science are only an indication of deeper underlying problems which the development of science as a whole has forced to the surface. The independent development of the university as an agent of science accentuates the dislocations in our present situation.

Within the university itself two contradictory themes are clearly apparent. One is the conviction of the impending doom of society, and the certainty that science will contribute to that doom. The other is the self-assured attitude that the university-based scientific community has matters well in hand. How is the university in fact handling itself in this atmosphere of impending crisis?

In speaking of the abstraction "modern university," we will try to delineate the dominating type by pointing out a few ideal-typical characteristics. The university in general appears to be an island of tranquility in the midst of turbulence.[2]

Or rather, it sits in gracious calm on top of a volcano. Heroism? Quixotism? Or just the conviction that this volcano really is nothing but a windmill, and the culture-pessimists are only windbags? Imminent downfall of culture? Come, come, the university says benignly, giving us an encouraging pat on the shoulder and a wink; we mustn't let ourselves be carried away by exaggerated reports from bilious melancholics and neglect the daily work that presses upon us. Let every man do his duty, as the day requires. No, a culture-crisis is most certainly not admitted within the reinforced concrete walls of the university. And so, in sharpest contrast to the keenly listening Middle Ages, which thought constantly to hear approaching hoofbeats of the apocalyptic riders, the modern sage pays no attention to

---

[2] Remember, this was written in 1951 E. B.

the pounding at the gates, and averts his head from the handwriting on the wall.

Has the cry "Wolf, wolf" perhaps gone up once too often, so that now when danger really threatens there is no one to listen? On the contrary, there has scarcely been any articulate cry of alarm to be heard, especially concerning the state of the university.[3] Those who attempt to speak are like voices crying in the wilderness. This failure to react hints of an intellectual inertia and spiritual poverty one would not expect from the university. The institutions of learning remain silent in every language.[4]

Is not the term "crisis" perhaps used too casually? Is it not rather the problem of that imperfection which dogs every human institution? Can we not confine ourselves to the constructive social criticism which every age requires? In our opinion, today's dislocations have completely shattered the normal frame of reference in respect to human efforts. This time something more and something different is at issue. It is no longer a simple question of the historic task of self-criticism and self-improvement, but a question of an enormous increase in effort in order to catch up with the times or to keep abreast of them. The very *raison d'être* of the university is threatened. The extent of this crisis can be measured in the three dimensions of the chasm that yawns between that which the university now is or is in process of becoming, and that which it needs to be or should be trying to become.

What *is* the typical modern university today?[5] A haphazard assortment of unattached areas of specialization, unattached colleges, unattached teachers, and unattached students.

The university is a factory. It produces spare parts for worn-out sections of the social machinery or builds new units for the computerized "scientific society." The product must of necessity be standardized. It is somewhat doubtful whether living human material is ever touched in this setting. In America particularly, where state

---

[3] The following two books ought to be required reading for all university scholars: Walter Moberly, *The Crisis in the University* (London: SCM Press, 1949), and José Ortega y Gasset, *Mission of the University*, (London: Kegan Paul, French, Trubner, 1946).

[4] Although the crisis of the university takes different forms in different countries, the crisis itself is an international phenomenon.

[5] By "typical modern" we mean the large urban universities. For smaller, regional, or denominational universities and colleges, these phenomena are as yet less pronounced.

universities have attained such a tremendous size, it has become a cliché to refer to them as diploma factories. But almost everywhere institutions of higher learning are being turned into centers of distribution of official passports entitling the bearer to put his brain at the disposal of the system.

The university puts its marketable products on display, and some have a greater variety than others. In America the specialities may include the undertaker's profession, novel writing, the beautician's art, landscape architecture, and interior decorating. But the basic principle is everywhere the same. How do I make an atom bomb, how do I handle personnel problems in my staff, how do I undertake a cost-accounting, how can I most effectively preach the gospel. . . . The answers to all these questions can be bought across the university counter, provided that it is listed in the catalogue. The buyer has free choice, but no one can obtain more than tiny scraps of the totality of knowledge. The students' opportunities for comprehension of the whole are steadily decreasing as the university pursues an ever-increasing specialization in preparing its apprentices to be useful in the megaloconcerns of modern society.

The university has sacrificed its *universitas* and made a mockery of itself as the great symbol of the indivisible totality of knowledge. As a rule it is nothing more than a collection of independent colleges under one name. The faculties have eclipsed the university. That which separates is more significant than that which unites.

The current trend toward superspecialization has made a euphemism of the so-called intellectual bilingualism in the sciences. No one knows any subject but his own specialty, and each man isolates himself behind the barrier of his own esoteric terminology. There are no accredited translators, and any attempt at translation is discredited. The only thing which the members of various faculties have in common, as a rule, is the town of residence, the institution which hires them, social position, and academic title. Occasionally, as chance wills, several of them may deal with the same student. But this is not a significant aspect of university life, for the modern university is much more a *Gesellschaft* than a *Gemeinschaft*. The broken contact cannot be re-established by meetings alone-these are in themselves one of the time-consuming evils of our age. Nor can it be remedied by personal interdisciplinary friendships. A heterogeneous collection of men of good will cannot weave academic splinters into an integrated whole worthy of the name "university."

The currently officiating representatives of the academic profession are themselves captive to the spirit of the times. They have

251

strengthened routine and immobility behind the bulwarks of tradition and conservatism. They suffer from the very disease they should be remedying. Instead of actively working against a further progression of the disease, they perpetrate *le trahison des clercs* and shape a learned barbarism.

The students also—however much they establish themselves in a network of associations—fall prey to the unattached state; the pieces are assembled only in the office files. The majority of students are known to their professors mainly through the class registration lists and the examination papers they turn in. Fellow students are more often competitors than *confrères*. How often does it happen that a student is really reached by his studies and leaves the university another (if not a better) man, capable of intelligent reflective thought and critical judgment?

The superman of our time is not the encyclopaedist, the generalist, the one who seeks universal knowledge, but rather the superspecialist. It is the man who knows more and more about less and less, until at last he knows everything about nothing. The student life was once considered to be a rather irresponsible one, and yet in their gay and carefree ways many students managed to pick up a little something from everywhere. The carefree aspect of student life has almost disappeared, to be replaced by the hardships of the student who must work his way through. And yet these restrictions on their freedom from care are not nearly as bad as the lack of an intellectual frame of reference of a universal character. The university imparts scattered fragments of science and knowledge and thus makes out of its student scatterbrained specialists.

There are feeble efforts on the part of the university to restore the *civitas academica*. The average student in the average modern university clutches his fragments of knowledge in his Faustian hand[6] as the university delivers him to society, a finished product of science. Thus cultural barbarism spreads like a weed through our society. Increasing specialization makes the problem even more acute. The long years of study are growing too short for cramming in everything

---

[6] *Dann hat er die Teile in seiner Hand. Fehlt leider! Nur das geistige Band.* Goethe was referring to the new techniques of analytic and increasingly differentiated research in chemistry (the so-called *encheiresis naturae*), and added, *Spottet ihrer selbst und weiss nicht wie.* Whether this is a fair criticism of chemistry I do not know, but as a general criticism of scientific development, particularly in the university setting, this strikes home. And yet Goethe had in all probability no inkling of coming developments in microphysics and the splitting of the atom!

which the superspecialist must know about his ever-shrinking field. That which the university should be is not something more, but something totally other. With Ortega y Gasset, I am personally convinced that only that university which endeavors in well-considered ways to achieve the cultural molding of its students is truly fulfilling its essential task. Such a cultural education would certainly include a systematic carry-over of the precious heritage of great thinkers out of the past into the future, and the furnishing of insight into the origin and development of the highest cultural values. It would include an orientation concerning the fundamental structural changes which have entered into our Western culture with corresponding changes in the image of the world and of society. Equally, it would include introducing all students to the burning questions of our day and to the divergent forms of *Weltanschauung* as man struggles for his present and future existence. In short, the camera lens of the university would be focused on that which moves the world.

Inseparably linked with this cultural transfer is the cultural preparation of students for the task of their own generation. This is a matter of training future leaders who are something more than specialists, who are individuals capable of transforming the subservient intellect into the serving intellect, who are free to contribute to the shaping of tomorrow.

Academic training in the best sense of the word sharpens the judgment and teaches how to discern where a Yes is called for in answer to society's needs and where a decisive No is demanded. This training should prepare the student to fulfill the indispensable function of an intelligentsia worthy of the name: to be the world's bad conscience about its cultural decline. In a word, what needs to be done is to undertake the selective transformation of as many students as possible into a new creative minority, wrested from the flood tide of massification. The university is now confronted with the crucial experiment which it must undertake to fulfill its cardinal function: it must contribute to the formation of this creative minority without which no culture can long survive.

For the university to fulfill, or even approach, the goal just outlined, requires nothing less than a full-scale rebellion of the creative minority of our generation, particularly its university contingent. This is the only answer to and counterbalance for the so-called rebellion of the masses, and is the necessary condition for the revival of genuine creative leadership in science. A spiritual revolution is called for to complement the Industrial Revolution.

A positive image of the future of and for the university can only stem from the premise that the university can itself have one of the most crucial functions of all to perform for the future. By its very nature it is a kind of transformer-station processing the ideas of yesterday into the ideas of tomorrow. Because of its function of intellectual mediation between preceding and following generations, it must ultimately produce thoughts which have not been thought before. The university cannot have any orientation to the future but a dynamic one. If it is not an intellectual and spiritual vanguard, it is nothing. We are far from asserting that the university has always answered to this ideal image in the past, but how the problem is of more significance than before. After the profound changes of the last 150 years, and in the face of the coming changes of the next 50 years (which promise to be far more radical), there is only one way open to the university: it must cut entirely new paths into the future, and do it while there is still time.

The Future of Science

While the situation of culture-crisis which we have been delineating is not generally recognized inside or outside the university, the earlier wholehearted faith that science can bring us within reach of our goals is now making way for a pronounced ambivalence of attitude.[7]

But even though two sets of values and attitudes are still encompassed in one system, there is at least a strong shift from the positive to the negative value-elements. A vague and indeterminate disquiet, evoked by historical, philosophical, and biological parallels, is on the increase as the fact of the antithesis between scientific civilization and a humanly worthy culture leaps more and more clearly to the eye. A few examples:

---

[7] This ambivalence is not entirely new. Ever since the Middle Ages there have been undercurrents of mistrust, running through Catholicism as well as through Luther, continued in such diverse figures as the romantic Rousseau and the mystic Goethe. There is the feeling that scientific pursuits will have negative effects on culture and religion, deriving either from a Mephistophelean inspiration (the Faust legend) or from man's rebellion against the supernatural (myths of Prometheus and Icarus; of Albertus Magnus, *doctor universalis;* and of Roger Bacon, doctor mirabilis). But after the Industrial Revolution, in the eighteenth and nineteenth centuries, the development of science became overwhelmingly identified with social progress.

254

1. The progress of military technology to the point where the potential exists for the total destruction of the planet earth and the species man.

2. The dissipation and exhaustion of the earth's sources of energy and its interior mineral capital.

3. Automation with the threat of mass unemployment and the prospect of ever-inceasing quantities of mechanized leisure.

4. Soil exhaustion as a result of the pressures of increasing world population, with the ultimate alternatives of hunger, world war, or both.

5. The moral dislocation of underdeveloped areas as a result of enforced transplantation of Western industrial civilization.

6. The expansion of technologically based totalitarian dictatorships, with the threat of the development of new, bestial human types.

7. The depersonalization of man and the technocratic mass-culture, in both East and West. The ascendancy of the mass un-man, and the decline of the Homo humanus.

8. The inadequacy of man's power over himself as he manipulates the microcosmos and the macrocosmos.

As far as the future of science is concerned, these dangers inherent in the applications of its findings do not alter the basic fact of unlimited possibilities. At many points the climactic developments are still far in the future. Both public and private capital investment in scientific research is continually on the increase. In spite of complaints that we already have too much of a good thing, the century of science has just begun.

The physical and social sciences do not stand in the same relationship to the changes we are discussing. The physical sciences concern themselves with distant time-spans whose astronomical remoteness leaves the present untouched. The social sciences are much more time-bound. They should precisely concern themselves with evaluating present developments in the light of future outcomes. But this age does not wish to hear itself judged. For this reason society has pulled the reins of positivism and empiricism very taut on the social sciences, giving this cradle of critical idealism and utopian reconstruction little opportunity for free movement. The intimidated social scientists maintain a rigid empiricism even while the very object of their studies crumbles visibly before their eyes.

The defection of the social sciences and the decline of culture are inextricably linked. The oft-discussed cultural lag—the incapacity of man to live up to the developments of human power over nature—is no more than a typical time-lag. The very use of the term "cultural lag" in this sense demonstrates the time-boundness of social science. No association is made with the future and with the vital forces at play in the dynamics of culture. Thus the social sciences take the lowly role of museum guide and no longer function as pathfinders exploring the future. We are told that at the Council of Nicaea no votes could be counted because the faces of the bishops kept changing, one into the other, and so the outcome of the vote could not possibly be determined. In the same way the face of reality is always changing as it is being studied. But if we are never finished with the sheer gathering of facts, performance will always lag behind pretension, and meanwhile the world changes—seldom for the better.

The science which developed at the hands of a creative minority with leisure time has now bestowed that leisure on the masses. The rebound of this action has robbed science of much of its own free time, which is its own life's blood. The Greek word for "free time," *schelè*, is not only the linguistic root of "school" and "schooling," but the psychological root of a free and fruitful pursuit of science. Modern science struggles under the heavy pressures and tensions of our time. Society holds a whip in one hand and a chronometer in the other, and the scientist fumbling at his forced labor must inevitably sacrifice quality to the Moloch of speed. There is no longer any time for writing (or reading) carefully wrought masterpieces which embody a lifetime of thought and study. A lifetime is now much longer than ever before, and yet much shorter. The essay replaces the major work, and the journal article supersedes the many-volumed book well filled with footnotes, appendices, annotations, and bibliographies, product of the great system-builders.

Scientific work that in earlier times would have been written out with great care, and discussed and rediscussed on the printed page, now remains unwritten, or at best receives a cursory scribbled note. How did the outstanding men of science of another era find the time for their tremendous correspondence with their colleagues, all written by hand, when today's scientist is always desperate for time simply to finish his own work? How was an encyclopaedic type of knowledge possible to earlier generations of scientists when we can scarcely keep up with our own specialties?

The exploitation of the subservient intellectual in this age exceeds that of the proletariat in the nineteenth century. Though he often comes in contact, in his work, with the problems of leisure time and culture, he has neither leisure nor culture himself. Subjected to this

256

permanent pressure, he is driven straight into the arms of the mass media and has his own opinions molded along with those of his less well trained contemporaries. And once he steps outside his own specialty he loses whatever claim he has to distinction and authority and merges into the anonymous majority.

This absorption of the creative minority into the masses is not simply a personal problem for time-pressed intellectuals. These sacrifices on the altar of the times will determine the future for all of us. A sufficient measure of freedom and leisure time is a *sine qua non* for the existence both of a creative minority and of a culture as such. The phenomenon of massification leaves society without the possibility of the development of a new minority able to do creative thinking.

At the moment two promising countercurrents against the prevailing trend stand out. The first might be called the reversal of "isms." There is a revolt against the domination of empiricism, mechanism, and rationalism. The rebellion has spread, sucking up strength from many old roots, until it represents a protest against all operations of the purely rational intellect. Other sources of acquiring a higher knowledge are put forward: art (Schopenhauer and Nietzsche), history (Dilthey), biology (Darwin, Goethe, Bergson, Spengler, Freud). More emphasis is placed on emotion as opposed to the rational faculties (romanticism), will (Schopenhauer, Nietzsche), intuition (Bergson, Husserl), utility (James), and being and becoming. Nietzsche is the central figure in this web of thought.

The two major trends in these philosophies are existentialism and anti-intellectualism. The growing influence of existentialism on the practice of science implies a further retreat of science into the security of empiricism. The converse of this is a retreat from values, goals, and ideals, and thus a retreat from images of the future. The anti-intellectual current is represented by such thinkers as Ludwig Klages *(Der Geist als Widersacher der Seele)* and Theodor Lessing *(Der Untergang der Erde am Geist).*

The second countercurrent to scientism originated in the circles of idealistic physical scientists animated by a lively sense of social responsibility. They are requesting an accounting for the current state of social disorganization and demanding solutions for social problems from social scientists, at the very time that the social sciences have been hiding behind empiricism. Having achieved freedom from values at the expense of so great an effort, should social science now sacrifice this hard-won scientific sophistication to naïve speculation on the future? The response of socal scientists to this appeal has been meager. They are most inclined to say, "We can describe and explain the social damage, but we cannot remove the causes or counteract the consequences."

Thus we see that while one countercurrent would call a moratorium on science, the other only serves to evoke the empiricist prejudice of the times.

Humanism

Humanism is selected here for separate analysis as an example of contemporary movements based on eschatological consciousness because it is the direct fruit of the utopian consciousness. The core-idea of humanism involves the self-elevation of man towards a higher type of manhood. It has a long history. Present in the socratic-platonic-stoic ideas of "Know thyself," of *eros*, *agapè*, and *paideia*, it turns up again in the duality-in-unity of *ramanitas* and *humanitas*, after having passed through Hellenic and oriental philosophic systems. Next it takes on the form of the Christian humanitarian ideal of charity and mercy. In the Middle Ages it lies behind the ideals of knighthood and womanhood. In the twelfth century it mutates in the new gospel of Joachim van Fiore. It is found in Cusanus, the transition figure between the Middle Ages and modern times, in his image of man as a microcosmos and a microtheos. It is found in Florentine humanism and in the Renaissance, as Pico's image of the *uomo universale* and *dignitas hominis*. It is found in Erasmus as biblical humanism. In the eighteenth century it is philosophically and ethically based in the idea of humanity as developed by idealistic thinkers ranging from Kant to Herder, Lessing, and Wilhelm von Humboldt.

Again and again we find as a constant element in this core-idea the concept of a rediscovery of man, resulting in his spiritual elevation through renewal. Twentieth-century humanism, however, opposes all philosophic dualism and idealism. Its methods are empirical and its concept of truth is pragmatic and utilitarian. Its social ethics, closely related to the Social Gospel movement, incline predominantly toward eudaemonism.

This modern humanism is inspired by the great minds of the past. That is as it should be. But does it represent a new countermovement to the trend toward despair? In order to live as a creative force for the future it must do more than stand up against the prevailing existentialism and philosophic nihilism. The tragedy of the present situation, as we see it, is that the more the humanist movement

258

grows in numerical strength, the more danger there is of a decline in spiritual strength. In trying to obtain a standing equivalent to that of the official churches, it is running the risk of a devaluation similar to that which the churches have suffered, that of becoming institutionalized and opportunistic. In seeking to relate itself politically to progressive socialism, it narrows its basis and limits its scope.

Historically, humanism knew scarcely any organizational ties other than those of the Florentine Academy or the international contacts between outstanding humanist scholars and artists. Here the old problem of the élite versus the masses with reference to culture-dynamics presses forward again. Must this organization submit to the *Zeitgeist* and take on the form and face of the times? Are not movement and direction subordinated to administrative mechanism? Is there not danger that its national and international organization will cause it to degenerate into a self-contradictory moment-ridden humanism? What is the position of the humanist movement with reference to the revival of rejected and abandoned expectations of approximating an ideal human society on earth? What is the humanistic image of the future? Will humanism build its own international organization, according to the temper of the times, or choose a more spiritual path and put its faith in the power of the idea?

Several of its leaders explicitly reject the historical form of humanism in respect to its optimism and proclaim the need for a realistic humanism. They feel that this changes nothing essential, but in our opinion it takes the very heart out of humanism, inasmuch as its ideal goal comes to be considered as a mere matter of historical form.

While the sixteenth-century and twentieth-century humanistic ideals may still be in essence the same, the carrier and agent of this ideal, man, is no longer the same. What can this new man do?

The neoliberal version of laissez-faire, in which the self-interest of the individual becomes the tool for the implementation of the general welfare, cannot be relied upon in the present situation either. History has taught us that complete freedom for some exists only at the price of absolute lack of freedom for others, and that the automatic harmonizing of individual self-interest and the general welfare is a pathetic illusion.

It is on this battlefield that humanism finds itself. It is caught between the forces at work towards the shaping of a new man, for whom everything human seems strange, and the powerful strategies that reject human dignity and initiative. Nevertheless, humanism's neoclassical image of man as an image of the future may play an important role in the regeneration of Western culture.

259

Chapter 21. A Modern Depth Psychology: Trigger or Barrier to Rebirth?

Post-Freudian psychoanalytical trends require special attention in this study. Carl Gustav Jung and his Swiss Circle laid the groundwork for a new trend, grounded in a fusion of Western and Eastern values, which claims the ability to revive religion and culture on the basis of its new insights, extending beyond the individual to the collective processes of mental and spiritual illness in our time. The publications of one of his influential but independent students, Erich Neumann of Israel, carry the Jungian ideas further.

Both Jung and Neumann attempt a renewing synthesis between religion, including its most archaic forms, and science, in its most modern form. This involves the construction of universal categories which will cover all religious experience from the time of the caveman to the present. By penetrating through to the archetypical forces of the soul, this psychology claims it can remove the cultural débris which is blocking man's way at present and once more tap the sources of human civilization. Let us examine the validity of this claim.

The Religious Ideas of Jung

Jung has written a great deal,[1] and has evolved his own special

---

[1] Works by Jung of special importance in this connection are *Answer to Job* (London: Routledge and K. Paul, 1954); *Essays on a Science of Mythology* (with Karl Kerenyi) (New York: Pantheon Books, 1949); *The Integration of the Personality* (New York: Farrar and Rinehart, 1939); *Modern Man in Search of a Soul* (New York: Harcourt, Brace, 1934); *Psychology and Religion* (New Haven:

terminology. A summary of his wealth of ideas is a perilous but indispensable undertaking.[2]

In answer to the orthodox view that God really exists "in and for Himself," Jung offers the following heterodox view. In the course of time the divine was evoked in different forms and shapes by man's inner being. It is a function of the human soul, more specifically of the unconscious which encompasses the individual and the collective (racial) unconscious. God's existence is not apart from or beyond man's existence in space and time, and is not independent of the historical unfolding of the human situation.

The divine receives its shape and becomes manifest through human psychic projection of mythical images which do not in themselves have reality, but which do flow from real experiences. The divine factor is creatively at work deep in the unconscious (of the individual and the collectivity). It is rooted in an unchanging foundation of archetypal patterns and trends that surge up out of the unconscious, molding and changing the conscious mind which, in its turn, again modifies the unconscious.

It is out of this mental process of interaction and self-realization that modern consciousness grows. Nurtured by the unconscious, it is nevertheless a process of liberation from the unconscious and its threatening powers over the weaker "I." For modern consciousness, God is only thinkable as a factor at work in the human soul. Man, in seeking the divine and finding it, encounters himself.

Jung has chosen a brand of mysticism all his own, a blend of Eastern gnosis, ancient Indic variants of mysticism, and medieval alchemy. Depth psychology claims to be an all-encompassing *Weltanschauung*, a reconciliation on a higher level of bipolar constellations: God and man, good and evil. The old projection of the perfect godhead is withdrawn as the human psyche develops toward a higher and deeper consciousness of the Self. Henceforth good and evil must coexist in the human spirit on equal terms, two sides of one and the same thing.

This implies the exit of traditional religious belief. As Jung says,

---

Yale University Press, 1938); *Psychological Types* (New York: Harcourt, Brace, 1923); *Psychology of the Unconscious* (New York: 1949); *The Secret of the Golden Flower* (New York: 1955). Pantheon Books, New York, has put out an edition of his collected works in English.

[2] We here gratefully make use of a summary of Jung's psychological-religious concepts by Buber. See his *Gottesfinsternis* (Zürich: Manesse, 1953), pp. 94—115 and 157—162 ("Anhang: Replik auf eine Entgegnung C. G. Jungs").

"the modern consciousness abhors faith and therefore all religions based on faith." In his Self man now finds again the divine power which is also satanic, and which joins the holy to the unholy. *Der Geist der stets verneint* is recognized as that basic divine-human element which necessarily negates every positive.

In a more recent work, *Aion*, Jung pursues the logical consequences of this line of thought with reference to evangelical Christianity. Christ himself has no other meaning than as a symbol of the Self. Jesus Christ as a projection of the unconscious also possesses, according to Jung, the divine-human double nature of a totality *welche sogar die animalische Seite des Menschen in sich begreift.*[3] This Christ has been forced back into the psyche of the human individual, and has become one with the *qualvolle Suspension des Ichs zwischen unvereinbaren Gegensätzen.*[4] This psychological approach necessitates the dismantling of all symbols and a complete demythologizing of the New Testament. Here modern psychology and modern theology meet.

The gnostic double-being which crystallizes out of this approach is a hermaphrodite, a fully conscious unity of intellectual man and instinctive beast, saint and sinner in one. In this way the great reconciliation between man and God, man and cosmos, is achieved.

Let us for the sake of the argument accept the possibility of the dethronement of reigning archetypes of the unconscious through their conscious unmasking, and the possibility of a liberation of the spirit through the progressive removal of unconscious restraints as man grows in self-awareness. Let us further recognize that from the point of view of individual psychology, these diagnostic insights may form the basis for a successful therapy.

We are primarily concerned here, however, with the more far-reaching claim to powers of cultural therapy, especially with reference to religious reconstruction and renaissance. We agree with Buber, although partly on other grounds, that such expectations are unjustified. The technique developed by this psychology contains a destructive rather than constructive spiritual tendency. Since Neumann carries both the arguments and the claims still further, and therefore demonstrates their untenability still more clearly, we will make only a few points here.

Gnosticism, in the modern dress which Jung gives it, contains as

---

[3] Aion, *Untersuchungen zur Symbolgeschichte* (Zürich: Rascher, 1951), p. 69.
[4] *Ibid.*, p. 74.

little perspective on a totally Other and better world as existentialism. This possibility is denied in principle. The wholly Other, and anything wholly Other, are anchored fast in the divine-human ambivalence of the Self. This God is incompatible with an eschatological hope of fulfillment for this world, and this man stands in contradiction to the utopian images of an ideal human society on earth.

On the individual level, a mere elucidation of the conflict in the personal unconscious may have a therapeutic effect. But does this mechanism also function on the social level? Is not such a transplanting in direct contradiction to the principle of individuation, that the modern consciousness can only be attained through self-liberation on the part of the individual mind?

Not only is the process of attaining consciousness accessible only to a small creative minority or élite, but its advantages to the masses are doubtful. The very attempt to popularize this process can lead to adverse results through a misunderstanding of the concepts involved. For the new-old, double-natured God is in every man, and so every man is always at the same time good and evil. What does this mean for the average mortal? The Old Testament image of original sin seems to be confirmed and strengthened in this new teaching, but without the counterbalance of divine redemption. May not this insight lead to pessimism and passivity?

The Religious Thought of Neumann

Erich Neumann builds further on the groundwork laid by Jung, using the same difficult jargon. He pieces together the many incomplete fragments of thought scattered throughout Jung's work and carries them through to their logical conclusions. However, there is one point of difference between them: Neumann regards himself as a left-wing Protestant, even though he is of Jewish origin, a convinced Zionist, and deeply versed in Hasidism. Thus the claim for a possible synthesis between science and religion narrows down to a compromise between modern depth psychology and the Christian faith.[5]

This comes out clearly in two recent books by Neumann, dealing

---

[5] This is also the case with other students of Jung, such as Hans Schar of Berne, who seeks a synthesis of theology and psychology.

respectively with the renewal of ethics and of culture through religion.[6]

Neumann's style is not always clear nor his terminology sufficiently precise. Nevertheless, we trust that the following brief summary of relevant ideas is fairly accurate.

Depth psychology is able to penetrate through to the primal sources of the human (individual and collective) unconscious, accessible in the collective archetypes and found in all forms of symbolism.

The central factor at work in this human unconscious is the numinous or the divine. The divine reveals itself solely as a force which acts in the depth of the soul. Theology is anthropology.

The divine is the transpersonal content within the uniquely personal Self of every individual. In the Self this non-I stands opposite the I as its hidden center of power, not metaphysical or *jenseitig*, but at the pole opposite to the conscious mind. It is in the empirical inner world of the Self that the human and the divine meet. Thus the divine can only be fathomed as polarity.[7] God reconciles all contrasts of being and not-being, good and evil. He is not the great unknown but the great generator, working simultaneously to create and destroy.

The attainment of consciousness by man implies the spiritual appropriation of this axiomatic duality of values inherent in all being. Awareness can come about in spiritually mature individuals through a psychic process of individuation and centroversion as man learns to absorb and assimilate, by suffering, the divine-evil powers generated deep within himself.

This understanding of man's double nature must result in a revolution in our current system of ethics and morals, based as it is on obsolete images from the unconscious. The present system has fulfilled its mission in a transition era, but its disappearance is a necessary condition of progress to a higher spiritual level. The fall of God must be accompanied by the dethronement of a heteronomous moral law. The new ethic must be autonomous, arising from the divine-human Self. The withdrawal of the divine from a supra-

---

[6] *Tiefenpsychologie und neue Ethik* (Zürich: Rascher, 1949); *Kulturentwicklung und Religion* (Zürich: Rascher, 1953). See also two publications in English: *The Great Mother: an Analysis of the Archetype* (New York: Patheon Books, 1955); *The Origins and History of Consciousness* (New York: Pantheon Books, 1954).

[7] *Tiefenpsychologie und neue Ethik* (Zürich: Rascher, 1949), pp. 157 ff.; *Religion, passim* (Zürich: Rascher, 1953).

mundane realm to the inner realm of the human soul involves also the transplanting of moral aspiration to psychic soil and sources, but these moral aspirations are now characterized by an essential duality of values. The most highly evolved man is he who recognizes the evil in his own bosom and acknowledges its equal rights with the good in his total humanity. Now at last the command "Resist not evil" can be grasped in its true meaning. If man behaves in full awareness of what he is doing, he will be able to serve society better and more responsibly than before.

This new insight implies a systematic revolutionizing of all religion and religious aspiration. Reduced to the briefest possible formulation, worship of God becomes worship of man himself. The encounter between man and God takes place in the Self, by way of dialogue between the I and the not-I. This dialogue is a dialectical art which can only be mastered by mystical man. Religion is mystical, mysticism is anthropology, and anthropology is rooted in depth psychology.[8]

Conscious insight into the basic psychic structure of the demiurgic god-devil and the sacral beast-man means spiritual self-liberation, the opening up of stagnant religious and ethical pools, and the inrush of the fresh waters of cultural creativity. This development could also go astray if emphases are misplaced, as Neumann recognizes. Its purpose is always the conscious renunciation of a one-sided striving toward ultimate perfection, and the recognition of ineradicable imperfection as a basic element of God and his human counterpart. But this consciousness, which is meant to bring about the realization of this duality of values, could swing man too far and drive him toward the opposite extreme of monism—not this time a monism of the over-optimistic All-Good, but that of a starkly pessimistic All-Evil. But, Neumann says, the recognition of this dangerous possibility is tantamount to its spiritual disarmament and so brings it under control. Rather, the growing realization of the dualities of man will finally drive men to voluntary association for the purpose of deliberate restraint of their own individual and collective evil excesses of power. Once every man knows himself to be no better than his neighbor in his own evil, then this blood-brotherhood and solidarity of evil will bring about a general brotherhood of man much more effectively than has hitherto been the case.[9]

The experience of unity of opposites which arises from man's

---

[8] See especially the third essay on "The Mystical Man" in *Religion*.
[9] *Ethik*, pp. 110, 159.

contemplation of his inner Self is comparable in Neumann's view with that which religion terms the gift of grace and art calls being gifted. These are regenerative powers of the unconscious to heal the sick world. Ultimately, they will provide a restoration of the social equilibrium whereby the current culture-crisis will be overcome.[10]

Neumann's view excludes all possibility of a fulfillment of history; because of the God within him, there is for man no Other time and no Other future. The eschatological perspective is utterly destroyed.[11] The question is whether precisely this perspective was not the very cornerstone of that Christian religion in aid of which Neumann's psychological renewal was meant to be applied.

As far as its value-content goes, the new ethic can only be bound to the autonomous human Self. All commands of a heteronomous morality are overthrown, from the Mosaic laws to the precepts of the Sermon on the Mount. There is no "ought." To recognize one's own evil and to commit it consciously is ethically "good."[12] Every man ought to seek a gentleman's agreement between the warring forces in his Self.[13] The pact between Faust and Mephistopheles provides an appropriate model for an "irreproachable" ethic.[14] One must have the "moral courage" not to wish to be better than one is.[15]

It is clear that Neumann himself wishes to call a halt at some point to the demons of destruction which he has summoned. But after this dethronement of value-systems, what ethical checks can there be on the sliding scale of dual values to prevent a slipping back to inferior values or to a state of valuelessness?

Man remains the image of God in Neumann's thinking, but, like God, he is profaned and perverted. Where the earlier deification of man was the product of an optimistic perspective, now a reification takes place which immortalizes suffering and evil without the prospect of any coming relief in history.

What is the individual to do who has accepted this new image of man? Is he to choose suicide, asceticism, alienation in the face of a meaningless existence, or the escapism of sensual surrender to wild desires? The contrast between our view of the split mental structure of man and Neumann's provides a mirror of the times which gives a

---

[10] These last ideas come from a series of lectures delivered by Neumann in 1954 at the International School of Philosophy at Amersfoort, The Netherlands.
[11] *Ethik*, pp. 95—96.
[12] *Ethik*, p. 132.
[13] *Ethik*, p. 86.
[14] *Ethik*, p. 135.
[15] *Ethik*, p. 127.

literal demonstration of our thesis.

We come directly to the heart of the matter through the definitions which Neumann uses for the concepts "culture" and "cultural development."[16] Culture is "the emergence of man through . . . confrontation with the mythical world." As for cultural development, ". . . the development of human culture, like that of the human mind, is a process of demythologizing." According to Neumann, the unreal mythical world built by the unconscious is one of catastrophic powers, of deadly loneliness, filled with despair.[17] The removal of this archworld of myth would therefore automatically imply a reversal in the direction of progress and hope.

Our own thought leads to the contrary position that certain demythologizing processes must be regarded as intimately related to the demolition of modern Western culture, with de-eschatologizing and de-utopianizing as decisive factors in the process. Since Neumann expressly bans eschatology and utopia, what is the basis of the claim that this view contributes to the revitalization of culture?

The doctrine of the "modern consciousness" is based on old images which have been patched up and polished—images drawn from ancient oriental gnostic movements which were persecuted and finally eradicated by a victorious Christian doctrine—but a host of other images has been added to these. The result is an ingenious mixture of ideal and mythical projections stemming from Iranian, Indic, Cabalistic, Hasidic, Egyptian, Hellenistic, Germanic, medieval, mystical, and even modern existentialist sources.

It would appear to us that Jung and Neumann, just as in another way Karl Mannheim, are too captivated by their discovery of mythical archetypes. They are misled into overextending their significance by presenting them as the primal forces of cultural dynamics which in dialectical fashion eliminate themselves as man comes into awareness. This progressive elimination is regarded as the main stimulant for the development of culture. They apparently fail to notice the fact just mentioned, that they introduce other (whether older or newer) *leitmotivs* in the place of those they eliminate. In consequence they overlook the two following aspects. First, they do not recognize that progress need not necessarily depend on the elimination of old concepts, but may equally depend on the simultaneous introduction of more adequate and reorganized ideas. Second, they fail to perceive the central role of images of the future with respect

---

[16] *Religion*, p. 109.
[17] *Religion*, pp. 90—92, 95, 121.

267

to cultural dynamics. Such images are contained in a number of older archetypical projections and have often been able to influence the growth of culture precisely because of their deep archetypical roots.

Furthermore, it is precisely the growing awareness of the untenability of naïve progress-optimism, arising out of the actual situation in the mid-twentieth century, which lies at the source of the current all-pervading existential pessimism. How then should a homeopathic cure of still more awareness concerning ineradicable evil lead to a turn for the better?

Depth psychology is nevertheless clear on what it intends and thinks it can do: nurse culture through its present crisis of illness and toward a healthy future. No one can doubt the intention, but we doubt the ability to carry it out. A psychology which establishes negation as an elementary constituent of the divine-human totality, has itself no "awareness" whatsoever of the psychology of negative thinking about the future.

The waxing of this depth psychology and the waning of our culture are but two aspects of the same phenomenon, and each explains the other. They ride on opposite ends of a seesaw balanced on the here-and-now.

Chapter 22. Art and Culture

*Die Künste scheinen heute wie durch das
Dasein gepeitscht; es ist kein Altar an
dem zu Ruhe finden, zu sich zu kommen,
wo ihr Gehalt sie erfuhlt.*

Karl Jaspers[1]

The sociology of art is the analysis of social and stylistic relationships between art and culture in specific historical periods.[2] Here we will examine certain parallel historical developments of art and culture with reference to the role of the image of the future in the process. We will begin by reviewing various attempts to trace functional relationships between art and culture on the basis of available research in art history and archaeology.[3]

---

[1] "Die geistige Situation der Zeit," *Sammlung Goschen*, Bd. 1000 (Berlin: 1949), p. 140.

[2] The sociology of art as a specialized field within cultural sociology has received little systematic attention. Johann Winckelmann, who concerned himself with the art of antiquity and was sharply attacked by Nietzsche, and Hippolyte Taine, author of *Philosophie de l'Art*, might be considered forerunners. Today, Sorokin is probably best acquainted with the field or at least is its most assiduous student. See Pitirim Sorokin, *Social and Cultural Dynamics*, 4 Vols. (New York, 1937—41); it includes an extensive bibliography. Other studies are: Max Dvorak, *Kunstgeschichte als Geistesgeschichte* (Munich: 1923); Walter Passarge, *Die Philosophie der Kunstgeschichte in der Gegenwart* (Berlin: 1930); and Herbert Read, *Icon and Idea* (Cambridge: Mass., 1955).

[3] Chapter 2 of Sorokin's *Social Philosophies of an Age of Crisis* (Boston: 1951) contains an excellent review of a number of outstanding theories and studies on this subject. It is one of the best and most reliable productions in the very comprehensive work of this author, who is as erudite as he is subjective, and who blends European and American approaches to scholarship. The following selection of hypotheses concerning the dynamics of and relationships between art and culture is taken almost entirely from Sorokin's resumé.

First, attempts were made to demonstrate that the development of art in all its forms is subject to historical laws of flowering and decline.[4] Moreover, sequences of alternatively dominant phases in art were assumed to coincide with similarly recurring phases of development of total cultures.

Next, art was treated as being subject to specific phases of development parallel to the phases of culture considered as a whole. This concept dates back to Hegel's *Aesthetik*, which lays down a three-pronged line of development: symbolic-classic-romantic.[5]

Other researchers, going a step further, conceive of a cycle of development which not only links art and culture in a pattern which must be repeated with every new culture, but also links them in a kind of "eternal recurrence," so that the same pattern repeats itself endlessly within every existing culture. Thus every culture would be programmed to repeat the trio preclassical-classical-postclassical in its music, and the triptych lyric-epic-dramatic in its literature.

It has been said that art is a highly sensitive culture-barometer. It is not only an indicator for the present, however, but a prognosticator of things to come. The image of the future presented by art is crucial in understanding future developments of a culture; in fact art *is* an image of the future.

Art and its Images

The dualistic structure of the human mind will be the point of departure for this discussion. The split and torn man, and no other, is able to conceive of another reality than the present. These distinctions were not at first made consciously; rather it was an intuitive

---

[4] In *The Revolutions of Civilization* (New York: Peter Smith, 1941) Flinders Petrie, the Egyptologist, maintains with considerable emphasis that all art forms do not develop simultaneously. On the basis of his considerable historical source-material, he suggests the following sequence: architecture, sculpture, painting, letters, and music. Paul Ligeti in his *Der Weg aus dem Chaos* (München: Callway, 1931) suggests another succession: architecture, plastic, graphic. Other writers, some of them specialists in one or another art form, suggest other sequences, but the idea of "lags" between developments in the differentiated art forms is common to them all. Usually architecture is considered to precede the graphic arts, and music mostly rounds off the list.

[5] The archaeolgist Waldemar Deonna proposes the thesis of a general dynamics of art according to a succession of archaic-classical-decadent, applicable to every type of culture. He brilliantly marshals support for his position from his extensive research in paleolithic, neolithic, Greco-Roman, and Christian art.

process. Therefore, precisely these capacities came into play which are the specific property of artistic natures. The capability for a splitting of space and time into the daily and the Other form the *conditio sine qua non* for the development of all artistic expression. Thus, culture gradually becomes differentiated from nature.

With the beginnings of culture one also finds the beginnings of art. Therefore we propose to take issue with the view of Plato and Aristotle that art is basically an imitation of nature. This view confuses the nature of art with the content of its representations. As we conceive it, even a meticulous copy of nature, if it achieves the stature of a work of art, is essentially a work of re-creation and transformation of the real into the Other and a beginning of all that is typically "cultural." This Other is the medium through which art places its world of semblance opposite the world of actual existence. *Art is artificial.* Through its spiritual power and ideational awareness, it distances itself from the existent and approaches the Other.

Thus, the split mentality forms the basis for all artistic activity—indeed, for all constructive cultural efforts. What is unique for art is the way in which it sets its own stamp on the representation of an Other reality, the specific manner in which it connects this with the existing world. How does art perceive the Other, where does the Other lead it, and in what form do these impulsions of the soul find expression? We will concentrate on answering these three questions, which fall particularly within the scope of this work. The positive, the image, and the future will be treated separately, but only taken together as an integrated whole do they become meaningful.

The Positive

How does the artist see the Other? It is a beholding with the inward eye, trained and sharpened by outward observation. This inward-directed seeing also includes a silent listening, an interception from other spheres, a sensitivity to and communication with the unseen. This intuitive perception generally precedes conscious reflection.

The Other reality is a living experience for the artist and therefore to him genuinely existent. The artist's gaze includes the not yet in the dimensions of time and space, in his own Kantian modes of perception.

The Image

The contemplation and realization of the Other realm find pregnant expression in the concrete image, the organic fusion of content and form, chosen and modeled by art for its appearance in this world. The image of art is a symbol in the literal sense of a "coincidence" of this and the Other world.

But the artistic image is more than a bridge between two worlds, more than a projection into the unknown; it is above all a prophecy of things to come. It is more in that it reflects not only what the mind's eye of the artist has beheld, but also his intention. The image, or rather the finished work of art, has covered the distance between the beginning and the end.

The Future

The contemplation of a union with the Other inspires the artist to his art. The Other is the primal source and also the ultimate goal. Art is the shuttle which moves constantly back and forth between the two poles which in the deepest sense are one, weaving its trends into the cultural pattern. True art splits the earth-bound atom and releases its energies for another order.

Before this artist can function as a transmitter of images, he must be able to receive them. Expressive creation follows upon introspective imagination. The reception of images out of nothingness touches the paranormal in a kind of telepathic transmission of higher and deeper psychic powers. One essential of all art is forward-striving; in its seeking and groping it reaches out toward the Other world.

If art is a directed movement toward the future, then we must reject the currently accepted view that art is essentially the purest means for expressing its time-period. Art may be this too, but only secondarily. On the contrary, true art of all times breaks through its own time.

For this reason, a true understanding of the language of art not only illuminates a specific historical period, but forms the instrument par excellence for the sounding out of the unfolding future. Art always contains in faint outline a prevision of that which is not yet. Eccentrically located on the farthest periphery of the times, art contains the heartbeat of the future.

The Positive Image of the Future

The image with which art works is a positive and ideal image of the future. Beyond expressing itself in symbols, art also expounds a deeper meaning; it offers a point of view through its symbols. The symbolism of the image and its ultimate intent or meaning are intimately related. In the last instance, all forms of art are "representational." Through its active idea of the Other, symbolically formulated, the artistic image possesses and expresses a norm of self-unfolding activity. As the horizon to the other is opened, a new perspective moves us towards it.

The introduction of perspective into the art of painting as a technical means of image-presentation is closely related to the perspective which all works of art contain as prospect of a coming time.[6] The complete realization of the perspective painting meant that it was possible to add a third and even a fourth dimension to an image projected on a flat surface. The canvas recedes into the background, the surface is hollowed out so that it has depth and transparency. One can now see through the painting as through a window. The representation itself is no longer a portrayal of an Other world in which man has no part; the spectator is now, through the medium of the eye, literally moved toward and brought into direct contact with the Other.

The alterations in dimensions and distances which perspective introduces result in the total picture becoming visually mobile, according to the position of the spectator. Without perspective, it is extremely difficult to give the impression of any kind of movement.

More than the quality of mobility is involved, however. The meaning of movement is more clearly defined as to its direction and goal. The images become visionary. The miracle visibly takes place in the psyches of the figures on the canvas. There is no better example of all this than Rembrandt. In the whole of his work a mobile and

---

[6] The presence or absence of perspective in art is certainly not a criterion for the evaluation of art. It is rather a criterion for symbolic and stylistic meanings. The elementary linear perspective was already known in antiquity, both theoretically and intuitively. It is no coincidence, however, that it was not fully developed until—and through—the Renaissance. The way was prepared during the transition from late Gothic to early Renaissance in the fourteenth century, especially through the frescos of Giotto and Duccio di Buoninsegna. Developed further in the fifteenth century through such men as Filippo Brunelleschi, Masaccio, Piero della Francesca, and the Van Eyck brothers, it was perfected by Alberti and Leonardo da Vinci, in respect to both mathematical-geometric foundations and the use of color perspective. The ensuing general spread of the use of dynamic-stereoscopic techniques of perspective in painting is closely related to the development of the new world-image and the new image of the future in this period of revival and rebirth, as contrasted with the world-image of antiquity and the Middle Ages, both in respect to space and time. The palingenesis develops before our very eyes in the forward-moving perspective.

supernatural light illuminates a gloomy world and disperses the shadows of space and time.

In the perspective of pictorial art a technique and vision have curiously emerged. But even the frozen movements of temple, cathedral, or sculptured piece, radiating tremendous pent-up energy, come to move through the technique of perspective. In their impassivity, history is made to pass. The perspective of painting and architecture can be compared with the depth which counterpoint provides in music.[7] Bach's *Art of the Fugue* brings this technique to its highest development in music. The transcending function and the futuristic aspect are practically the same. Specialists will be able to point parallels for other art forms.

Art Shapes the Future

The intimate relationship between the dynamics of art and the dynamics of culture is located in their images of the future. Thus, shifts in the kinds and styles of art are structurally related to shifts in the cultural image of the time and the future.

Now we will examine the twofold position that the current decline of culture, or of its components, particularly through a systematic mutilation of images of the future, will in all probability be ascertainable in a general derangement of art, and that an eventual decline of the artistic image of the future could have fatal consequences both for the future of art itself and for the future of culture.

Art's Image of the Future

Traditionally, aesthetics has been one of the foremost branches of metaphysics. A clearly marked transition has taken place in modern

---

[7] Dr. R. Mengelberg, in *Muziek, Spiegel des Tijds* (Rotterdam: W. L. & J. Brusse, 1948), states that new dimensions have been added to music in Western culture, especially through the chord, the harmonic triad, and the new rhythms utilized in instrumental music. In the field of sociology of music, Max Weber was once again the pioneer, with his essay on "Die rationalen und soziologischen Grundlagen der Musik," published in *Wirtschalt und Gesellschaft* (Tübingen: 1925). Also of importance are the essay by Kurt Blaukopf on "Musiksoziologie" in *Soziologie und Leben*, edited by Carl Brunkmann (Tübingen: C. Brunkmann, 1952), and a separate work entied *Musiksoziologie, Eine Einfuhrung in die Grundbegriffe mit besonderer Berücksichtigung der Soziologie der Tonsysteme* (St. Gallen: Zollikofer, 1950), and the study by Andreas Liess, *Die Musik im Welbild der Gegenwart* (Lindau: Werkverlag, 1949).

times away from all-inclusive metaphysics and towards specialized fields of science and philosophy: the history of art, the science of art techniques, the philosophy of art, the psychology of art (T. Lippe, Johannes Volkelt), and the sociology of art (Jean-Marie Guyau). Metaphysical aesthetics has been largely superseded by the modern methods of science.

Tracing the parallel development of religion and art, it is obvious that the iconoclasm of orthodox Protestantism and the continuing disintegration of eschatological representations cannot remain without profound effects on all art which has religious experience as its source of inspiration. A declining church membership, agnosticism, or an impersonal faith all reflect patterns of thought and behavior which turn art away from an Other reality and toward the present. Religious emotion and aesthetic emotion should certainly not be equated—in certain respects they are even antithetical—but the weakening of both can have its origin in the same life sapping forces of cultural dynamics. The analogy lies in the progressive hollowing out of the metaphysical-religious and of the aesthetic images of the future.

In its own time, almost all great art has stepped outside its period and been misunderstood. But this does not mean that all "modern art" is for that reason a sign of artistic health. It is difficult to avoid on the one hand the trap of reaction, perennially set for all modern art by the philistine, and on the other hand the trap of revolution set by the nihilist, out to destroy all past and future art.

It is suggested that the modern art of our day (wrongly but unavoidably considered as a whole) is basically different from the greater part of the modern art of previous ages. The defenders of today's modern art can point to suspicion and prejudice and resistance which stemmed from the misplaced application of old norms or current values to new art forms, so that critics were drawing upon an outmoded image-terminology even while a new and deviating vocabulary of images had already developed. We must always be aware of this danger and be honestly willing to learn to understand the newly emerging language of art with its different expressions.

The fact cannot be altered, however, that a renewal of art may overshoot its goal and that not all resistance may be disqualified in advance on historical grounds. This seems to us to be particularly true with reference to modern nonrepresentational art. When we have a situation not only where one image-vocabulary is replaced by another, but where the image representation in its stylistic unity is radically rejected as such, then the question at once arises, to what extent does this art still contain a meaning?

One of the major modern developments in painting which took place in the last decades of the preceding century is impressionism. This art concentrates on quasi-photographic instantaneous exposures, on the capture of the fugitive moment. All art of the moment is in basic contrast to an art of the future, just as the transitory and the eternal are always in conflict. The development of this style is one from the imaginary to the purely sensory, from the visionary to the merely visual.

Realism deliberately opposes the idea of the transcendent. Whether or not it develops further into neorealism or surrealism, it remains primarily oriented toward immanent reality. Volatility and lack of depth characterize it; it remains on the surface.

This led, in the first quarter of this century, to a new reversal to the other extreme, expressionism. Attacking the purely sensory rendition of momentary impressions, it appeared to aim at the rehabilitation of the supersensual, the ideal image of the future.

The tragedy was that time would not permit a simple setting back of the clock. At the same time, the reaction against the purely visual style of the preceding school of painting was so strong, and such extreme views were held about freedom in regard to the difference between appearance and reality, that a violent shift took place in favor of the ideal content at the expense of the plastic form. Finally the image itself was sacrificed to the basic idea. Generalizing about these two movements, it can be said that impressionism eliminates or curtails the future, and that expressionism eliminates or curtails the image; thus the image of the future was crushed between the hammer and anvil of movement in time.

Expressionism is more than a specific pictorial art-style, since it assigns a radically changed place to the artistic image. Therefore it is of interest to review briefly the ideas of various schools of expressionism. A number of trends developed under different labels: cubism and dadaism, divisionism and constructivism, futurism, archaism and surrealism, abstract and absolute art, and, especially in architecture, the *Neue Sachlichkeit.*

Cubism seeks to express the supersensual in the mathematical essence of simplified cubes, segments, and prisms. The resulting image is an imitation not of nature but of science.

Dadaism attempts a similar simplification, particularly through studied näiveté and primitivity. reproducing the feeling of pictures by small children.

Divisionism is based on the analysis of complementary colors, including light and shadow. The images show an abundance of dots (pointillism) or mosaiclike arrangements of elementary colors.

Constructivism is equally technical in its design. Constructions are mechanized, and as a rule the image actually contains machines or parts of machines.

The movement toward renewal in art next moved in two currents: futurism and archaism.

Futurism appeared at first to hold real promise for the image of the future, but it overstrained its original idea, its optimism became puerile, and it turned into hysterical excess. Finally, futurism became diverted into fascism and fizzled out in politics.

Archaism, on the other hand, went to an extreme of simplification and schematization, through an innovation which went back to the so-called primitive cultures and arts. In the image this is expressed in the first place by a return to a two-dimensional rendition. Perspective is banished. Works of art became childlike and wooden; forms and figures were flat. If futurism was too dynamic, archaism lacked dynamism. *Alles schon da-da gewesen.*

Archaism further developed into a kind of neonaturalism which painted nature as it "actually was," without the varnish of civilization—and it was taken to be "primitive:" uncultured, vital, and brutal.

In this form archaism merged with surrealism. The surrealist artist does not paint what is observed consciously and with the senses, but projects onto the canvas that which is hidden in the subconscious.

The striking resemblance of these works of art to pictures made by mental patients has frequently been pointed out. These trends clearly culminate in negativism and nihilism.

In abstract art, all ties with space and time are severed. Rather than irrational, these works become hyperrational, a series of formulas. Logically, they culminate in a void, in a colorless single plane (white or black), or in a single line or point. This is the ultimate expression of the dehumanized and dedeified All-One.

Neue Sachlichkeit had its beginning in modern architecture with Le Corbusier and others. Here too, sensory perception makes way for abstract essences. The new image is hard, cold, and efficient. The concrete is combined with the abstract, and utility is more important than beauty. The future is swallowed up in the order of the day.

Recent analyses of trends in modern art reflect an increasingly pessimistic point of view on the part of writers as diverse as Karl Jaspers, Ernst Junger, Nikolai Berdiaiev, Ortega y Gasset, H. E. Holthausen, and Sorokin. The outstanding features mentioned in current cultural appraisals of a pessimistic nature can be summarized as follows:

The nonsensical: the representation of the meaningless and the irrational as the normal face of human society. Analogies with neurosis, narcosis, and nightmares. The portrayal of the fundamental disintegration and incoherence of human life.

The existential: the ultrarealistic answer to the challenge of current trends of thought. Identification with science and technology. Utilitarian, calculating attitudes. The portrayal of man as completely alone, forsaken by God and his better self.

The perverse: the preference for the morbid, the obscene, and the ugly. The salacious portrayal of excess and abnormality.

The demonic: the evocation of the forces of darkness and evil. The regression of humanity to bestiality: *Satan conduit le bal.*

The negative: development of the themes of chaos, wasteland, and death. Images of damnation and moral impotence.

These five appraisals may be reduced to two: modern art is chiefly characterized by the loss of an ideal image of God; modern art has brought about the loss of an ideal image of man.

Modern art, thus assessed, robs the world of radiance. God is dead, and man is at best a robot, made up of lines, surfaces, angles, and spheres, without life and without soul.

We think it can be demonstrated that in modern art, at least of the Western variety, the formerly underlying ideal image of the future has been destroyed—in part consciously and in part unconsciously. The current attitude of mind is more and other than merely anti-Christian and antihumanist; it is overtly anti-idealistic and antifuturistic. Some examples follow.

Flatland—No perspective: the deliberate flattening of the pictorial perspective—the once-precious fruit of centuries of artistic development cannot be other than the mirroring of the symbolism of modern society. The reduction and liquidation of perspective in the practice of art is the counterpart of a general spiritual shift and indicates a lack of resistance against this spiritual sickness. Art has abolished perspective as misleading. Perspectiveless painting leads the way in what it supposes is honesty and a critical sense of reality, of which the world stands in dire need. In so doing, it believes itself to be doing a service to the culture of its day, but it does not point the way to a culture of the future.

278

Chaos—No structure: from an existential point of view, there is but one reality, no matter how one twists and turns it about. The world may be turned upside down, but it remains the same unredeemable world in the indifferent universe of space and time. This aspect of the negating of the earthly image of the future is also reflected in the forms which art has adapted for its use.

The remarkable blurring of the difference between "above" and "below" in modern plastic art is of significance here. The possibility of turning a painting in any direction and holding it upside down if desired, without altering its message to the observer, is a popular subject for jokes. The deeper meaning is anything but funny. The deft obscuring of the distinction between above and below corresponds to that of existentialism with reference to the past and the future, which constantly meet in the now. All former distinctions and positions have been overturned in the consciousness of our time. Life is approaching death. The supernatural is completely explicable in natural terms.

Underworld—The eruption of surrealism: the human figure in modern art bears witness to a deep self-disdain. The mask and caricature have always played a role in art, but even the most monstrous portrayals were balanced by irony or humor. Surrealistic man, hurled to the canvas, is no longer a lord of creation. Surrealism is basically not superrealistic but infrarealistic. Its people are subhuman.

In its images of man, surrealism carries out the task set forth by Nietzsche: *Der Mensch ist etwas, was überwunden werden muss.* Man is spiritually flayed, rendered lifeless, stripped of every shred of dignity—not only as a reality, but as an ideal.

Iconoclasm-Graphic devaluation: the discarding of the image of man as a *christopheros* (Christbearer or lightbearer) also implies his end as a participant in one of the most sublime activities of the human spirit, as a bearer of art. Modern art in consistent and true to itself in launching a direct attack on this art with its tradition of future-oriented norms and values. It attacks the artistic values of the "beautiful and good," the *kalos kaiagathos;* it attacks the roots and rules of humanistic-religious aesthetics. Baudelaire's *fleurs du mal* have quickly reproduced themselves and bear abundant fruit. The "revaluing of all values" of Nietzsche, a lover of art and beauty, is tragically pursued to the art-deadening extreme of the anti-Nietzsche.

Decadent Art: Measure and Matrix of Cultural Decline

If it were possible to isolate art and let it be *l'art pour l'art*, if it could be maintained that art is an independent field of human activity which need not consider nonartistic problems of culture and human society, then all that is described above need have no further consequences. However, art in all its forms is not only a mirror of its period but also a prereflection of the future. Works of art are of historical import because they influence future history. In addition to its acknowledged diagnostic and prognostic function, art also has a constitutive and regulative function.

Formerly art was to a great extent merged with the reigning style of life and thought. It was natural that it contributed to a clear expression of the *Zeitgeist's* expectations for the future. This is why art's specific role in creating the future has so seldom been noticed. However, now that art is submerged in the present it still exerts influence through its transmission of images, in a nihilistic way. Modern art is more than a prophet of woe. It has responsibility for the woes which may come.

Modern art of that kind has no message and no promise. The artist has become both enslaved by and addicted to his age, repeating what the times dictate. Art itself has adapted to the tempo of our modern times, overstraining its dynamic to remain up to date. It has to present new models at ever shorter intervals.

The development of modern art demonstrates a daemonic trend of self destruction. It is daemonic in that art itself regards its own death agonies as the growing pains of a youthful life-force. Each new direction in rapid succession is proclaimed to be a countermovement against decline and decay.

Naturally there are those among the pioneering renewers of modern art whose genius shines through any style and whose art cannot be disguised by even the strongest time-bound trappings. These artists still manage to give shape to the shapeless, to make the crudest material immaterial, to create a mystery in the midst of the ear-and-eye-splitting manifestations of the times. But we are referring here to the more impersonal, symptomatic currents and trends which characterize modern art as a whole. And these seem to us to be caught in a vicious downward spiral.

The three main turning points in this development may be described respectively as the transition in art from idealism to all kinds of manifestations of realism, the introduction of various iconoclastic procedures, and the development of expressionism as a countermovement to impressionism.

From Idealism to the New Realism

The transformation of idealism into realism (of whatever style) reduces original art to copy-art, and dilutes its inner symbolism to a photographic snapshot. Art can only flourish as a moving dynamic if it is moved by the tension between the poles of idea and reality. Thus we are faced with the justified countermovement of surrealism. It seeks for the idea behind observable reality. It is thus a protest movement against mechanization and against the misrepresentations of the truth as it is experienced by the conscious mind.

Nevertheless surrealism is a sham maneuver. Where does surrealism look for the hidden idea which underlies reality? In the unconscious and subconscious of an unreal and irrational dreamworld, in a Nietzschean will to power. What a fateful self-deception!

Surrealism in the last analysis remains within the framework of the here-and-now and does not overstep its bounds. Its idea is an alluring illusion. The same insane world which was first consciously observed returns at a gallop via the subconscious. It is the same reality, only still cruder.

From Images to New Functions

A second line of development, if carried to its logical extreme, results in a voiding of the intrinsic meaning of the image of art, specifically where its form of expression is concerned. All the expressive imagery by means of which the Other can be symbolically revealed is radically rejected: harmony, melody, symmetry, perspective, and color. The new artistic image is atonal, abstract, or functional. All this is done in the name of an idea, reasonable *Sachlichkeit.*

This style may hold its own in industrial design, but when it comes to art, the logical outcome of this approach is a series of horizontal and vertical lines and black-and-white planes, imageless images, without inspiration and without communication.

From Impressionism to the New Primitivism

Seemingly the most hopeful movement to appear on the scene after sensory impressionism, was the revolutionary countershift towards expressionism. Here the explicit desire was at work to go back to older values by leaping forward. In futurism a new image of the future developed only to become embroiled in political developments. This dismal outcome set in motion futurism's counterpart, archaism, which turned back to a primitive world-image.

Again we find self-deception! For this primitive image of the world was seen through the sharply focused lens of the modern world. The willful abandonment of perspective and the quasi-naïve representation on a two-dimensional plane, without the enriching matrix of living inspiration which the fine art of so-called primitive people always had, can only produce a pseudoprimitive, contentless art.

Nevertheless, this trend towards a would-be primitivism is hailed as the long-awaited revival of Western art. It is so regarded not only in art circles but also among cultural sociologists. One of the most important cultural sociologists of our time, F. S. C. Northrop, actually presents a weighty argument in defense of the thesis that the crisis of Western culture can be resolved through primitivism.[8] His contention is that all Eastern culture, especially that of China and India, is based on an aesthetically intuitive approach to knowledge, while Western culture is based on an intellectual, theoretically systematic approach. The cleavage between East and West is the great problem of our time, and arises out of opposed, exclusive and equally one-sided culture constructions. In order to achieve the necessary synthesis, the West—whose artistic creativity has been destroyed by intellectualism—must accord more place to the spontaneous, naïve, and aesthetically primitive world-view of the East, and the East must in turn take over more of the scientific and technological approach of the West. The revival of Western culture, seen from this point of view, requires a conscious shift to unconscious primitivism.

These three countercurrents leading to modern art all have the same negative result. The reversal from idealism to realism has broken off communication between the artist and an Other realm. The symbolic representation is banished, its revelation in meaningful compositions forbidden. The turning to expressionism has only achieved a sophisticated fixation in a primitive past. So all three contribute to the destruction of the positive idealistic image of the future, lifeblood of art.

The revolution in the value-system of art was not exactly a silent

---

[8] See his *Meeting of East and West, an Inquiry Concerning World Understanding* (New York: MacMillan, 1946). A summary of criticism of this argument is also to be found in Sorokin's *Social Philosophies* (Boston: Beacon Press, 1950).

revolution, but even so it has taken the public by surprise. Works in the traditional style of *beaux-arts* and *belles-lettres* are now denounced as old-fashioned and boring. Only the very newest can find grace as pure art. We must pity the artists of this midcentury generation, who now have every eye upon them and are the subjects of so much praise and serious analysis, while in another decade, if not sooner, their art will no longer be *the* art—or perhaps not even art at all. The experimental "isms" of the art of even very recent decades are now practically forgotten, and have nothing to say to our time. Nevertheless, Sartre's oft-repeated cry that all must be "actual," "engaged" in the situation of our time, has become an accepted code of art. The modern artist strives for the highest measure of actuality and originality in order to be up to-date. He sees only the present, which applauds him, and not the future, which will bury him because he has ignored it. If modern art no longer creates for future generations will future generations be able to create art? Or are we on the brink of an era which will only be creative in science and technology?

A defuturizing art is an important causal factor in the threatening decline of a dehumanized, futureless culture. Art is both measure and matrix of culture. It is at once the crystallization of a developing culture and the chrysalis of a coming culture. Not only is degenerate art the fruit of a culture in decline, but it engenders further decay.

The cycle can be broken, however. There are creative artists in all fields whose work is charged with a positive symbolism concerning the future; there is also a special, if shrinking, public that consciously appreciates this aesthetic testimony, staunchly refusing to let Stravinsky dwarf Bach or Picasso overshadow Rembrandt.

Notes on Modern Music and Poetry

Those who are acquainted with modern art are well aware that the various arts are closely interrelated and demonstrate striking similarities in development, especially with reference to the trend from impressionism to expressionism. Expressionism is now typically found in architecture, theater, literature, music, and poetry. We have chosen the plastic arts, and particularly the art of painting, as our main illustration because the numerous trends are most clearly differentiated there, and because nothing can throw a clearer light on the elimination of the functional essence of music and poetry than the banishment of spatio-temporal perspective from painting.

In music, this modernism takes the form of a radical rebellion against existing norms of style, harmony, tonality, instrumentation, and so on. Apart from certain neoromantic and neomystical trends, the greater part of modern music belongs to that genre which seeks renewal in demolition, pandemonium, and cacophony, without any original creative power, and without positive symbolism. Nevertheless, this modern amusical music is chosen for performances, praised by critics, and spread over the Western world. If one considers this new-fashioned laboratory sound-product in a milder mood, as an experimental transitional stage, one must do this on the basis of a faith in a dialectical but unhistorical development of art which would make the beautiful spring forth out of the ugly.

If music is by its nature a field of imponderables, poetry, that other invisible and impalpable art, may provide a clearer view of these same trends. Moreover, poetry's case is more accessible to the general public than that of the other arts because it is more given to explaining its intentions in detailed self-analysis: probably no other group writes so much about poetry as modern poets themselves.

Poetry has at times been called the art of arts. Aside from the question of whether it must be considered aesthetically the highest form of art, it can be said that it is the most spiritualized in the sense that it expresses itself without the use of any material or instrument, but addresses itself directly to the human imagination. It literally speaks in images, symbols, and meanings. The poetic image is the seedbed of all artistic images. Poetry paints, draws, sculpts, decorates, builds, dances, gestures, and makes music; it has line, color, sound, and style; it is characterized by rhythm, timbre, tempo; it presents its own image of harmony and symmetry, of dimension and perspective. The art of poetry contains something of all the arts, and yet it remains distinct.

In the last half-century poetry too has passed through the international currents of surrealism and expressionism.[9] The intentions of modern poetry can be fully appreciated. Modern poetry has the same spiritual root and wells up out of the same split human mind as the utopia. It is the protest of the revolted spirit against all that is unjust, superficial, and hypocritical. It expresses the protest of the artist against a society that is wholly unworthy of man. His artistic spirit seared by two world wars, his sensitive imagination clutched by fear

---

[9] Examples from different countries: Ezra Pound, T. S. Eliot, André Breton, Paul van Ostayen. The latter's work was recently reprinted in full, including expressionistic typography.

of a third orgy of destruction, his body and mind drawn into the vortex of a mounting dehumanizing technocracy, the artist's protest is raised against everything and everyone.

This protest of poetry, in itself so understandable, finds expression in an explicit rejection of all existing poetic forms and images. Thus the protest is not only against common usage in punctuation, syntax, and symmetry, but against rhyme, rhythm, and meter; against ordered prosody and melodious harmony; and above all against the coherent structure of a rationally or at least intuitively comprehensible whole. In outward form, poetry has been shredded into unrelated image-fragments, detached word-and-sound combinations, a stream of vibrations which does not crystallize as a melody, a series of image-flashes juxtaposed in deliberate disorder. Each separate image is eloquent enough, but together the images are a triumph of inarticulateness.

But whatever may be the case in the other arts, in poetry it is quite impossible to impair existing modes of expression without seriously affecting the content. Therefore the protest against the form of the poetic image inevitably turns into a protest against its intrinsic meaning. This makes of modern poetry a keynote of the whole of contemporary art and culture, the ideal-type of unconscious and unintended self-destruction.

For the modern poetry of our time it is the meaningless which provides the only natural and existential meaning. Conversely, the meaningful is unnatural and false. Honest art, according to this view, portrays reality as it basically is, reflected in man's subconscious images and in the unchangeable conditions of existence: fear, suffering, and despair. In all the meaninglessness of the times which it glorifies, nothing finally appears as meaningless as its own rebellion, culminating in a sterile art which contemplates its own navel. This is the new freedom imagism has brought us. The sole meaning of the poetic image is now located in the one-dimensional present.

.The elements indispensable to true poetry—sensitivity to images and tone, fantasy, word mastery, creative emotions, and dynamism— are still to be found in the work of promising experimental poets. But other, equally essential elements are lacking. For the modern poet is possessed by the daemonic present; his inspiration is too exclusively drawn from the drama of the irremediable human situation.

Where is the way out?

Chapter 23. Socio-Cultural Dynamics

*The choice is no longer between Utopia and
the pleasant ordered world that our fathers
knew. The choice is between Utopia and Hell.*
William Beveridge[1]

*The construction of Utopias used to be
despised as the foolish refuge of those who
could not face the real world. But in our
time social change has been so rapid, and so
largely inspired by utopian aspirations, that
it is more necessary than it used to be to
consider the wisdom or unwisdom of dominant
aspirations.*
Bertrand Russell[2]

The relationship between society and culture is not only a structural one, but above all a dynamic relationship of continuous interaction. Social and cultural patterns grow, develop, and change as
they mutually influence each other. Although these interdependen-
cies have been recognized, the area of socio-cultural dynamics has
remained largely unexplored.[3]

We will confine ourselves to three aspects only of this neglected
field, with special regard to their orientation to the future: capitalism, socialism, and politics.

---

[1] From a talk by Beveridge, quoted in his autobiographical *Power and
Influence* (London: Hodder & Stoughton, 1953), p. 355.
[2] Bertrand Russell, *The Impact of Science on Society* (London: Allen & Unwin,
1952), p. 85.
[3] The chief pioneering work in this field has been done by Mannheim and
Sorokin.

286

Capitalism and Socialism

The rise and development of capitalism, and its transformation and decline, have since the time of Marx been seen chiefly as a dialectical process of self-disintegration, a point of view greatly reinforced by the crisis of the thirties. The Marxist-Leninist doctrine remains the official basis of Soviet international politics. But independently of the Russian dream, this doctrine has been subject to renewed socio-economic analysis during and after World War II, and powerful supporting arguments have again been presented. Two books stand out here, both written by Austrian emigré economists in the United States: Karl Polanyi and Joseph Schumpeter.[4]

Since Schumpeter has already so well described the self-destroying effects of capitalism, and we know of no authoritative refutation of this argument, we would like to take Schumpeter's analysis as our point of departure. We will translate his conclusions into the categories and concepts made use of in this book.

His general argument runs as follows. Capitalism is not destroyed by its failure, but by its success. The numberless limited-liability and joint-stock companies, with their salaried managers and expanding technology-based enterprises no longer dependent on private initiative and personal risk, destroy the earlier phenomenon of new entrepreneurial combinations set up by profit-seeking capitalists. Capitalism itself undermines its own protective bulwark, the bourgeoisie; it attacks the position of the farmer, the small business man, the middle-class shopkeeper, the trades, and the professions; above all, it devalues the function of the bourgeoisie as such in society. Its own extreme rationalism gives rise to a critique of bourgeoisie as such in society and to a critique of bourgeois values, which finally extends to the values of capitalism itself. This weakens the unique institutional conditions of private property, free competition, and freedom of contract, and creates an atmosphere which is increasingly hostile to itself. Its own rational, bourgeois, and antiheroic mentality leaves it defenseless against attacks by labor and a discontented

[4] Karl Polanyi, *The Great Transformation* (New York: Tarrar and Rinehart, 1944); Joseph Schumpeter, *Capitalism, Socialism and Democracy* (New York: Allen & Unwin, 1943). Polanyi's contribution is his delineation of how the historical flowering of liberal capitalism in England, through the first Industrial Revolution, already contained those forces of self-destruction which did not become evident until the twentieth century. Schumpeter, on the other hand, takes the present as his point of departure. Each work complements the other to produce a historically adequate whole.

intelligentsia. Thus, it actually contributes to its own reshaping and to the transition to a collectivist social order.

Leaving aside any discussion of the validity of this analysis, let us compare, on the socio-psychological level, the functioning of the capitalistic image of the future in the two periods of peak and decline. Polanyi makes the main contribution here. Arguing from the development of the poor laws, he shows how industrial capitalism in England was able to flourish thanks to a dominant and vigorous image of the future which itself nullified the corroding side-effects of economic industrialization. Numerous currents converged in this image of the future: liberalism, classical economics, biology, Social Darwinism, the social philosophies of physicalism and mechanism, Spencerian sociology, and even theology.

All strands come together in the idea of the survival of the fittest, and the harmony between self-interest and the general interest (the "hidden hand" doctrine). The free functioning of the market would lead to the optimum of prosperity and justice. The evils of hunger, poverty, and unemployment suffered by the working proletariat, seen from the point of view of the general welfare, became subsumed under a positive good. Thus, capitalistic entrepreneurs who were enriching themselves by grinding the faces of the poor could be considered the nation's benefactors.

The capitalist image of a future of progress and prosperity collapsed as much as a result of its social failure (Polanyi) as of its economic success (Schumpeter). In spite of ultraliberalist revivals on a theoretical level, such as those of Ludwig von Mises, Friederich Hayek, Wilhelm Ropke, Lionel Robbins, and John Jewkes, and the neoliberalism of John Maynard Keynes, there is no longer the unconditional faith in evolutionary development once symbolized by the gold standard. Today's entrepreneurs do not adore any such golden calf—they mostly lack the self-confidence to live for such an image of the future, much less die for it.

The increasing social regulation instituted to restrain the activities of capitalism, has been met with decreasing resistance by capitalism itself, and is now accepted as a matter of course. Some of the measures have had the effect of further weakening the liberalist image of the future. Schumpeter correctly singles out two phenomena which reflect this impairment of the essence of capitalism: the decrease in the average size of the family and the decrease in accumulation of capital through individual saving. A good deal of attention had of course already been given by others to both these phenomena, and it is certainly true that both—formation of family

288

and formation of capital—are intimately related to the expectations for the future which men cherish. The number of children and the number of bankbooks speak, each in its own way, the language of anticipation. As far as I know, however, no one has attempted systematically to relate these specific anticipations to the general, cultural image of the future.

The interaction between these changing anticipations and the socio-economic framework of different societies and cultures would be of great interest, but here we must confine ourself to an analysis of events within the framework of Western European culture. We will see the same regression which we have observed in other areas of culture: a driving back of the future, accompanied by concentration on and consolidation of the present.

Let us first consider the decline in the average size of the family in the West. Historically, the size of the family has wavered between the two poles of a faith that God would provide, and the bitter wisdom of Malthusian abstention. From the late Middle Ages on, children were, for the proletariat, assets which helped balance the budget; for developing industries, factory fodder; for the expanding nationalist, cannon fodder; and for the Church, so many souls for the Kingdom. A large family was both necessary and good, particularly in view of the high rate of infant or child mortality. Now, on the contrary, the leveling of income and property has led to the leveling of time. This leveling of time has worked out, as we will try to show, into a reduction of family size and a shrinking of the age-span between the oldest and youngest child, and between parents and children.

Taxation and inheritance laws leave no prospect for those who are well off to make future capital provisions for a large number of children; at the most they can provide for one or just a few. Social regulation and cultural pressure have eliminated the role of children as economic assets for the less well off. Rather, each additional child means a downgrading of the family standard of living. This is also true of the farm population as the countryside becomes mechanized. Limiting family size increases opportunities for parents and children alike, for women as well as men.

In some European countries the childless household is no longer uncommon, and in middle-class families the one-child or two-child family predominates. The continuing increase—with ups and downs—of the divorce rate changes the traditional family unit into a temporal, contractual relationship between part-time bachelors with as few bonds as possible in the form of children. Parents are no longer posterity-minded.

These phenomena are closely related to the accumulation of capital through sober living and thrift. More than ever before the accent falls upon enjoyment of this earthly life. A revolution at the expense of individual saving habits has taken place in favor of mass consumption. The traditional private saving has been replaced to a significant degree by compulsory mass saving through social security systems and voluntary types of insurance, whose farthest time horizon is the old-age pension. Thus, the future is already laid down as of today.

There is an unmistakable shift in our time from the the uncertainties of capitalistic adventure towards a protective security of existence from cradle to grave. It is a shift from independent work to a salaried appointment.

Add to this the fact that independent entrepreneurs are more and more giving way to salaried directors and holders of preferred stock, and that the philosophy of expansion is making way for one of consolidation. Industry is often protected by high tariff walls; the relationship between employers and employees is largely regulated by collective contracts; and, finally, contemporary government seeks to stabilize the business cycle and achieve full employment through a planned economy.

The tremendous potential of the laissez-faire image of the future, capitalism's source of energy, has evaporated. This age is the age of neomercantilism and mixed forms of central planning. Is the capitalistic image of the future being succeeded by a socialistic image of the future? Schumpeter suggests the unavoidable transition from a capitalistic to a socialistic order. This does not necessarily mean the replacement of one image of the future by another—it can indeed mean the opposite.

Socialism, like capitalism, is a social movement, moved by the spiritual force of a positive image of the future. Both images are utopian. Equally utopian is Marxism, wavering between the evolutionary views of liberalism and the sharp dialectic of the class struggle.

We have tried to demonstrate in our historical survey that each movement and socio-cultural trend has derived its effectiveness from its particular projection of the future, and that these projections have pushed and pulled the ongoing stream of events towards the future they foreshadowed.

On the other hand, we have also come to the conclusion that any once-powerful historical movement which no longer possesses genuine images of the future, faces spiritual decay. Social movements are

290

particularly liable to this kind of decay.

Western socialism, in all its ups and downs, runs a course almost painfully parallel to the general course of socio-cultural development from utopia to counterutopia.

Marx and his followers resisted the nonrevolutionary reformist socialism, despising it as "utopian" and bourgeois. In the end, they succeeded in destroying true utopian socialism, at least in the West, and it was replaced by bourgeois socialism. The Marxist brand was to result in a paradise of a classless and stateless society of workers. In the following discussion of Western socialism, we refer to socialism in its broadest sense as a general spiritual current and the socio-political movement.

The fruits of modern socialistic political action, such as full employment, social security, public health programs, and a just distribution of income, are for a large part the harvest of the seed sowed by utopism in previous centuries. Where are the new utopian ideas preparing the way for further changes in the direction of a socialistic image of man and society? The social proletariat and the socialist idea have changed places: the proletariat has risen, the idea of the totally Other has declined.

Just as the liberal's evolutionary image of unhampered progress has led to a concentration of economic life in extensive monopolistic organizations, so has the socialistic revolutionary image of systematic intervention led to similar patterns of vast socio-economic organizational networks: on the one hand a metamorphosis of independent entrepreneurs into many-headed megaloconcerns, on the other hand, a metamorphosis of socialistic pioneers into massive administrative bureaucracies. The capitalistic apparatus now has its managers and anonymous stockholders, and the socialist apparatus has its managers and masses.

The combined effects of the technical revolution and increasing government regulation enforce a further elaboration of the socialistic apparatus. What will be the effect of the increasing size and complexity of the Socialist Party on the future of the socialist movement which gave it birth?

Let us assume, for the sake of argument, that challenge and reponse are similarly structured for the two opposing movements. What does this demonstrate? Does this in any sense reduce the tremendous difference of ideology and program between capitalism and socialism? Or is this difference not rather sharpened now that the protagonists can meet each other with equal forces at their disposal?

291

The possibilities for the further development of socialism stem not from its special nature but from the nature of any mass party. A nascent socialism, with minimum machinery, had a more critical eye for future developments than the flourishing socialism of the present day. At that time, large-scale political bureaucracies formed a fine target for the fire of socialist opposition. But gradually it has become clear that the development of a powerful political machinery is indispensable to the realization of socialistic ideals. Now comes the test of a social growth and maturity.

The political sociologist Robert Michels, in his 1910 study, *Zur Soziologie der Parteiwezens*, develops the hypothesis of the iron law of oligarchy on the basis of his study of the S.P.D. (German Socialist Party). One can argue with Michels, but it must be admitted that his general prediction concerning the antidemocratic implications inherent in the building up of large and powerful political parties is correct.

Updating Michels's argument, it can be said that at present no large political party can do without strong smoothly-functioning party machinery if it wants to exert influence in the political arena. This in turn presupposes strict party discipline. By implication, the highest value is no longer placed on human individuality. Conformity and obedience are prized instead.

At its best an oligarchy may be run by conscientious and skilled specialists, but it will also by its very nature exercise a strong attraction for less capable, power-hungry "managers." Great parties which have fought for self-government of the masses are driven by the requirements of large-scale organization along the road of progressive concentration of power in the hands of a centralized administration.

In general, the above holds true more or less for every major party. Changes in the social structure seem to have made this development inevitable; the mechanization of culture is reflected in the mechanization of political and social organization. At what point must the line be drawn between a Yes for what is just barely acceptable and a No that may no longer responsibly be suppressed? A survey of actual party behavior indicates a gradual dulling of the social conscience and a tendency to accede to the so-called exigencies of circumstances. What is exceptional about socialism is that it, of all parties, can least tolerate these typical characteristics of a modern large party without irreparable damage to its essential nature.

The machinery of socialism is increasingly (and to a considerable extent unwillingly) approximating a historical counterpart of liberal capitalism. The power and abuse of power of the hated capitalist have now both been transferred, at least in potential, to the collective body with its army of anonymous employees and officials, and its hierarchical caste system.

If it can be said that the socialist movement is becoming bourgeois, the paradox must be kept in mind that this is happening through excluding the individual as an active bourgeois, burgher, or citizen. Instead, he becomes a small cog in the gigantic machinery of automated politics. Increasingly passivity and even apathy go hand in hand in the modern state and the modern party. A fixing of the *status quo* is accompanied by the enfeeblement of a progressive striving towards a *status ad quem*.

How far can realistic political conduct deviate from ideal principles? The answer varies, but it can descend to the very bottom of the scale. Socialist policy can travel the whole way back to *status quo* conservatism. With scarcely noticable transitions, socialism inclines toward a recognition of the existing powers: the throne, the altar, the army, and commerce. In the process it makes considerable gains, but also irrevocable losses.

In portraying this political transformation, we do not mean to imply that it represents only regression and no progress. Obviously, it represents a more realistic political attitude which has resulted in much positive good that could not otherwise have been achieved. We are not faced here with simple alternatives of good and evil. We are rather faced with complex and problematic basic questions of man and society.

We are here not concerned with historical valuation, but with assessing chances for future development. However high a value one places on the very respectable sum of socialist achievements in the past, one may nevertheless entertain less hopeful expectation with reference to future developments. Even the most firmly convinced socialist must thoughtfully ask himself where the recent developments will lead socialism itself.

The greater the success socialism achieves in the parliamentary and governmental sphere, and the more it becomes absorbed in this, the less it can retain its independence against the forces dominating the actual situation in political reality. And so socialism, revolutionary in its European origins, very gradually and seemingly of its own free will grows moderate with maturity and wisdom, and under the burdens of practical responsibility develops a dispassionate and realistic policy which is more political than socialist.

It is neither academic nor premature to ask what now remains of the original, vital socialist idea. Many see the extension of political power, combined with material welfare and social security for the workers, as representing in essence the realization of the socialist idea. Of course, the very fact of partial realization of old ideals through political channels must inevitably diminish their dynamic power in equal measure. If we compare future prospects today with the future as it looked when socialism was first coming into its own, the outlook appears definitely less favorable. Yet the challenge from the future to our generation is more compelling than ever before. Therefore, this retreat from the future and the outspoken preference of modern socialism for the reality of the present must have deeper reasons than the fact of realization of older dreams; it must be anchored in a deeper layer of modern thought. If even socialism, which was always intrinsically utopian and futuristic, is indeed subject to this uniquely contemporary delimitation of perspective and scope of activity, then the question arises whether socialism has not paid too high a price for political power.

Unfortunately, it is almost impossible for the leaders of now-powerful socialist parties to believe in any signs of inward decay, and to see any further ahead than their own time. Let us consider the sad story of the Socialist Party in Germany. The S.P.D. at its zenith and in its fall provides a classic illustration. Not only did this party surrender its enormous and hard-won power (and thus its future) in the course of a few decades and without a blow, but the effects were felt in a political situation which gave rise to the two world wars; the effects even extend to the development of the third, cold war. In each decisive period—in 1914, in 1918-20, and in 1925-33—the S.P.D. failed spectacularly.

Not the image of the future, but the party was at fault. In spite of the facade of power, the party was inwardly rotting away, at the very time when other political parties were hammering on the voters' doors with competing prospectuses for the future. Through persistent nearsightedness, it paved the way for a national socialism obsessed with the idea of a pan-Germanic world of the future.

Socialism must also carry a share of the responsibility for the flowering of communism, through failing to respond to the challenge of the times. A fatal aspect of contemporary socialism is antifuturism. We have already encountered this in our discussion of Hayek, Toynbee, Popper, and others. They all plead for the restoration of an *ancien régime*, or, at the least, for progress with the brakes on.

Having begun the nationalization of production and the means of

294

production, socialism has itself in the meantime also become nationalized. The Fichtean nationalistic anti-utopia, which exchanges the categories of time and space, has sowed its bad seed in socialism too, and the idea of an international socialism has nearly vanished.

What then remains as typically socialist? Science, technology, and rationalism are after all available to all political groups. There are few promising creative developments in present-day socialism. One could point to the independent left wing of the British Labor Party, but this may at some time split off into an independent party without this representing a primarily socialist movement. A drive toward world community could express itself in other forms and movements, such as world federalism, without being specifically socialist.

Other ways, with other names, may be as good or better. But if socialism can not project a course of its own after having pioneered for so long, then it loses not only its traditional leadership in this direction but also its own unique significance and *raison d'être.*

Is the demise of socialism inevitable? Personally, we will continue to put our faith in the fundamental socialist idea, albeit against our own better judgment; we believe in the possibility of a timely rebirth of the socialist idea. The current unrest in the socialist parties of all countries is an encouraging sign.

Politics and Culture

If present-day conditions of socialism seem to represent a denial of its heritage and its goals, it must not be forgotten that this reversal fits into the framework of modern culture and is part of a greater social change.

The new look in politics is well illustrated by the symptomatically titled *Politik ohne Wüschchbilder: Die konservative Aufgabe unserer Zeit,* by Dr. Hans Mühlenfeld.[5] Apart from the apparently inescapable German preoccupation with self-exculpation *(Wir haben es nicht gewollt und nicht gewusst)* in reference to national socialism—the supposed offspring of the union of liberalism and socialism—it contains a double plea for politics without images of the future and for conservative thinking.

The books pleads for exactly those things which are in fact

---

[5] Dr. Mühlenfeld was one of the early members of the German Bundestag. He was Ambassador from West Germany to the Netherlands at the time this work appeared (Munich: Oldenburg, 1952).

undermining socialism. Politics, like science, should turn away from the ought and confine itself exclusively to the existent. All the misery in the world is due to the irrational drives let loose by ideologies. The question is whether this argument for a pure *realpolitik* is really a challenge to action or simply a description of the actual state of affairs.

Too little attention has been paid to the consequences of the so-called managerial revolution for the form and structure of politics. There is little doubt that a new managerial caste is developing which is providing leadership in key places in government, industry, and political parties. These managers are the prototypes of the social engineer. The specialist has difficulty in focusing on the far horizon, and conservative thinking flourishes in the managers' bureaucracy. Thus, while the tempo of social change makes higher demands than ever before on responsible government officials, these leaders themselves operate within increasingly limited mental horizons. It is not at all unusual for a statesman completely to retract, verbally or in writing, former positions on even the most essential points, within a short period of time. His "Here I stand" may shift locus with lightening rapidity and scarcely be noted.

From the point of view of domestic policy within Western lands, both socialist and capitalist images of the future have spent their force. Workers are only a little less conservative than the entrepreneurs, and they often combine in oppression of the unorganized middle, including the intelligentsia thus driven either to the extreme right or the extreme left. The bitter class struggle of an earlier day is fortunately over, but its valuable aspect of building up long-range visions in both groups of antagonists has been lost. Instead we have a trivia of competing, short-range interests and a dearth of creative leadership.

That modern foreign policy suffers from the same evils need scarcely be documented. The times of a Jean Jaurès, Walther Rathenau, Thomas Masaryk, Jan Smuts, Woodrow Wilson, or Theodore Roosevelt are over. At the same time that social changes are giving rise to problems of a worldwide nature, we are producing leaders who are immature and irresolute, unable to see ahead. The historian of the twenty-first century, if he is indeed able to write freely then, will surely award a boobyprize to this age.

It is easy enough to scorn the endless petty rituals of diplomacy. What is more serious is the mediocre staffing of the foreign service at all levels and in all countries, great or small.[6] Exceptions can always be found, but it would be difficult to maintain that the finest flowers of the land are to be found in the foreign service, in spite of the fact that men like Keynes and Toynbee put in their stints in this service before they became well-known. Diplomatic functionaries above all men must be able to think broadly in terms of time-spans and space beyond the national borders of the present; yet they live as spiritually hand-to-mouth as the rest of us, perpetually surprised by the events of the day after tomorrow.

The only long-range planning is to be found in the field of economic development and applied social engineering—the Marshall Plan, the Schuman Plan, the Common Market—in such organizations as NATO, born of the fear of Communist aggression. But while there is an abundance of partial plans, the visionary plan which offers a genuine perspective on the future of Western culture is lacking.

There remains one more area within the field of political affairs: cultural policy. In the present force-field of socio-cultural dynamics, this ought to be a crucial factor in terms of long-run effects. However, the member of our managerial class, half-barbarians that they are, lack the necessary perception and breadth of vision to develop such a policy. Measured by economic outlay and in terms of the population as a whole, there is indeed in some respects more culture-consciousness and more political activity on this behalf than would earlier have been acceptable or possible. But in the face of our present need, it is far too little. Universal suffrage, parliamentary democracy, codified law, and social legislation all have their sources in the daring conceptions of earlier ages. The continuation and defense of this culture is a life-and-death matter for Western politics, too. But even while Western politics and culture may in the future die together, they are certainly not at present living together, at least not without grave discord.

Today a sudden interest in culture arises only when expenditures have to be cut, and cultural programs appear as the most expendable budget items. What remained of the world-states of antiquity, once

---

[6] Bertrand Russell found in high officials of the British Foreign Office an "ignorance unsurpassed except by their conceit" (*The Impact of Science on Society*, p. 51) (London: Allen & Unwin, 1952). This complaint is naturally neither new nor confined to England. We are again reminded of Axel Oxenstierna's words of over three hundred years ago: "Don't you know, my son, with what a minimum of sense the world is governed?" However, in our day the consequences of a lack of understanding are much graver than ever before.

their culture had fallen into decline?

The cultural blindness of modern politics is extreme. The politicians of today are for the most part equally prisoners of the *Zeitgeist*, whether they stand in the ranks of the conservatives or the progressives. Who will sound the warning bells?

Chapter 24. New Perspectives

For here we have no lasting city, but
we seek the city which is to come.
Hebrews *13:14*

As we look back over the route traveled in this book, we cannot fail to see a pattern in the complex workings of the civilizations we have traversed. The pattern unfolds in a panorama that includes both past and future. We can see proscopically right through this world into the Other behind it. The numerous little pieces of the jigsaw puzzle of culture fit together in an intricate and subtly patterned cultural mosaic. The many-colored fragments adhere and produce a steroscopic three-dimensional projection of Western culture: one world in the foreground, the Other in the background.

In every sphere that we have examined, there has been no escaping the symptoms of the frantic effort of man to wall himself up in the now. In the end, all streams of culture flow together, and the towering banks of the mighty present shut off all possibility of meandering currents exploring new river beds. Meanwhile our civilization sits in sickly narcissism, motionless at the riverbank, spellbound by its own image reflected there.

Is a culture more than its component parts? Exactly the same process which injured the imaginative and forward-thinking capacities of each individual facet of culture is at work on the whole; the course of development is completely analogous. One can speak of a general decay of positive and creative cultural awareness.

Once we see that the same key fits both individual cultural phenomena and the total structure of culture, and recognize that the key has three parts—past, present, and future—we get a new perspective on our own time. Before examining the synthesizing functions

299

which the image of the future may fulfill, we will review the other three functions discussed in our analysis of culture so far. First, we found the positive image of the future at work in every instance of the flowering of a culture, and weakened images of the future as a primary factor in the decay of cultures. The image of the future has been represented as itself subject to a dialectical movement between the poles of optimism and pessimism.

Second, we found that the potential strength of a culture could be measured by measuring the intensity and energy of its images of the future. These images were seen to act as a barometer indicating the potential rise or fall of a culture.

Third, the concept of the image of the future has made it possible to move from diagnosis to prognosis. This is possible because of the intimate relationship between the image of the future and the future.

The image of the future can act not only as a barometer, but as a regulative mechanism which alternately opens and shuts the dampers on the mighty blast-furnace of culture. It not only indicates alternative choices and possibilities, but actively promotes certain choices and in effect puts them to work in determining the future. A close examination of prevailing images, then, puts us in a position to forecast the probable future.

Any culture which finds itself in the condition of our present culture, turning aside from its own heritage of positive visions of the future, or actively at work in changing these positive visions into negative ones, has no future unless strong counterforces are set in motion soon. This view is of crucial importance for practical policy. It opens up new vistas for policy-makers in the areas where they still have freedom of planning and action.

We must first deal with the question of why a new swing of the pendulum in regard to images of the future cannot be taken for granted. If history is indeed a long chain of dialectical movements, why do we not assume that this particular reversal, a trend towards more optimistic images of the future, will also take place in due course?

It is not simply a question of any reversal of trends at any time. It is a question of the right reversal at the right time. We have reached that critical stage where the need for time is the primary need of the times. Images of the future are not so easily constructed. After the iconoclasm of the last half-century, the images of the future out of past centuries scarcely exist as such any longer, and probably could not be forced into a new life. This is why it is not possible now to revive old images of the future. Neither is it possible, however, simply to pull new images of the future which can inspire and motivate a society out of a hat.

Our contemporary culture negates just those qualities which would be virtually necessary in giving new life to our culture, such as faith in man's essential worth in spite of social cataclysms. There must be some basic certainty that in spite of the current dehumanization of man there can be some radical reversal of the existing order. Is there still a real possibility for the maintenance and revival of our Western culture, in terms of a general spiritual rejuvenation and a new vision of the future? At the moment, Yes, but the time may come, even within the next half-century, when it will no longer be possible. The time is short, and therein lies our greatest handicap. We are fighting an unequal battle with the passing hours.

How are we to weight the relative strength of man against time? His greatest problem is his crippled awareness of the Other. Though the crippling may be serious, time has not yet run away with us. Not yet. What is the extent of the damage? Although we have made it clear that all areas of culture are affected, they are not in fact all affected equally. In terms of the major distinction we have made between utopian and eschatological approaches to the problem of man in society, which of these approaches to the problem is currently the more vital, the more productive of new thinking? Eschatology is without a doubt very seriously weakened, owing to the profound secularization of Christianity itself. Furthermore, Western culture is no longer primarily a Christian culture. Thus, to make the fact of Christianization the condition for the continued vitality of Western culture is the same as deliberately to choose to further weaken both Christianity and Western culture.

The Middle Ages, which had a thriving eschatological image of the future, will not return. Neither will the period of revolution and rationalism, when the utopian image had its heyday. Our age has turned against both images alike. In this period of rejection, those who are concerned for these images must let the accent fall on the unity which is present among their diversities. The claims of the eschatological image have lost their meaning within the religious sphere, especially as these claims maintain themselves in the face of the pseudo-eschatology of modern myth and ideology. The utopian image is basically concerned with another sphere, the dynamically interacting human society on earth and its earthbound goals. In a strongly secularized world the cultural task of the utopian image is more indispensable than ever—paradoxically enough—in part because it alone can in our time maintain the cultural base for religion.

Eschatological and utopian visions, ultimately sprung from the same spiritual source and now threatened by the same social forces, must learn to understand and fulfill one another.

The choice for modern man is no longer between this image of the future and that, but between images of his own choosing and images which are forced upon him by outside pressures. The empty void between today and tomorrow cannot withstand the magnetic pull of tomorrow, especially not while a new kind of image of the future from Eastern Europe is flowing like white-hot lava over large parts of Asia and Africa.

Our hopes for cultural survival lie in a blending of utopian and eschatological images, or even in predominantly utopian images. Christianity has as much at stake in supporting such images as does any part of our civilization. The task before us is to re-awaken the almost dormant awareness of the future and to find the best nourishment for a starving social imagination. For Western Europe, this means finding its own way out, without resorting to imitation of either Russian or American patterns. For America, its means considerable soul-searching regarding the vitality of the American dream, which has for so long been taken for granted. It is not too late to do this. Man has not yet been degraded to animal or machine. One fortress remains to him. His capacity for dualism has not yet atrophied, and thus the chief condition for construction of positive images of the future remains. The mental process of splitting reality continues, although frequently in inappropriate and grotesque ways.

Man knows better than ever, thanks to modern technology, how to create something Other which is different from day-to-day reality. This type of creation no longer represents an ideal tension between present and future, however, but a strictly ultilitarian escape from tension through a splitting of the present into two parts: daily life versus synthetic experience. The latter represents diversion in the truest sense of the word: diversion away from the future and the task of building visions.

But this same mental capacity can be used in another way; it can serve the regeneration of culture. We are standing at what may be the last fork in the road. If we take the low road and follow the vision of the negative utopia, there can be only one end to the journey: the abyss for our civilization. A new civilization may arise, but there may be a long interim period of chaos and barbarism for man.

We have striking evidence that the capacity to choose the high road has not disappeared. The fact that the Russian image of the future has commanded such a widespread following and elicited such remarkably dedicated—if ill-fated—behavior on the part of its disciples, including those outside Russia, indicates that man is still able to choose and work for a high and difficult goal. That the Russian vision is based on some fundamental illusions regarding social reality does not change the fact that many men have given devoted service to this vision. Part of the European intelligentsia is even willing to invoke self-destruction on its behalf. The whole tragedy of "Holy Russia," and therefore of our modern world, is that her zeal could not serve a holy vision.

The evidence from America regarding the vitality of existing images of the future is somewhat mixed. The European observer sees a tremendous dynamic potential still active in this country, and at the same time discovers what seems to be a dangerous social apathy. America is a land of extremes. The greatest visions, and most daring experimentation with the farthest limits of the potentialities of the human mind and the natural environment, exist side by side with the crassest materialism and preoccupation with a tomorrowless now.

Although much of our thinking about the future today is inevitably in terms of choosing between the two competing images of the future which the East and the West have set before us, we must in the long run pass beyond these dichotomies which paint the future in black and white. Neither Russia nor America alone can spawn the future. The image of the future, at its best, has always been universal in character, a vision to serve and foster the growth of all mankind. At a time when the lack of such a vision seems to be driving us to self-destruction, it is well to remember that one of the most potent and enduring visions in the history of man has been that of a Thousand Years' Reign of Peace. This is a vision which is never entirely absent from the hearts of men and women who come together to bear children and build a home. If the man leaves home and wife and child to go forth to war, as he has so often done in the past, it is only that he may in the end return and continue building in peace. If the woman endures hardship bravely and finds ways to survive when there seems to be no hope of survival, it is only that the child of her womb may live to build a better world. The sparks of this universal vision lie in every human spirit in every land. A vision of the future which falls short of this universality will in the end leave the earth a smoking ruin. The same tool cannot serve simultaneously as sword and ploughshare, and the scope of the vision will determine the final use to which the tool is put.

With Eastern Europe galloping at top speed after a chimaera, Western Europe frozen in despair, and America chasing her own tail in a rather confused state of mind, we can still take courage for the future, for we know that the capacity to create and follow visions has not been lost. We have already indicated that there are hopeful signs both in the Russia and in the America of today. We must look to what we have. Our first challenge is to examine the basic foundations of our existing visions, to analyze their contents, scope, and direction. Analyzed in these terms, how did the Russian go so far astray? Why are the traditionally full-speed-ahead Americans bogging down? Are they indeed bogging down? These two questions lead straight into two major projects which social science must undertake, the theory and dynamics of image formation and propagation, and field studies of current images of the future in action. This book and its companion, *Prognostics*,[1] represents an opening up of the field, but much remains to be done.

For the social scientist, an adequate study of the image of the future, both theoretical and descriptive as in case studies of existing societies, means drawing on knowledge and techniques from every branch of social science and achieving a working integration of this knowledge. For others—thinkers, artists, engineers, and activists alike—it means not only examination of their own vision, but an examination of their attitude toward visions. The adjectives "utopian" and "visionary" did not always have a derogatory meaning. We need a new generation of Founding Fathers to father a new age—men of the same breed as that first generation of Americans, hard-headed visionaries who knew how to make dreams come true.

Perhaps we should ask whether we still have creative leadership in our democratic society. Or has the thinking élite—the very term inspires horror in the democratic mind—been absorbed into the passive mass-mind as a result of its own idealistic fraternization with it? The answer is No, certainly not yet. The very ideals which have prompted the fraternization can rescue both leaders and masses if awareness comes in time. The thinkers, leaders, and creators of our age still have all the wealth of the uncensored past and the vast reservoir of the open future to draw upon in creating new visions, plus the opportunity to bring the great mass of the citizenry into responsible partnership in fulfilling these visions. The same educational system and mass media which now threaten to deaden the mind of the average man can also be used to awaken it, if we know what we are doing.

---

[1] Abridged edition transl. in English (Amsterdam: Elsevier, 1971)..

If we can arouse our own creative leadership in time, are our ideals and values good enough for the task ahead? If we are honest we must confess that there are many shriveled husks lying around in our culture, husks of once-vital ideas which have somehow dried up. Existentialism has been busy sweeping up these husks in order to provide itself—and mankind—with a tidy, if barren, room. It is not too late to gather them up. Though dead, they contain living seed. If they are planted and tended, mankind will not go hungry at harvest time.

Everyman, look to the harvest! It is the layman's responsibility to be aware of his own aspirations and those of the group to which he belongs. It is for him to choose the vision he will follow and to take responsibility for carrying it out. Society offers him not just one role, but many. Through his performance in these roles—in the family, in the community, in his vocation—he stands answerable for the vision he chooses.

No man or woman is exempt from taking up the challenge. Social scientist, intellectual, artist, leader, middleman of any breed, and the Common Man (and Woman) to whom, after all, this century belongs—each must ask himself, what is *my* vision of the future? And what am I doing about it?

God forbid that we should end this book on a note of self-study! If Western civilization does go down, irrevocably, the last figures to be seen above the floodwaters will have pencil and notebook in hand, as they busily conduct an investigation of what is happening. No. We need to understand our ailing visions in order to know what to reject and what to accept in them, but all our study is only a preliminary clearing of the decks for the urgent vision-work of creating tomorrow. Self-analysis is only meaningful if it liberates us to choose our own destiny. Man has the capacity to dream finer dreams than he has ever succeeded in dreaming. He has the capacity to build a finer society than he has ever succeeded in building. We have always known this. Must this knowledge paralyze us? Here lies the real challenge! There are among us even now dreamers and builders ready to repeat the age-old process of splitting the atom of time, to release the Western world from its too-long imprisonment in the present. Then man will once again be free to "seek the city which is to come."

Author Index

308

Subject Index